106 MORTGAGE SECRETS ALL BORROWERS MUST LEARN— But Lenders Don't Tell

106 MORTGAGE SECRETS ALL BORROWERS MUST LEARN— But Lenders Don't Tell

Second Edition

GARY W. ELDRED, PhD

John Wiley & Sons, Inc.

Published by John Wiley & Sons, Inc., Hoboken, New Jersey.
Published simultaneously in Canada.

Wiley Bicentennial Logo: Richard J. Pacifico

For general information on our other products and services or for technical support, please contact our Customer Care Department within the United States at (800) 762-2974, outside the United States at (317) 572-3993 or fax (317) 572-4002.

Wiley also publishes its books in a variety of electronic formats. Some content that appears in print may not be available in electronic formats. For more information about Wiley products, visit our web site at www.wiley.com.

ISBN 978-0-470-15286-7

Printed in the United States of America.

10 9 8 7 6 5 4 3 2 1

Contents

3   Slash Your Cost of Interest   43

4   The Risks and Rewards of ARMs   73

5   Perfect Your Credit Profile   97

6 The Lowdown on Low Downs 121

7 Win Big Savings with Seller Financing, Foreclosures, or REOs 147

8   Beware of Those Fine Print "Gotchas"   183

Preface to the Second Edition

During the past 10 to 12 months, the media have flooded us with news about the so-called mortgage meltdown, a doubling or tripling of delinquent mortgage loan payments, the dramatically increasing rate of property foreclosures, the tragic stories of people who now suffer payment shock, and more generally, the millions of borrowers who paid far more for their property loans than they would have paid had they shopped, compared, and negotiated wisely instead of merely relying on the supposed good faith of their loan representatives.

William Poole, president of the Federal Reserve Bank of St. Louis, was recently quoted in *The New York Times* (July 27, 2007) as saying, "Driven by the prospects of high fee income, mortgage originators have persuaded many borrowers to take out these [expensive and unsuitable] mortgages." Or, more bluntly, disaffected borrower Jennifer Hintz says, "I feel we got totally screwed" ("Nightmare Mortgages," *BusinessWeek*, September 11, 2006).

Isolated incidents? Hardly. The U.S. Congress and the attorneys general of more than a dozen states are holding hearings and conducting investigations that clearly reveal widespread fee gouging, unsuitable loan products, nondisclosures, deceptive advertising, bait-and-switch practices, and other malfeasance by loan reps and mortgage lenders.

So, it is within this context that my editor, Laurie Harting, suggested that we bring out an updated edition of *106 Mortgage Secrets All Borrowers Must Learn*. Although any reader of the first edition would have been forewarned against the abuses that are now coming to light, this new edition sets out in more detail how borrowers go wrong—plus, it emphasizes how to make financing property one of the the most rewarding transactions of your life.

When you learn how to loan shop with savvy, explore alternatives, and stay alert for ill-advised borrowing, the United States offers the best mortgage system in the world. Many loan reps will work diligently to help you own your own home and build wealth through investment real estate. These loan reps and lenders deserve fair compensation for their help.

Nevertheless, as a borrower, you must assume nothing. You must question intelligently; you must know how to distinguish the fake from the genuine. You must understand that maybe you shouldn't even use a lender to originate a new mortgage; rather, you might ferret out seller financing or an assumable mortgage (yes, contrary to popular belief, lenders still write a million or more assumable mortgages every year), or you might consider a "subject to," a wraparound, a lease option, or a blended-rate refi. Or you might snag a bargain through buying a foreclosure or a lender REO.

The first edition of *106 Mortgage Secrets* was widely praised by homebuyers, investors, and consumer advocates. It was often condemned by loan reps who want to keep you in the dark. One such reader trashed the book and claimed, "There are no secrets here; your lender has to tell you all of these things." The recent outpouring of media coverage firmly disposes of that nonsense. Lenders and loan reps—even those who display honesty and competence—try to get you to buy the product(s) they sell. Few, if any, will explain those many financing or buying opportunities that they do not offer.

That's where this new edition of *106 Mortgage Secrets* comes to the rescue. Unlike any other book on property financing, this new edition of *Mortgage Secrets* steers you away from those loan choices that will lose you money—and shows you how to find, structure, and negotiate the lowest-cost financing that leads you to maximize your ownership and wealth-building possibilities.

I wish you the best in your quest for property ownership. Should you discover questions, insights, or anecdotes that you would like to share with me, please give me a call at 352-336-1366 or visit my website, garyweldred.com.

Introduction: Use OPM to Achieve All That You Really Want

In this book, you will discover how to arrange the best deal when you finance your home or investment properties. But you'll gain much more than that. *Mortgage Secrets* goes beyond "the best loan for the lowest cost" type of discussion and shows how to achieve multiple objectives. For example, how many of these goals appeal to you?

- Own your own home?
- Trade up to a larger home?
- Refinance an existing property?
- Buy properties at bargain prices? Foreclosures? REOs?
- Strengthen your qualifying ratios?
- Overcome cash or credit problems? Boost your credit scores?
- Own a home or investment property that you think is priced beyond your means?
- Own rental properties that yield positive cash flows and high rates of appreciation?
- Reduce borrowing costs by tens of thousands of dollars?
- Buy property with little or no cash out of your own pocket?
- Avoid predatory loan reps, loan terms, and loan costs?
- Learn to live "on the house"?
- Build millions in wealth and enjoy a life of financial freedom?

Yes, in this book you will learn the best, the easiest, and the least costly ways to finance real estate. But you will gain much more than that. Most importantly, you will discover how to use credit (Other People's Money, or OPM) to create wealth. You will learn to think about money and financing in ways that will change your life. Before you borrow, you must always answer these two questions: (1) Will this loan help build my net worth? Or, (2) might this loan diminish (or maybe destroy) my financial future?

Banks and finance companies want you indentured to them. Unless you resist, they will load you up with car loans, credit card loans, home equity loans, boat loans, vacation loans, and other types of monthly payments that zap your financial strength. Although such loans enrich the banks, they deep-six your ability to create a secure and prosperous future for your family and yourself.

So, read *Mortgage Secrets* to discover the best way to finance the properties you want to own. But also, think big. Let *Mortgage Secrets* guide you toward the financial goals that will bring about the life you would really like to live. To win the money game, outsmart the banks. Learn to cheaply borrow productive debt. Say no to high-cost consumer loans. Steer clear of consumer debt that swamps you in a quicksand of monthly payments.

Think of OPM not just as Other People's Money. Think of OPM as Our Productive Money. When you learn the secrets of leverage and productive borrowing, you learn the secrets of the millionaire mind. You learn the secrets of living well.

CHAPTER 1

Affordability Depends on You—Not a Lender

You've heard the advice, "Before you shop for a property, meet with a lender and get preapproved for a loan. The lender will tell you exactly how much you can afford to borrow."

That advice seems right. Why pore over the menu at the Ritz Carlton when your budget says McDonald's? But here's the problem—and the opportunity.

SECRET # **1**

Affordability depends on you.

In the world of property finance—for homebuying and investing—the loan market offers thousands of lenders and hundreds of financing techniques. Plus, interest rates, closing costs, credit standards, and underwriting guidelines vary among lenders.

Read through the following list of 65 affordability techniques; these techniques only sample your loan alternatives. Because you enjoy a cornucopia of choices, no loan rep (or anyone else) can tell you exactly how much loan (or how much property) you can afford until they work through these and other possibilities. If one lender (or seller) says, "No," you say "Next."

Selected Sources and Techniques to Achieve Affordability

Accessory apartments

Adjustable rate mortgages

ARM assumptions

ARM hybrids

Balloon mortgages

Blanket mortgages

Buy a duplex, triplex, or quad (tenants pay mortgage)

City down payment assistance

Co-borrowers

Co-ownership

Co-signers

Community reinvestment loans

Compensating factors

Contract-for-deed

County down payment assistance

Create value/fixer-uppers

Employer-assisted mortgage plans

Energy efficient mortgages

FHA assumable w/qualifying

FHA Title 1 home improvement loans

FHA 203(b)

FHA 203(k)

FHA 203(b) mortgages

FHA 203(k) mortgages

Fannie Mae affordable mortgage programs

Fannie Mae Community Home-buyers programs

Fannie Mae Start-up Mortgage

Fannie 97

Financial fitness programs

Freddie Mac central city mortgage programs

Gift letters

Government grant money

Habitat for Humanity homes

Homebuyer counseling centers

Homebuyer seminars, fairs, classes

HUD/FHA foreclosures

HUD homes with easy financing

Interest rate buydowns

Interest rate buy-ups

Interest only mortgages

Lease-options/lease purchase

Lease-purchase agreements

Mortgage credit certificates (MCCs)

New home builder finance plans

Not-for-profit grant money

Option ARMs

Owner will carry (OWC)

Pledged collateral

Private mortgage insurance (PMI)

Reverse annuity mortgages

Second mortgages

Self-contracting

Shared equity

Shared housing/housemates

State mortgage bond programs

State VA mortgage programs

Subprime mortgages

Sweat equity

Tenant-in-common (TICs)

USDA Rural Development Loans (formerly FmHA mortgages)

VA assumable w/qualifying

VA mortgages

VA REOs with VA financing for non-veterans

Wraparounds

For the Answers You Need, Go Beyond Automated Underwriting

Some unthinking loan reps just plug your financial information into their computer AU system (automated underwriting) and provide an easy answer. Loan reps who follow a quick and simple approach not only fail to explore all choices, they slight you in a more seriously deficient way. Their "one size fits all" mindset ignores contextual data that explicitly reviews where you are now, where you would like to go, and the best way to get there. Never accept an AU-generated response, until you answer questions such as the following:

- What are your goals to build wealth?
- How do your household expenses differ (positively or negatively) from the affordability assumptions imbedded in the AU computer software?
- Do you spend, save, and invest to achieve your life priorities?
- How long do you plan to own the property?
- How can you improve your credit scores?
- How can you improve your qualifying ratios?
- What percent of your wealth should you hold in property?
- What types of real estate financing (other than those offered by the lender you're talking with) might best promote your goals for cost savings or wealth building?
- What types of real estate financing (other than those offered by the lender you're talking with) might best enhance your affordability?
- What type of property (fixer, foreclosure, duplex, fourplex, single-family house, condo, apartment building, commercial, and so on) might advance you toward your financial goals?
- How much would a larger down payment save you?
- Should you use a fixed-rate or an adjustable rate mortgage (ARM)? Given your situation, what are the risks and opportunities of each? Which choice offers the best trade-off of risk and return (quickest buildup of property equity)?

Although savvy loan reps can help you answer life-planning questions, the majority will not. The majority lack time, knowledge, and incentive to guide you. Loan reps are like car salesmen. They encourage you to buy product(s) they are selling. Would you expect unbiased auto advice from the sales agent at the Honda dealer? No? Then why would you expect unbiased advice from the loan (sales) rep at the Old Faithful Mortgage Company?

Recall the theme of *Mortgage Secrets*: First, take measure of yourself. Learn your choices. Arrange your property purchase and financing decisions to advance your life goals. A majority of borrowers err because they attempt to minimize their monthly payment rather than maximize their wealth.

Most lenders compare income to monthly payments, but you need more depth, more vision. Decide for yourself: Should you buy more (or less) property than an AU system suggests? Should you borrow more (or less) than this lender's guidelines recommend?

Practice Possibility Thinking

The folks who urge you to get preapproved for a loan rarely mention that you can choose from hundreds of loan products. Each of these products may vary as to interest rate, down payment, credit standards, monthly payments, mortgage insurance premiums, qualifying ratios, closing costs, eligible properties, occupancy standards, and many other terms and conditions. In fact, banks and mortgage brokers may not offer many of the best purchase and financing possibilities.

Sometimes you can even design and create a financing plan. Though most borrowers choose some off-the-shelf loan product, some lenders (and many sellers) will customize specifically—if you know how to ask, and what to ask for.

As you read through *Mortgage Secrets* and reflect upon the ins and outs of property finance, ask yourself, "Would this idea work for me (us)?" Today, financing options exist for nearly everyone who wants to own a home, refinance a home, or buy an investment property. Know the possibilities. Cut wasteful personal spending. Shape up your credit profile. Lift your credit scores. Look for ways to reduce the costs of your loan. Explore the many paths that lead to alternative financing.

As you will see, possibility thinking pays big returns.

SECRET # **2**

How you choose your property and arrange financing can add (or subtract) tens (or even hundreds) of thousands of dollars to (from) your net worth.

Do you think you want to own a single-family house, a condo, or coop? Before you decide for sure, answer this question: Would you instead be willing to live in a fourplex for three to five years if that choice plumped up your wealth by $100,000 or more?

Own a Rental Property; Boost Your Affordability and Wealth-Building

For purposes of loan "preapproval," most loan reps assume that you're buying a single-family house or condo. The loan rep might say that, based on your income and monthly payments, the bank would loan you $200,000. If you've got $50,000 for a down payment, you could look at houses (or condos) in the $250,000 price range.[1]

Now see how much more you could afford to borrow if you bought a fourplex, lived in one unit, and rented out the other three. Since your rental income from three units will expand your borrowing power, you could buy a property worth say $600,000 (instead of $250,000).[2]

If each of these potential properties appreciates at 4 percent per year, and if after five years the mortgage balance on each falls to 92.5 percent of the original balance, you can see in Table 1.1 how your equity would build with each property.

The part home, part rental fourplex expands your affordability and boosts your net worth by $173,250 (vs. $70,000 for the house). The fourplex more than triples your original cash investment. Although specific property

---

[1] Don't concern yourself with the specific dollar amounts used in this or other examples. Focus on the idea or technique. Naturally, your finances and the property prices in your area may run higher or lower than the numbers used as examples throughout *Mortgage Secrets*.

[2] *Mortgage Secrets* discusses the exact numbers in Chapter 2.

Table 1.1 **5-Year Equity Buildup**

	Single-Family House	Fourplex
Purchase price	$250,000	$600,000
Amount financed	200,000	550,000
Appreciated value @ 4 percent p.a.	305,000	732,000
Mortgage balance year five	185,000	508,750
Equity	120,000	223,250
Original down payment	50,000	50,000
Investment gain	70,000	173,250

results vary, this example shows the powerful wealth-building effects of leverage (OPM). With the fourplex, you employed other people's money to create your productive money.

Other Wealth-Building Ideas

Later chapters further show how your property purchase and financing decisions will impact your net worth 5 to 20 years in the future. You will learn to evaluate mortgage prepayments, short-term mortgages, fix-up properties, bargain-priced properties, foreclosures, real estate owned (REOs), and low-interest-rate financing.

Few homebuyers or investors compare thoroughly. Most people figure that their property will appreciate. Eventually they'll make a fair amount of money. No doubt, history proves them correct; however, history also shows that buyers who weigh and consider a range of property and loan choices can build much larger investment gains.

SECRET # **3**

Separate the emotional from the financial.

Avoid emotional impulses. Identify, clarify, and separate emotions from your financial goals and motives.

Personal versus Financial

Did you quickly dismiss the idea of buying a fourplex? Was it a gut emotional decision, such as "I don't want to call an apartment building home—even if I am the owner"? Or, did you look at the money that you could make and decide that even with an extra profit of $100,000, it's not worth it?

Subtle Distinction

Emotional decision makers quickly decide an issue according to their whims of superficial likes and dislikes. They pass by future fortunes for present comfort. For example, do you know people who drive new or nearly new cars with big loans but can't afford to save or invest in property? How many people turn down bargain-priced fixers because they don't want to make the repairs? How many renters remain long-term renters because buying would give them a longer commute or place them in a neighborhood that seems less desirable than where they currently live?

Just recently, I erred along these lines. (Yes, even pros can make mistakes—especially when they forget to follow their own buying rules.)

Emotional Delay (or Withdrawal)

In this case, the pro was me. I evaluated an investment property (a single-family house). The owner agreed to finance the property with just 5 percent down. The property was located in a neighborhood of professionals; it suffered no problems of disrepair or deferred maintenance. However, notwithstanding these advantages, a couple of features in the house turned me off. I hesitated to make an offer. Rather than quickly weighing all advantages and disadvantages, I focused only on what I didn't like.

That was a big mistake. The next investor who looked at the property bought it. My failure to quickly size up the opportunity cost me an excellent property that was offered with terrific seller financing.

Avoid Mistakes Similar to Mine

Separate the financial from the emotional—only then will you judge fairly whether the decision exposes you to more cost than benefit. As humans, we seem to be hardwired with emotional response. Yet, to build your financial future you can't let emotions control. Persistently weigh and consider. Yes, identify what you like and don't like, what you want and don't want. Then attach a dollar price tag. Don't think here and now. Think of your future returns.

Throughout *Mortgage Secrets* you'll discover dozens of property purchase and financing techniques. Each of these offers trade-offs. Some require effort, inconvenience, or discomfort that at first glance may seem unappealing. Please, though, leave that possibility in view until you've examined it closely. Do now what most people won't do. In 10 years, you'll do what most people never can.

SECRET # **4**

Align self-talk with your priorities.

Are you reading *Mortgage Secrets* to learn how to deal with shaky credit, low cash, affordability, and so on? Good! You'll find more creative financing ideas here than anywhere else. Yet to focus on creative financing begs the ultimate question: Why do you confront such financial issues? Are you managing your money as well as you could?

Self-Defeating Self-Talk Destroys Wealth-Building

Dr. Shad Helmstetter explains that we create our own difficulties (financial and otherwise) through self-defeating self-talk (*What to Say When You Talk to Yourself*, Pocket Books, 1987). Do any of the following statements creep into your self-talk?

- I can't remember names.
- I'm always running late.
- I can never get organized.
- I'm always short of money. I just don't know where it goes.
- No way could we ever save enough for a 20 percent down payment.
- No way could we ever afford a property in that neighborhood.
- Get qualified for a mortgage? Not with my credit.
- At the rate we're putting away money for retirement, I'll probably be working until I'm 75.

◆ I don't believe that infomercial hype. I know that I could never raise enough cash to invest in real estate.

◆ I just can't seem to lose weight.

According to Dr. Helmstetter, none of these self-descriptors actually states a fact. But they do determine your future. "The more you think about anything in a certain way," Helmstetter writes, "the more you believe that's the way it really is." And when you believe "that's the way it really is," you do nothing to solve the problem.

The complaint denies your ability to change your behavior. Self-denial vanquishes potential improvement. Now, here's how to bring about the results you really want.

Reprogram Your Thoughts to Deliver Self-Fulfilling Messages

Reprogram your self-talk. Erase your self-denying complaints. Never describe your behavior in self-demeaning ways. Give yourself a jolt each time you let self-denying assertions short-circuit your search to improve.

As you eliminate self-defeating self-talk, replace it with goal-promoting self-talk. Ask yourself questions. Brainstorm answers. Adopt attitudes and habits that advance you toward the life you would like to live.

For example,

◆ What are six ways that I can save more?
◆ What are six ways I can cut spending?
◆ What are four ways I can stop running up credit card bills and start paying them down?
◆ What are four ways that I can work toward a $1 million net worth within 15 years?
◆ How can I use real estate to help build wealth?

Ask questions that point to where you want to go. Invite solutions into your thoughts. With solutions in view, you motivate yourself to advance toward your goals. Determine how you must change. Create promises to yourself. Live those promises.

Does Self-Talk Work?

Absolutely! I rely on positive self-talk to help avoid all health problems; to maintain a vigorous program of diet, fitness, and exercise; to improve work productivity; and, yes, to save, invest, and spend wisely. Self-affirming, goal-directed self-talk gives you a promising outlook on life. Don't just take my word for it. Go to Amazon.com and search for Shad Helmstetter. His book has accumulated more than 50 reviews with a near perfect five-star rating.

Get Started Now

Review your spending, borrowing, saving, and investing. Where does your money go? Will your current money practices transport you to the life you want to live 5, 10, 20 years from now? Or look at it like this: At current rates of interest, each $100 per month you cut from your spending and instead devote to financing a property can add $15,000 to your borrowing power, and up to $50,000 (or more) to your future net worth.

Look at Table 1.2 and fill in the monthly amounts in each category. Do your spending, borrowing, and saving demonstrate a happy outlook for mortgage qualifying, property investing, and lifetime accumulation of $1 million (current dollars) or more?

If you doubt that money habits can power your wealth building, read *The Millionaire Next Door*, by Thomas J. Stanley and William D. Danko (Longstreet Press, 1996). You'll see that most people who become millionaires do so through saving and investing—not because they earn six-figure salaries.

Suggested Improvements

Do your spending habits show fits of extravagance, excessive borrowing, too little saving, and a general mismatch with your priorities? Yes? Then match your behavior to your self-made promises. Use these techniques:

- *Think priorities*. Think reward. Realign your money habits to promote your highest values. What do you want most for the next 10, 20, or 40 years?

Table 1.2 **Your Spending Profile**

Rent	$_____
Electricity	$_____
Gas	$_____
Cable TV	$_____
Internet charges	$_____
Online charges	$_____
Telephone(s)	$_____
Car payment no. 1	$_____
Car payment no. 2	$_____
Gasoline	$_____
Automobile insurance	$_____
Groceries	$_____
Child care	$_____
Clothing	$_____
Electronics	$_____
Lunches	$_____
Dining out	$_____
Entertainment	$_____
Tobacco	$_____
Beer, wine, liquor	$_____
Other vices	$_____
Health club	$_____
Magazines	$_____
Newspapers	$_____
Furniture	$_____
Appliances	$_____
School expenses	$_____
Health insurance	$_____
Weekend trips	$_____
Vacations	$_____
Housekeepers	$_____
Personal care	$_____
Credit card interest	$_____
Other	$_____
Total	$_____

- *Stop paying rent.* For most people who don't yet own their own homes, rent wastes money. Can you eliminate or reduce rent payments? Can you switch to a lower cost apartment? Can you house share? Can you find a house-sitting job for the next 3 to 12 months? Can you move back with your parents or stay rent free with relatives or friends? Bank your rent money for 6 to 12 months, and for the rest of your life you'll never pay rent again.

- *Cut your food bills in half.* Eliminate restaurant meals. Bring brown bag lunches. Buy unbranded foods in bulk. Prepare your food in large quantities and freeze portions in meal-sized servings. Locate a remainder and closeout grocery like Canned Foods, Big Lots, or Drug Emporium. Food prices in discount stores run 20 to 50 percent less than in big name supermarkets. When you find bargain-priced items that you use regularly, buy them by the case.

- *Cut your credit cards in half.* Stamp out credit card addiction. Throw away your needles. Adopt a strict cash diet. You will spend far less when you count out real cash. Besides, credit card balances zap strength from your constructive borrowing power. By the time you pay off your credit card balances at 18 percent interest, you pay back two (or more) dollars for every dollar you originally charged— and that's in after-tax, take-home dollars. Since you only take home 65 to 80 percent of what you earn, you have to earn more than $2,000 just to pay back every $1,000 you charge on your credit cards

- *Don't put the car before the house.* If you own a car that's worth nearly as much as a down payment on a house, sell it. Get rid of those cash-draining car payments. If the car(s) is (are) mostly paid for, a sale provides a good part of the cash you need to finance a property. If you are thinking about buying a more expensive car, stop! Until you can afford your perfect home, until you have built up the wealth you want, drive the least expensive, dependable car you can find. Use debt only to acquire appreciating assets. If property prices in your area do not offer a great risk/reward ratio, invest in other parts of the country—or the world.

- *Eliminate costly vices.* How much do you spend on cigarettes, beer, liquor, drinks at restaurants, clubs, or bars, illegal drugs, or other wasteful habits? Vices can easily squander $2,000 to $4,000 a year (or more).

◆ *Buy clothes in thrift shops.* Even if you're an up-and-coming investment banker on Wall Street, shop for bargains. How about an $1,800 Armani suit for $695 or an Emprio Armani silk paisley tie priced at $40? Both of these (and many comparable bargains) were available at GENTLY Owned in Atlanta. And these fashion items were new, bought at closeout. With recycled clothing, you can save much more. In her newspaper column, *Dress for Less*, Candy Barrie writes, "I'm a big fan of these [consignment and thrift] shops for their fashion bargains. . . . You'll discover we're not just talking about 20, 30, or 40 percent discounts. Sometimes you can get clothes for 90 percent off retail. Rather than give away their expensive clothes, some wealthy people place them in consignment and thrift shops."

Want to save money? Locate the recycled and closeout clothing stores in your area or a nearby big city. Whatever your tastes and price range, you'll find that you can slash your clothing costs by 50 percent or more. (Of course, you pocket even more savings when you resist buying all those clothes you don't need—regardless of their bargain price.)

◆ *Buy "preowned" furniture.* As with cars and clothing, many people who dream of building wealth spend too much too soon for furniture. And, instead of paying cash, they buy on credit. They chain themselves to years of payments at high interest rates. (Or increasingly, they are lured into those "no payments, no interest for six months" types of promotions that make slipping into a quicksand of debt all too easy.)

Most furniture depreciates in value faster than it depreciates in condition. You can find terrific preowned bargains. I have bought many beautiful pieces of high-quality furniture at prices far less than the cheap particleboard stuff that the discount stores carry.

When you buy clothing, cars, or furniture, let someone else suffer the depreciation. Pay only for the usefulness of a product. The less money you waste on depreciating assets, the faster you build wealth through home buying and other property investments.

SECRET # **5**

Envision the property(ies) you would like to own 5, 10, or 15 years from now.

At age 21, I bought my first "home." It was a large old house that had been converted into four apartment units and the garage converted into a fifth unit—which is where I lived. It was owner-financed with 10 percent down and a 5 percent interest rate land contract. At the time, my friends had fun kidding me about the "dump" and my "slumlording." (Actually, the property wasn't *that* bad.)

However, six years later, while enrolled in my PhD program at the University of Illinois, I owned (among other properties) a four-bedroom, two-bath, brick house that had previously belonged to the professor who chaired my doctoral dissertation. (Incidentally, he even financed it for me at 7 percent interest and 10 percent down.) Where were my friends living? Most lived in rental apartments. None lived in (much less owned) a home anywhere near as nice as mine. (I am not bragging—just trying to show the power of knowledge, goals, and action.)

What's the Moral?

As real estate prices throughout North America (and throughout the world) have skyrocketed during the past five years, many potential first-time buyers and investors feel frustrated. They hesitate to buy and invest. But if you hesitate, you will only lag further behind.

Renters: Make Ownership Your First Priority

Had I continued to rent when I was age 21, I would not have been able to own the upscale house I bought at age 27. Your best chance today to own the home you would like in, say, 5 or 10 years is to first become a property owner as quickly as possible. Weigh carefully the advantages of buying a property that makes you some quick cash (rental income, fixer-upper, bargain-priced foreclosure).

Do not complain that prices have gone through the roof (remember, push aside the self-denying, goal-defeating self-talk). Instead, create a financial plan that places you on the fast track to the property(ies) you really want.

Gain a Great Tax Break

Since 1998, tax law has permitted homeowners to sell their homes every two years and pocket their profits tax free (up to $250,000 for singles and $500,000 for married couples). This tax break means that you can buy a bargain-priced fixer-upper, renovate as you live in it, and then sell for a profit (the economy willing) in two years; then repeat as necessary or desired.[3]

Want to earn an extra $100,000 to $250,000 (more or less) in tax-free gains during the next four to six years? Weigh buy, renovate, and resell fixer-upper properties.

Summing Up: You Control Your Buying/Investing Power—Not the Lender

The "tell you exactly how much you can afford" approach to "preapproval" gives a snapshot photo of your property buying power—but only with that lender's camera. Instead, think of your life as a moving picture. You not only star in this movie, you write the script, direct, edit, and determine the ending.

Do you want to own your own home? Do you want to own investment properties? Do you want to structure the best way to finance your acquisitions? Would you like to seriously improve your net worth? Would you like to live free of destructive debt? Would you like to achieve financial independence? Yes.

Then start now. It's your movie. It's your move.

---

[3] For more on this technique, see Gary W. Eldred, *Investing in Real Estate*, 5th ed. (John Wiley & Sons, 2006) and *Make Money with Fixer-Uppers and Renovations* (John Wiley & Sons, 2003, 2008).

CHAPTER 2

Increase Your Borrowing Power

O kay, you realize that, to a much larger degree than most people believe, your borrowing power and your buying power depend on the knowledge you gain and the decisions you make. No genetic code predetermines your financial future.

If one lender or loan program doesn't work for you, choose from multiple other possibilities. If your current finances show weak spots, reshape them to strengthen your borrower profile. If your income falls short of what you need, figure out ways to earn more.

SECRET # **6**

10,000 lenders set their own standards.

Some loan advisors claim that the big national mortgage companies, Fannie Mae and Freddie Mac, set underwriting standards for nearly all mortgage loans. Fannie and Freddie actually account for less than 40 percent of the residential real estate financing issued throughout the United States. A big number, yes, but hardly all-powerful. Moreover, Fannie and Freddie do not perfectly mirror each other. Both Fannie and Freddie publish underwriting *guidelines*, not edicts.[1] Lenders who sell loans to Fannie and Freddie remain free to apply a reasonable degree of flexibility.

Portfolio Lenders

Lenders who don't sell their mortgages to Fannie, Freddie, or other players in the secondary mortgage market are called portfolio lenders. Portfolio lenders include many banks, savings institutions, credit unions, pension funds, and life insurance companies. Although Fannie/Freddie-affiliated lenders may exercise flexibility if they choose to, portfolio lenders can design any type of loan they like.

These portfolio lenders sometimes review Fannie/Freddie lending standards. Then they develop differentiated loan products for some targets of borrowers—for example, low credit scores, self-employed, no-documentation, low-documentation, stated income, stated assets, jumbo amounts over $417,000 (for single-family residences, multi-units provide higher conforming limits), no mortgage insurance, balloon notes, high qualifying ratios, income properties, farm land, rehab and renovation loans. Some portfolio lenders structure financing to meet the special needs of a single borrower—especially for investment properties.

Government-Backed Loans

Government-backed loans include a variety of loan programs that mostly (but not exclusively) appeal to homebuyers (and sometimes investors) who might face obstacles in borrowing from Fannie/Freddie or most portfolio lenders. Some of the more popular government-backed loans include:

- *Federal Housing Administration (FHA)*: The FHA specializes in low-down-payment, easier qualifying loans. FHA can issue loans where borrowers need no cash of their own for a down payment.

---

[1] Fannie and Freddie do set limits on the maximum amount of loan they will buy from their affiliated banks, savings institutions, and other mortgage lenders.

- *Department of Veterans Affairs (VA)*: The VA offers easier qualifying, no-down-payment mortgages to eligible veterans. The VA sells its foreclosed properties to investors and offers vendor financing on attractive terms. (At present, you can buy and VA finance with as little as 5% down, 6.5% interest, 30-years.)
- *Rural Development Administration (USDA)*: As part of the United States Department of Agriculture, this agency helps low- to moderate-income families buy homes with low down payments and low interests rates.
- *State mortgage bond programs*: These programs offer low-down-payment, lower-interest-rate loans. They target first-time buyers. First-timers include anyone who hasn't owned a home within the past three years.
- *Community development loans*: Many states and cities encourage homebuyers (and sometimes investors) to buy and fix up properties in designated neighborhoods. To achieve this goal, community re-development agencies frequently offer purchase and fix-up loans on favorable terms.

What All of This Means for You

With this quick trip through some common types of lenders and loan programs (more details in later chapters), I want to again drill into your consciousness that lenders differ, loan programs differ, and qualifying standards differ. No loan rep can ever tell you how much property you can buy, or how much money you can borrow. Specific loan reps can tell you how much (if any) money their funding sources will loan you. Never think of mortgage loans as peas in a pod. They're more like large baskets of mixed fruit with at least a few poisoned apples.

You can even get different answers from different loan reps who work for the same lender and are working with the same loan program. How well the loan rep packages your personal information, and how effectively the rep responds to underwriter (or computer) queries can make the difference between a no and a yes—as well as in the loan amount, terms, and costs.

SECRET # **7**

You can make your qualifying ratios look better.

For many (but not all) loans, lenders judge your borrowing power through their use of two qualifying ratios: the housing cost (front) ratio, and the total debt (back) ratio. Both the housing cost ratio and the total debt ratio give lenders a way to measure whether your income looks like it's large enough to cover your mortgage payments, monthly debts, and other living expenses (see examples below).

Run-of-the-mill loan reps will merely plug your financial data into their AU program. Savvy loan reps will do a "first review" and then, if desirable, suggest ways to improve your financial profile. The average loan rep approves or rejects. The savvy loan rep says, "Here's what you can do to make your ratios look better."

Calculating the Ratios

With the use of AU (automated underwriting), most loan reps no longer calculate ratios per se. Nevertheless, qualifying ratios matter a great deal. Only now, the math is hidden in the underwriting software program.

If you reduce your qualifying ratios, you raise the odds for loan approval and increase the amount the lender will loan you. Low ratios may also slice your interest rate and mortgage insurance premiums (if any).

Housing Cost (Front) Ratio

Figure your housing cost ratio with this equation:

$$\text{Housing cost ratio} = \frac{(\text{P\&I}) + (\text{T\&I}) + (\text{MI}) + (\text{HOA})}{\text{Monthly gross income}}$$

where: P&I represents principal and interest (the basic monthly
            mortgage payment).
         T&I represents the amount you pay monthly for property taxes
            and property insurance.

MI represents the monthly mortgage insurance premium you
may have to pay if you put less than 20 percent down.
HOA represents the monthly amount you may have to pay to a
condominium or subdivision homeowners association.

To keep things simple, say that your household income equals $7,000
per month. You need a loan of $235,000 to buy the property you want.
You prefer a 30-year, fixed-rate loan, which (based partly on your credit
score) is available at 7 percent interest. This loan will cost $1,563 per month
(235 × $6.65). See Table 2.1. Property taxes and insurance on this property
total $400 per month. No mortgage insurance applies, but you must pay
the homeowners association $125 per month to maintain the community

Table 2.1 **Monthly Mortgage Payment for Each $1,000
Borrowed at a Variety of Interest Rates and Terms**

Qualifying Interest Rate	15-Year	30-Year	40-Year
4.0	$7.40	$4.77	$4.17
4.5	7.65	5.07	4.50
5.0	7.91	5.37	4.82
5.5	8.17	5.67	5.16
6.0	8.44	6.00	5.50
6.5	8.71	6.32	5.85
7.0	8.99	6.65	6.21
7.5	9.27	6.99	6.58
8.0	9.56	7.34	6.95
8.5	9.85	7.69	7.33
9.0	10.16	8.05	7.71
9.5	10.45	8.41	8.10
10.0	10.75	8.78	8.50
10.5	11.06	9.15	8.89
11.0	11.37	9.53	9.25
11.5	11.69	9.91	9.68
12.0	12.01	10.29	10.08
12.5	12.33	10.68	10.49

swimming pool, tennis courts, and clubhouse. Here's how to calculate the housing cost ratio for this example:

$$\text{Housing cost ratio} = \frac{\$1,563 + 400 + 125}{\$7,000}$$
$$= \frac{\$2,088}{\$7,000}$$
$$= .298 \text{ or } 29.8\%$$

Because the lender with whom you are talking has set a housing cost guideline ratio of 28 percent, your numbers look reasonable. Next we figure the total debt ratio.

Total Debt Ratio

The total debt ratio includes housing costs plus your monthly payments for your installments (such as auto loans) and revolving (credit cards, department store accounts, and so on) debt. At present, your BMW hits you for a payment of $650 a month; the Impala adds in $280. Your credit card and department store balances total $8,000 and require a minimum payment of 5 percent of the outstanding balance per month ($400). Here are the figures:

$$\text{Housing costs + installment debt + revolving debt}$$
$$= \frac{\text{Total debt ratio}}{\text{Monthly gross income}}$$
$$= \frac{\$2,088 + 650 + 250 + 400}{\$7,000}$$
$$= \frac{\$3,388}{\$7,000}$$
$$= .484 \text{ or } 48.4\%$$

With this loan program, the lender prefers a total debt ratio or 40 percent or less. Whoops. Looks like you've blown through this ratio. But does this mean you won't get the loan? Will you have to settle for a smaller amount? Not necessarily.

If your credit score (see Chapter 5) looks strong, your loan may gain approval. If that possibility fails, lift your qualifying income, reduce your monthly payments, or talk up your compensating factors.

(Note: In the easy-qualifying loan markets that prevailed from 2000 until early 2007, lenders would often approve total debt ratios of 45, 50, or in some cases 55 percent. Currently, in the face of increasing foreclosures, some lenders are tightening their qualifying standards. Yet, no matter where a maximum debt ratio sits, you strengthen your borrower profile and increase your ability to negotiate approval, interest rate, and costs when you reduce your debt ratios to the lowest percentage possible.)

SECRET # **8**

Lift your qualifying income.

We previously *assumed* that your qualifying income totaled $7,000 a month. That was simple. In the real world, lenders qualify you according to a variety of actual and potential income sources such as:

- Salary
- Hourly wages
- Overtime
- Bonuses
- Commissions
- Scheduled raises
- Alimony
- Welfare/ADC
- Pension
- Tax-free income
- Child support
- Social Security income
- Unemployment insurance
- Self-employment
- Moonlighting/part-time job
- Tips
- Disability insurance

- Dividends
- Interest
- Consulting
- Rents (received from rental units you own or are buying)
- Annuities

Look through this list. Is your total income set precisely? Consider overtime, bonuses, commissions, self-employment, and tips. Over months or years, these amounts could jump up or down.

Or think about unemployment insurance. How could someone who's unemployed (or expects to become unemployed) hope to qualify for a mortgage? Well, I know a savvy loan rep who routinely gets unemployment insurance counted. His borrowers work during summer stock theater for good wages. Then during the off-season they collect unemployment. So, their qualifying income includes both their earnings from theater and their regular checks from the state unemployment insurance.

Remember, too, if you buy a two- to four-unit property, a lender will count 60 to 100 percent of your potential rent collections as part of your qualifying income. Typically, though, to count rental income you will need to provide the lender copies of the leases the existing (or to be) tenants have signed. For larger rental properties, lenders use a debt coverage ratio (DCR). To calculate DCR, divide a property's yearly net rental income (i.e., rents less property taxes, insurance, and operating expenses) by the total annual mortgage payments.

For example, assume a rental property's rental income (net of operating expenses) is expected to equal $50,000 per year and mortgage payments will total $40,000 per year. In this example, the DCR would equal 1.25 (50,000 ÷ 40,000 = 1.25). Typically, lenders prefer DCRs—depending on the type and quality of the property—in the range of 1.1 to 1.5.

Regular, Stable, Continuing

Lenders will count any income that you can show as stable, regular, and continuing. Usually, a two-year history with a realistic future is enough to satisfy a lender. On the other hand, what if during the past five years you've typically earned sales commissions of $4,000 a month, but during the past 12 months your income jumped to $6,000 a month? Now, you must persuade the underwriter that your more recent earnings better reflect your future earnings.

Or consider alimony or child support. You possess a court order that requires your ex-spouse to pay $1,500 per month. But sometimes you get paid; sometimes you don't. So, what amount will the lender count? This is a judgment call. How well can you explain away your ex's past irresponsibility? How persuasively can you show your ex will forever after pay as required?

Future Earnings

Sometimes lenders accept future earnings that may lack a past or a present. Imagine your spouse has just taken a new job in Topeka. You previously worked as a teacher but, for family reasons, took a leave of absence for the past two years. After your family gets settled in this new community, you again plan to teach full-time. Will the lender count these future earnings? With a good argument and evidence of intent, you can probably get at least part of this potential income included. In fact, Fannie/Freddie both issue liberal guidelines for "trailing spouses."

Recent college graduates or recent graduates of professional schools such as nursing, law, medicine, business, or engineering can also secure mortgages without immediate past or present income or employment. A contract for a new job may work to establish your qualifying income.

When Current Income Doesn't Count

For the past 12 years, you worked as a master mechanic at the local Ford dealer. You earned $5,350 a month. Then, six months ago, you got hooked on Amway products. You quit your job at Ford, and became an Amway sales distributor. Business was slow at first, but during the past three months you've cleared close to $25,000.

Will this income qualify? Sorry, your newfound success would not impress *most* lenders. They would tell you to reapply after proving your Amway sales skills for another 18 to 24 months.

Maximize Your Qualifying Income

To secure loan approval and maximize borrowing power, present your income history, current earnings, and future prospects as optimistically as possible. You must anticipate and respond effectively to any negative signals that may cause the lender to doubt the amount, stability, or continuing nature of your income.

Overcome the Negatives

If your earnings fell last year because you went back to school to gain education that will lead to a raise or promotion, make sure you tell the loan rep. If you earned $60,000 last year, but as of October 1 of this year you've taken in only $40,000, show the lender that your big earnings season runs from October to December. Provide evidence that typically you earn 40 percent of your yearly commissions during these three months, so you will actually exceed last year's income.

If self-employment earnings complicate your income, explain thoroughly. For complex situations, enlist your accountant. For example, show that your tax losses are matched by positive cash flow or strong business profits. You might point out that you draw a small wage or salary from the business to minimize your personal income taxes. Some loan reps won't understand these issues unless you guide them to the result you want.

Without a guide, some loan reps will figure your income too conservatively. They follow rules such as, "When in doubt, leave it out." Or, consider the two earnings patterns shown in Table 2.2.

Each of these earnings patterns shows average annual earnings of $45,000, and, respectively, recent earnings of $50,000 and $40,000. Common logic might hold that lenders would use a consistent method to calculate qualifying income from each of these patterns. But no. Without persuasive evidence from each borrower, the lender would probably qualify Jack using the three-year average of $45,000; and to qualify Jill, the

Table 2.2 **Earnings Patterns**		
Year	Jack	Jill
2001	$40,000	$50,000
2002	45,000	45,000
2003	50,000	40,000

loan rep would use the most recent income of \$40,000.[2] Why? Play it safe—unless you provide a realistic rationale.

Put Positives in Writing

Talk is cheap. Explanations sway hearts and minds only if put on paper. Lenders follow this rule: "If it's not in writing, it doesn't exist." Loan reps and underwriters need "protect your job" paperwork piled higher and deeper.

A paper trail doesn't just protect the frontline lending personnel. It protects lenders against repurchase requirements that Fannie, Freddie, or the mortgage insurer (or guarantor such as FHA, VA, or PMI) may impose on them. If a lender strays too far from secondary market guidelines, the buyer of the loans it sells may toss the losses back to the careless lender.

Also, nearly all lenders today monitor loan quality and file data integrity through internal audits. Without the paperwork necessary to justify their loans, the lender could run into trouble with regulators, stockholders, or bank insurers such as the Federal Deposit Insurance Corporation (FDIC). If you want a lender to view your past, present, and future income more favorably than it would otherwise, write out and deliver your evidence—before the loan rep and the underwriter formally review your application.

SECRET # **9**

Reduce your debt.

Can you easily manage your monthly loan payments? Or do you often run out of money before you run out of month? From the following list, total your current required minimum monthly payments.

- ◆ Car #1   ——
- ◆ Car #2   ——
- ◆ Car #3   ——

---

[2] Lenders would probably use income from the past two years and the year to date. However, this example illustrates the principle.

- Motorcycle —
- Jet ski —
- Power boat —
- Furniture —
- Student loan(s) —
- Appliance —
- Credit card #1 —
- Credit card #2 —
- Credit card #3 —
- Credit card #4 —
- Medical bills —
- Alimony —
- Child support —
- Merchant account #1 —
- Merchant account #2 —
- Merchant account #3 —
- Judgments/liens —
- Personal loans —
- Mortgage #1 —
- Mortgage #2 —
- Other —
- Other —
- Other —
- Other —
- Other —
- Total monthly debt repayments = $__

What to Count, What to Leave Out

To calculate the total debt ratio, lenders usually divide your monthly payments into two types: (1) installment debt, which includes self-liquidating debts such as autos, boats, medical bills, and student loans; and (2) revolving (or open) accounts which include Visa, Mastercard, AmEx Optima, Home Depot, Heloc (home equity line of credit), and any other types of credit lines that remain open until you or your creditor closes them.

Not All Payments Count

Most lenders delete payments for *installment* debts that are scheduled to be paid off within 6 to 10 months. However, if your auto lease will expire shortly, those payments may still count against you. The lender assumes (unless convinced otherwise) that you will continue to pay this expense because you soon will sign a lease for a new car to replace the old one.

You do, however, get a break for qualifying when lenders look at your revolving debt. Even if you regularly pay hundreds of dollars more per month than your minimum payment(s) due, most lenders will only count your payment as 5 percent of your outstanding balances. Or when less than 5 percent, your actual minimum required payments—providing you ask the lender to do so.

Prepare Well in Advance

As with proving your qualifying income, prepare your desired debt profile as soon as you can. Not only will this tactic lift your qualifying ratios, it *may* also boost your credit scores. Here are some tips:

- *Consolidate bills:* One payment of $280 a month will hurt you less than four payments of $125; however, don't close three accounts and then run one up close to its credit limit. Credit scoring doesn't like high balances relative to card limits.
- *Pay down debt:* If your installment debt has only 11 or 12 months to go, prepay two or three payments. That pushes those debts off the table and out of sight—under the rules followed by many lenders.
- *Pay off debt:* If you can swing it, get rid of as much debt as you can.
- *Avoid new debt:* The less your debt, the better you look. Even if you can afford them, avoid new loans.

Remember, destructive debt destroys your ability to build wealth; it destroys your ability to borrow constructively to finance wealth-producing assets such as real estate. You cannot achieve financial freedom if you enslave yourself to car loans, credit cards, and other degrading types of debt.

SECRET # **10**

Use compensating factors to justify higher qualifying ratios.

In this age of automated underwriting, some loan reps forget that the qualifying guidelines within their software programs do not rule absolutely. If you fail some "standard" loan rule, you can still gain mortgage approval if you stress your compensating factors.

Types of Compensating Factors

What types of compensating factors will lenders consider? Virtually anything positive that reasonably demonstrates that you will faithfully pay your monthly obligations. Here are a dozen examples:

1. Your rent payments equal or exceed the after-tax cost of your proposed mortgage payments.
2. You save every month. You spend less than you earn. You shun destructive debt.
3. You are traveling the fast track in your career. You frequently receive promotions and raises.
4. For your age and occupation, you've built a high net worth.
5. You maintain cash reserves to cover financial setbacks.
6. You or your spouse earn extra income through part-time work, a second job, tips, bonuses, or overtime.
7. You owe little or no monthly installment debt. No monthly payments often permits a higher housing cost ratio.
8. You've been through a homebuying counseling program that helps homebuyers develop a realistic budget. FHA, Fannie, and Freddie lenders give special deals to first-time buyers who complete such programs. Many last only four hours, and they're well worth the time.
9. You will make a down payment of 20 percent or larger.

10. Your employer provides excellent benefits: auto, cash reimbursement for a home office, a superior health and dental insurance plan, large contributions to your retirement account, and so on.

11. You earn an above average income. Budget-conscious people whose earnings exceed $4,000 or $5,000 a month often enjoy the financial flexibility to devote more money to housing than typical qualifying ratios indicate.

12. Your nonhousing living expenses sit below average. You explain that you can afford a higher mortgage because: The home is energy efficient; you can walk to work or just drive a short commute; you reject costly vices (smoking, drinking); you spend conservatively: you backpack for vacations, drive a cream puff 2002 Chevy, and buy clothes at outlet stores; you're handy with tools so you can perform your own household maintenance; your food costs are low because your parents supply you from their garden with all the fresh and home-canned vegetables you can eat.

Write Out Your Compensating Factors

After you list your reasons why you can afford the mortgage you want, don't just tell your loan rep. Explain in writing. Get supporting letters from your employer, minister, landlord, clients, customers, or anyone else who can vouch for your good character, creditworthiness, job performance, or personal responsibility.

Sometimes, too, it's a good idea to write out a family budget. Show your lender that your monthly income exceeds your monthly spending. (VA loans may actually require this step.) Then back up your budget with proof: financial records, cancelled checks, letters, and all of the compensating factors you can think of. With convincing written evidence, you'll break through qualifying guidelines that deter or delay ill-prepared borrowers.

These efforts do not merely help homebuyers; they also help beginning investors. Such preplanning conveys persuasive information about your ability to pay back the funds you borrow. It further shows the loan rep (and underwriter) that you prepare diligently and responsibly. You're not jumping into this investment without thinking it through.

SECRET # **11**

Never fib to a lender.

To stretch their buying power, more than a few borrowers stretch the truth. "Everybody fibs a little," they say. "Besides how's the lender going to find out?" Verifications, that's how. Even stated income or stated asset loans require that you state the truth. (If you prefer to avoid stating the truth, use a NINA (no stated income, no stated assets) product.)[3]

Verify, Verify, Verify—Then Audit

Most surely, except for "low doc" or "no doc" loan products that carry higher costs, lenders will check your income, assets, and debts. They may also want to see your divorce or separation agreement, where you're getting the money for your down payment, any gifts you claim to have received, bank and investment account balances, and virtually any other fact that stands material to your loan application.

Verification of Income

To verify income, your lender may call or write your employer, inspect your pay stubs, ask to see copies of your tax returns, and/or request your permission (Form 4506) to contact the IRS directly. To perform these checks the lender will compare all numbers obtained through third-party sources with each other and with those provided on your loan application. Should the lender discover (nontrivial) discrepancies, it will delay or deny your loan.

Confirm the accuracy of the figures you provide. Prepare to explain anything that a critical eye might view suspiciously.

Verify Debts

To verify the amount of your debts, the lender will obtain credit reports from the three major credit repositories (see Chapter 5). In addition, the

---

[3] This chapter tells how to best qualify for full-documentation loans. To avoid verifications (and pay a higher interest rate), request a "low doc" or "no doc" loan.

lender may ask you to provide your most recent monthly bank account statements. The lender may also run a separate check of public records to look for outstanding judgments or liens against you. Because discrepancies among debt balances are common, take care to provide evidence that the figures you show on your application reflect the truth.

For example, you may have paid off your car loan two or three months ago, but Experian still shows a balance of $1,400. If you can't get Experian to quickly correct its error, give the lender a copy of your auto title, lien satisfaction, and canceled check.

Other Verifications

To make sure you do not (improperly) borrow funds for your down payment, lenders may require you to provide bank statements from the past three months. If you're separated or divorced, previous joint debts with your (ex-) spouse will still show up on your credit report. Make sure you list these debts on your application. Likewise, should your divorce agreement saddle you with financial obligations, declare these, too. Even if they don't show up in your credit file, the lender will likely discover them by obtaining a copy of your executed divorce (separation) agreement.

The Application Itself Reveals Your Integrity

Most lenders carefully review your loan application. They search for numerical discrepancies, missing information, gaps in dates, inconsistencies, and any whiffs that smell fishy. "Hmm," the lender muses, "You say you've been out of college only three years, but you list no debts for student loans and you report cash savings of $25,000. How did you manage that feat?"

Experienced loan reps and underwriters have examined hundreds of loan apps. Their eyebrows raise easily. If your life story evokes an air of mystery, don't leave the loan rep in the dark. Turn on the light. Provide firm evidence that you're traveling the straight and narrow. Even innocent lapses in your application can spell trouble if you do not satisfactorily explain them.

Justify hard-to-believe items. Do not try to slip by an application that intends to deceive. The best lenders would rather solve your income, debt, or credit problems than loan money to someone they do not trust.

In testimony before Congress, the great banker J. Pierpont Morgan was asked:

Q. "Is not credit based primarily on money or property?"
A. "No sir, the first thing is character."
Q. "Before money or property?"
A. "Before money or anything else. Money cannot buy credit. Because a man I do not trust could not get credit from me on all the bonds of Christendom."

Take J.P. Morgan's advice. Don't play games with the lender. Report all income and debts truthfully. Not only does honesty result in greater borrowing power over the long run, it will keep you out of jail. Lying (or misrepresentation) on a mortgage application subjects you to thousands of dollars in fines and a lengthy visit to federal prison. (In recent years, many commission-hungry loan reps have conspired with borrowers to create "liar's loans." We will discuss this dangerous trend in a later section.)

SECRET # **12**

Can't qualify? Enlist a cosigner, co-borrower, or co-owner.

Okay, you've strengthened your borrower profile (income, debts, credit) and still your borrowing power's too weak to finance the property you want. Maybe you should bring in a cosigner, co-borrower, or co-owner. Here are some examples of how these techniques have helped first-time homebuyers—but they can also be adapted for use by investors.

Cosigners, Co-Borrowers, Co-Owners

"I'm not sure about this one," says loan officer Tiffany Lane to homebuyers Paul and Cindy Jackson. "Even counting both your incomes and 75 percent of the rents from the garage apartment, your qualifying ratios are high and your credit shows two 30-day late payments on your car loan during the past 12 months. I want you to get your home, but I'd feel more confident forwarding your application to the underwriter if we could get one of your parents to cosign your mortgage."

A cosigner guarantees to make your mortgage payments when you fail to do so. Usually a cosigner is a parent or other close relative. For borderline applications, a cosigner could tip the mortgage underwriter in your favor. Cosigners (sometimes called guarantors) can't change a flat turndown into an enthusiastic yes, but, in marginal cases where you look pretty good—but not quite good enough—a cosigner might strengthen your borrower profile enough to move your loan toward approval.

Co-Borrower (Co-Investor)

But what if your buying power needs more help? Then look for a co-borrower. Whereas a cosigner figures marginally in a loan approval, a co-borrower fully participates in the mortgage application process. Do your qualifying ratios blow past the loan program's limits? Add a co-borrower's income to your ratio calculations and bring them safely back into approval territory.

Use a co-borrower when, in the eyes of a lender, your *qualifying* income alone doesn't look like it will support the amount of money you want to borrow; however, the co-borrower need not actually help pay for the property or your monthly loan payments. If you can come up with the payments—by using housemates, accessory apartments, second job, self-employment, tight budgeting, or whatever—that's all right. The lender won't care where the monthly payments come from, as long as you make them on time.

Often, to obtain lender's approval, beginning real estate investors bring in co-borrowers or co-investors. The beginner might contribute the work of finding a good promising property; the experienced money partner gives the lender confidence that the deal makes sense.

Co-Owners

Lifelong renter, Mary Mills (age 74) had ruled out the possibility of owning her own home. Especially now, she believed herself too old and too short of income. But one day she read a flyer distributed by a Shaker Heights realtor, Frank Berry. This flyer explained a technique that Frank calls "co-op buying." Frank says, "It was something I stumbled upon. . . . I stumbled on it by talking to people. I learned that with so many people unable to buy houses by themselves, some do it as a team. Relatives and nonrelatives alike sometimes go together to buy their homes."

Intrigued by this idea, Mary Mills called her daughter-in-law. Yes, she, too, wanted to become a homeowner, but didn't think she could afford it by herself. So together, they contacted Frank to see if he could help them. Well, Frank was the right person to call. Within several months, Mary and her daughter-in-law became first-time homeowners. By combining their incomes, they were able to buy and move into their own duplex. Co-owning can work for homebuyers as well as investors.

Equity Sharing

Although for homebuyers co-ownership usually occurs among family or friends, some Realtors specialize in matching professional investors with homebuyers. This technique is called equity sharing. In exchange for part ownership of a property, tax shelter benefits, and appreciation potential, an investor will contribute a down payment, borrowing power, and sometimes part of the monthly payments. The homebuyer and the investor negotiate the exact terms of the agreement.

Many beginning (as well as seasoned) investors also use a variation of this technique—especially for fix and flip properties. One investor contributes cash and/or borrowing power. The other contributes time and talent.

SECRET # **13**

Let tenants pay your mortgage.

In my 1996 book, *Stop Renting Now!*, I advised, "To increase borrowing power, let tenants pay your mortgage. Choose a two- to four-unit rental property and live in one unit for a few years. Collect rent from the other units." Anyone who followed this advice would have multiplied their original investment many times over. Although Secret #4 introduced this topic, let's revisit this possibility.

Should You Buy a Two- to Four-Family Home (or Larger)?

"I'm trying to buy my first home, but without success," writes Lorrain Stark to real estate columnist and investor Robert Bruss. "My problem is that I do not earn enough to qualify for a mortgage. [Do you think] I should buy a two- or three-unit rental property . . . to provide income to help pay the mortgage?"

Bob Bruss responds that he thinks it's an excellent idea. In fact, that's how he got started in real estate. "My first [home]," Bob answers, "was a triplex where I lived in one unit. . . . The rental income provided the money for my mortgage payments. . . . My triplex wasn't my dream house . . . [but] few of us can afford to buy our dream home when we start out. Eventually, though, we can build equity and then move up to the home we really like." (As mentioned earlier, I got my start in real estate with a multi-unit property/home. That partly explains my enthusiasm for this approach.)

How to Finance a Two- to Four-Family (or Larger) Home

Every property financing technique you will learn throughout *Mortgage Secrets* is available for two- to four-family, owner-occupied properties. You can finance these multi-unit properties through FHA, VA, conventional (Fannie/Freddie), portfolio lenders, or seller-assisted financing. In fact, sellers help finance rental properties more readily than single-family homes. You can buy a two- to four-unit property with five percent down or less. If you can't pull the needed up-front cash from your bank account, bring in a co-investor as a partner. Investigate this alternative. You may find it easier to finance a two- to four-unit property than a single-family house.

Most five-unit (or larger) properties, however, and some nonconforming two- to four-unit properties can prove difficult to finance through a typical mortgage lender. If you locate a tough-to-finance property, the fact that lenders shy away from it—or maybe require a 20 to 30 percent down payment—could work to your advantage. The more difficult it is to finance a property through a financial institution, the greater the chance that the owner will offer seller-assisted financing.

Prices and Rents Vary by City and Neighborhood

If you live in Berkeley, Queens, or Georgetown, a well-kept fourplex might cost $1,000,000 or more. In Pittsburgh, Peoria, or Paducah, you can buy small multifamily investment properties for $200,000 or less. As to the relationship between rents and price, these, too, vary significantly by city and neighborhood. In Detroit, $100,000 multi-unit properties might generate $1,000 a month in rents. In Miami, a four-family unit that generates $2,500 a month in rents might sell for upwards of $500,000.

Nonetheless, no matter where you live, a two-, three-, or four-unit (or larger) investment permits you to venture into real estate at a much higher price than you could otherwise afford. You will build wealth faster through both amortization (paying down the mortgage balance) and price appreciation.

Lower Monthly Costs

An income property can boost your power to build equity in another way. Even though you may pay a higher price for a two- to four-family or larger property, you may pay less out-of-pocket for your own housing expense. To illustrate: Say a four-unit property costs $2,300 a month for principal, interest, property taxes, insurance, and upkeep. If you give up $750 a month from your building's rent collections of $2,750 a month because you move into one of the four units, the other three units will still pay you $2,000 a month.

Subtract that $2,000 of rental income from your outgo for mortgage payments and operating costs of $2,300 a month. You personally spend just $300 each month. You save $650 a month as compared to the $950 a month you would spend on a single-family house. Over five years, these monthly savings would total close to $40,000. If you raised rents each year and banked your housing cost savings, you could probably accumulate more than $50,000 over five years. Add these savings to your equity build-up. In many instances, you will have multiplied your original down payment three to five times over.

Share with Housemates

"My biggest accomplishment in Washington, D.C.," writes Doreen Bierbrier, "was buying a house and creating a management system for it that worked." Doreen describes her experiences in her book, *Living with Tenants: How to happily share your house with renters for profit and security* (McGraw-Hill, 1986).

"When I bought my first home," Doreen explains, "I was earning a modest salary. . . . I decided that the only way I could buy a house in a good neighborhood was to find one large enough to accommodate a couple of housemates who paid rent. If everything worked out, the rental income would cover more than half of my house payment and two-thirds of my utilities. Adding in tax advantage and appreciation, I figured buying a home would actually make me money. Even better, some time later when the house was paid off, I would own a valuable asset free and clear. . . . It's amazing how things fall into place [even when you think] you have no choice."

Generate Income with Your Single-Family Home

As Doreen points out, you can generate income from a house even if you choose to pass up a two- to four-family property in favor of a single-family. This sharing technique has been popularized in a dozen or more books with titles such as *Homesharing and Other Lifestyle Options*; *Housemates: A Practical Guide for Living with Others*; and *The Complete Roommate Handbook*. The latest U.S. Census reports that 8.3 million homeowners now share their homes with non-family members.

This idea worked so profitably for Doreen Bierbrier that she quit her modestly paying job and, within a year and a half, bought three more houses that she organized as houseshare room rentals. In fact, Doreen bought her second property using a VA assumable mortgage and borrowed the down payment from her father. Unfortunately, today, most lenders won't permit housemate rents to count as qualifying income, so, you may have to talk to a savvy mortgage broker who could find a willing lender. (Or you can use a co-borrower.)

John Walker jumped over the qualifying income problem. He asked his mother to come in as a co-borrower on his mortgage. That got him past the lender's scrutiny. After moving into his property, he found two housemates to pick up over half of his monthly mortgage payments. John's mother never paid anything.

Realtor Mary Rodriguez tells of one of her buyers who bought a house that was then rented by three women. Instead of evicting these tenants, the new buyer moved in with them. "He didn't even ask for the master bedroom," Rodriguez recalled. Although few lenders like to count housemate income in your qualifying ratios, many will count rent generated by a leased house (or condo)—if you can provide the lender a copy of the lease. So, you could buy and finance such a house and then, after you close, move in and share as did Mary Rodriguez's buyer. That could navigate you around the co-borrower issue.

Choose Your Property Carefully

If a houseshare could work as part of your investment strategy, buy a property that adapts itself well to roommate living. Privacy, security, location of entrances, noise, parking, as well as kitchen and bathroom access greatly influence appeal and livability. Before you buy, pose as a potential tenant and meet with other homeowners who advertise for housemates. Identify those house features that would appeal to you if you were to live as a roommate in someone else's property.

Also, size up the rental market to learn which features and locations pull the highest demand and rental rates. In expensive cities, room rents often range between $400 and $800 a month. Houseshare income can add $5,000 to $20,000 to your yearly income.

Personal Experience

I've seen this housesharing strategy work well firsthand. During the time I taught at the University of Virginia, I spent many weekends in Washington, D.C. To avoid hotels when in D.C., I participated in a houseshare. The fellow who was buying the house collected enough from me, his girlfriend, and one other housemate to cover two-thirds of his mortgage. And this house was no slouch—a $300,000 (16 years later, $1.3 million) Georgetown three-story townhouse. Although skeptical at first, I found the experience fun.

Likewise, Doreen Bierbrier enjoyed the personal side of housesharing. "For me," Doreen explains, "the advantages of sharing my house with tenants overwhelmingly outweighed the disadvantages. Housemates [not only] made it possible for me to buy and maintain a house at a time when most people told me my salary was too low to consider buying, [but also] tenants provided countless hours of companionship, laughter, and insights into everything from Republican fund-raising to Vietnamese cuisine— things I never would have discovered had I lived alone."

Accessory Apartments

Maybe you prefer not to share with housemates or buy a two- to four-unit property, but you do need more income to stretch your borrowing power. Then buy a house with an accessory apartment. These units are commonly known as a granny flat, garage apartment, carriage house, studio, efficiency, in-law quarters, or basement suite. In Vancouver, British Columbia, more than 100,000 single-family houses include basement suites. These so-called suites not only add to owner borrowing power, they somewhat ease the tight rental housing market in Vancouver.

An accessory rental allows you to share a house without disturbing your life. And it won't require the same level of management and upkeep that some multi-unit properties require. An accessory apartment can add $4,000 to $10,000 to your yearly income.

Create Your Own Accessory Apartment

If you can't find the property you want already equipped with a rental unit, create your own. That's what freelance artist Andrea Pogue did.

Andrea bought a three-story fixer-upper and converted the lowest floor into an accessory apartment that she rented to two sisters for $550 a month. When Andrea realized the income potential of her house, she carried her idea further. After the tenant sisters moved out, Andrea moved up to the third floor. She renovated the lower floors into two private units and rented each one for $750 a month.

"I don't earn much," says Andrea, "and I doubt that I'll ever become another Andy Warhol and make a fortune. So it's great to receive the rent checks. I'm now taking in $1,500 a month. That's enough to pay my mortgage and cover part of the property taxes and homeowners insurance."

— 41 —

Zoning and Inspections

If you intend to add an accessory apartment, find out whether zoning or building regulations might restrict your rights to operate the property as you have planned. Likewise, just as some houses work much better than others for houseshares, so, too, do some properties adapt more readily to apartment conversions. As you evaluate properties, visualize how well they might work for the rent-producing use you have in mind.

SECRET # **14**

Don't change your loan status.

Many borrowers believe that once their loan approval goes through, they're home free. Not true. The lender may continue to verify your employment (income) and monthly bills up to the time of closing.

A job change, a new car lease, or new kitchen appliances charged to your Sears credit card could give the lender the right to revoke your approval, yet still charge you for various mortgage costs such as application fees, appraisals, surveys, title checks. Even changes that you consider positive (such as a new job with a raise in salary) might cause the lender concern. "Is your new job really secure?" the lender might ask. Once you submit your application and the loan rep likes it, leave well enough alone. For an account of a humorous—yet frustrating—loan status dilemma, see Gary W. Eldred, *The 106 Common Mistakes that Homebuyers Make* (John Wiley & Sons, 2006, 4th ed.).

CHAPTER 3

Slash Your Cost of Interest

You know the drill, "Shop until you drop. Call lenders and search for the best rate. An interest rate just one-half percent lower than the competition can cut thousands of dollars from your total mortgage costs."

What's Right and What's Wrong with This Advice?

First, what's right. No question, save one-half percent on your mortgage interest rate and you put thousands into your pocket. Do shop for your financing and compare interest rates and other costs (see Chapter 9). However, dialing for dollars to find the best rate on a 30-year, fixed-rate mortgage (as most borrowers do) won't necessarily get you the lowest rate you are quoted.

Rate Quotes

No loan rep can know the interest rate a lender will charge you until after you've submitted your application for a loan. Interest rates for 30-year fixed-rate mortgages will vary according to your credit score, qualifying ratios, cash reserves, amount of down payment, type of property, and other variables the loan reps won't learn until they see all of your financial data. Moreover, mortgage rates change daily. No loan rep can confirm the rate you will pay until the day you lock or the day funding occurs (if you choose not to lock).

Loan reps who offer a lowball rate quote may set you up for bait and switch or other disreputable sales tactics (see Chapter 9). However, telephone rate quotes aren't the only problem. Many borrowers mistakenly assume that they should originate a new 30-year fixed-rate mortgage before they've fully explored their other financing alternatives.

Alternative Terms and Sources of Financing

Always compare interest rates and fees (as well as other terms discussed later) among a variety of loan products. Mortgage markets change. The best loan yesterday may differ from the best loan tomorrow. Plus, how long you plan to keep your loan should affect your choice. To slash your cost of interest, weigh the costs and benefits of a variety of loan products.

You save money when you locate a 30-year loan at a lower rate. But you can sometimes save far more when you select another type of loan.[1]

SECRET # **15**

Many borrowers who want a fixed-rate loan should choose 15 years, not 30 or 40.

For four decades, the 30-year, fixed-rate mortgage has ranked as the most popular loan product because it permits you to obtain larger amounts than a loan of shorter duration (though many lenders offer 40-year fixed-rate loans, few borrowers choose this product). With this "lower payment" advantage, the 30-year loan pleases most homebuyers and investors. More recently, though, many borrowers have begun to question this longstanding, often automatic choice of loans. Investors have favored adjustable rate mortgages (ARMs) and interest only products to enhance their cash flows. Homebuyers—especially those over age 40—have been choosing 15-year terms.

The High Costs of 30-Year Loans

Historically, not more than one out of five potential borrowers has carefully calculated the costs and benefits of 15-year as opposed to 30-year

---

[1] For purposes here, I'm ignoring the costly practices and loan programs of predatory lenders (see Chapter 8).

Table 3.1 Save with a 15-Year Loan: Interest Costs of 15-Year vs. 30-Year Loans at Currently Available Interest Rates

	15-Year Term	*30-Year Term*
Mortgage amount	$200,000	$200,000
Interest rate	5.9%	6.5%
Payment frequency	Monthly	Monthly
Monthly payment amount	$1,676.92	$1,264.13
Total interest paid	$101,846.91	$255,088.92
30-year extra cost		$153,242.01

mortgages. In thinking 30 years, borrowers focused on affordability. But they did not calculate their total interest costs and equity build-up.

Total Interest Costs

You will pay an astonishingly higher amount of interest with the 30-year loan relative to a 15-year loan. Your savings on the 15-year plan result from two sources: The 15-year loan can slice .25 percent up to .6 percent off the rate you might get on a 30-year loan, and you pay interest for half as long. Compare the interest costs shown in Table 3.1. These figures show you will pay $153,242 more for the pleasure of taking twice as long to pay off your mortgage—a pretty hefty cost disadvantage.[2]

(Note: I again emphasize that interest rate spreads for maturity risk (i.e., term of the loan) and default risk (quality of the loan/borrower) fluctuate. No consistent rules of mortgage selection apply. That's why you must compare a variety of loan products and loan terms. The loan/lender that looked best last week, last month, or last year may not still look best at the time you're originating (refinancing) your loan.)

Equity Build-Up

Now, think how your choice of financing will add to (or diminish) your future net worth. Look at Table 3.2. Not including appreciation, the figures

---

[2] To calculate and compare precisely, figure in principal reduction and tax deductions. These complexities won't significantly change the results for most borrowers.

Table 3.2 **Equity Buildup Due to Mortgage Paydown: 15-Year vs. 30-Year**

	15-Year Term	(Balance)	30-Year Term	(Balance)
Original loan	$200,000	($200,000)	$200,000	($200,000)
Total paydown @ 10 years	113,048	(86,952)	30,466	(169,534)
Total paydown @ 15 years	200,000	(−0−)	54,898	(145,102)

show that the 15-year mortgage grows your equity much faster. After 15 years, you've paid off the full $200,000. But with the 30-year loan, after 15 years you still owe a whopping $145,102.

Alternative Use of $412 per Month

If you're a savvy investor, you may say "Hold on here. The cost and equity advantages illustrated in these tables ignore the extra $412 a month that I will have to pay to reap these interest-saving advantages." You may figure that you could invest $412 each month and earn (over the long term) a rate of return of 10 percent a year. After 15 or 20 years, your pile of investment funds would outweigh the interest savings and equity build-up that the 15-year borrower receives.

Indeed, many property investors select their financing to maximize their annual cash flows and use of leverage (OPM). These investors try to build portfolio equity, not max out their equity in any one property. This strategy can yield big returns—and in my early days of investing I followed this path. It does, though, create more investment risk.

We go through some calculations along these lines in Chapter 10. For now, recognize that the 15-year benefits shown result without risk. Choose investments that promise yields of 10 percent, 12 percent, or higher and you could end up with lower returns or even lose your principal. Home equity typically offers more security than stocks, bonds, or rental properties (see *Mortgage Secret* #98).

Equity Build-Up with Appreciation

True, 30-year (or 40-year) terms help you qualify for higher priced properties than 15-year loans. Nevertheless, if you buy a lower-priced property,

Table 3.3 Equity Buildup Due to Mortgage Paydown of $151,000: 15-Year vs. 30-Year (no assumed appreciation)

	15-Year Term	(Balance)	30-Year Term	(Balance)
Original loan	$151,000	(151,000)	$200,000	(200,000)
Total paydown @ 5 years	35,502	(114,498)	12,799	(187,201)
Total paydown @ 10 years	65,578	(85,422)	30,466	(169,534)
Total paydown @ 15 years	151,000	(−0−)	54,898	(145,102)

Both loans require a payment of $1,264 per month.

the wealth effect may favor that choice. Say you want to pay $1,264 a month for principal and interest. That size of payment and a 15-year, fixed-rate loan amortizes $151,000. Yet, you may still build equity faster with the 15-year term (see Table 3.3).

Now assume that you plan to trade up properties in five years. With either mortgage/property, you would place $20,000 down. This means that with the 15-year mortgage, you bought a property priced at $171,000; with the 30-year, a $220,000 property. Each property appreciates at 3 percent a year. Table 3.4 shows how your total equity would grow.

Or, what if we assume a 5 percent per year rate of appreciation (see Table 3.5).

Again, even a 5 percent a year appreciation rate builds equity quicker with the less expensive house and a 15-year mortgage versus a more expensive property and a 30-year term. In this example, you would need an

Table 3.4 Total Equity Buildup (3% Appreciation) @ 5 Years

	15-Year Term	30-Year Term
Purchase price	$171,000	$220,000
Appreciated value @ 3% p.a.	198,531	255,420
Mortgage balance @ 5 years	114,498	187,201
Total equity	$84,033	$68,219

Table 3.5 **Total Equity Buildup (5% Appreciation) @ 5 Years**		
	15-Year Term	*30-Year Term*
Purchase price	$171,000	$220,000
Appreciated value @ 5% p.a.	219,393	282,260
Mortgage balance @ 5 years	114,498	187,201
Total equity	$104,895	$95,059

8 percent annual appreciation rate before the 30-year mortgage actually gave you a larger equity after five years.

Common advice says buy the most expensive property you can afford and you will build wealth faster through leverage and appreciation. But this advice can err. For many borrowers in many cities, the 15-year term, even on a lower-priced property (holding payments the same) can provide larger and safer returns.

Please note. *Mortgage Secrets* does not specifically encourage you to use a 15-year fixed-rate term. But before you automatically decide on a 30-year term, ask a loan rep to work through the numbers with you. From a wealth-building view (other things equal), the 30-year, fixed-rate loan on a higher-priced house proves superior only during periods of high rates of appreciation.

(Remember, for this example, we have assumed that you make the same sized monthly payment regardless of the mortgage/property you choose. Naturally, in terms of wealth building, the 2- or 4-unit property, when financed with a 15-year loan, grows your equity faster than a single-family property would.)

SECRET # **16**

Lower interest rates mean big savings.

You already know that lower interest rates save you money, but do you know how much? Look at Table 3.6. See the striking difference in total interest costs between 15-year and 30-year loans. Also, recall that lenders sometimes charge about one-half percent less for 15-year rates. If, say,

Table 3.6 **Total Interest Costs per $100,000 @ Selected Interest Rates**

Rate (%)	Monthly Payment ($)	15-Year (Total Interest, $)	Monthly Payment ($)	30-Year (Total Interest, $)
4.0%	740	33,128	477	71,864
4.5	765	37,628	507	82,376
5.0	791	42,326	537	93,248
5.5	817	47,060	568	104,372
6.0	844	51,884	600	115,820
6.5	871	56,798	632	127,520
7.0	899	61,784	665	139,508
7.5	927	66,860	699	151,712
8.0	956	72,008	734	164,132
8.5	985	77,246	769	176,804
9.0	1,014	82,556	805	189,656
9.5	1,044	87,956	840	202,544
10.0	1,075	93,428	878	215,900
12.0	1,200	116,018	1,028	270,296
14.0	1,332	139,706	1,185	326,564

All figures are rounded.

market rates were 6.0 percent (15-year) and 6.5 percent (30-year), the loans would cost $51,884 and $115,820, respectively—a savings of nearly $65,000 for the 15-year term (per each $100,000 borrowed). For a historical comparison of interest rates and maturity spreads, Google "Treasury yield curve."

Even when you compare the 15-year or 30-year terms at the same interest rate, you still might save a pile of $1,000 bills.

SECRET # **17**

Lower rates magnify borrowing power.

You know that lenders look closely at your income and debt levels to determine how much they will lend you. High debts or low *qualifying* income can reduce your borrowing power. In addition, rising interest rates will slice your borrowing power because they increase your monthly payments per dollar borrowed. See these relationships in Table 3.7.

If, after looking at your income and bills, a lender says you can budget $900 a month for your mortgage payment (principal and interest), you could borrow $150,300 at 6 percent interest, but only $102,600 at 10 percent. The figures in Table 3.7 again reinforce this point: To increase borrowing power and slash interest costs, find lower rate financing. How do you do that? Here are eight possibilities that you will learn in this and later chapters.

1. Consider an adjustable rate mortgage (ARM).
2. Call state and local housing finance agencies to find mortgage bond money.
3. Search for a lower-rate mortgage assumption or "subject to" purchase.
4. Buy from a builder or developer who offers below-market interest rates.
5. Weigh the benefit of paying points as a trade-off for a lower interest rate.
6. Ask the seller to pay for an interest rate buydown.
7. Use a wraparound or a blended rate mortgage.
8. Use lower rate/costs seller financing.

Table 3.7 **How Much Can You Borrow at Various Interest Rates and Monthly Payments?**

Monthly Payment (P&I, $)	4% ($)	6% ($)	8% ($)	10% ($)	12% ($)
400	83,800	66,800	54,500	45,600	38,900
600	125,800	100,200	81,700	68,400	58,300
750	157,200	125,200	102,200	85,500	72,900
900	188,700	150,300	122,600	102,600	87,500
1,000	209,600	166,900	136,200	114,000	97,200
1,250	262,100	208,600	170,300	142,500	121,500
1,500	319,100	250,400	204,400	171,000	148,800
2,000	425,466	333,783	272,465	227,943	198,350

Term = 30 years.

SECRET # **18**

ARMs sometimes offer greater borrowing power and lower costs, with risks you can manage.

To help borrow a larger amount, many people rely on ARMs. In practice, (though Freddie Mac, regulators, and critics—who think ARMs attract too many people who borrow more than they can afford to repay—are pushing for restrictive changes), an ARM will qualify you for a larger loan than a fixed rate (other things equal). However, besides the qualifying advantage, ARMs may also save you substantial interest costs.

At first you might think, "No way would I take an ARM. Rates may head up. I want to sleep well, not toss and turn worrying about skyrocketing mortgage payments."

Yet, after you figure the benefits, costs, and risks, you might find that some types of ARMs clearly beat the 30-year fixed-rate mortgage.

Caveat: No set cost-benefit relationship prevails. Sometimes ARMs look attractive relative to 30-year, fixed-rate mortgages; sometimes their advantages narrow or disappear. Terms and rates also vary among lenders. Rather than sell to Fannie Mae or Freddie Mac, some lenders hold ARMs in-house. These *portfolio* lenders set their own rules and rates rather than follow the standards issued by the secondary mortgage market. So, shopping for ARMs may turn up a bargain. Consider the experience of the Klar family from several years back.

The Klars Save a Bundle

Through smart shopping for their one-year, adjustable-rate mortgage, Neil and Eileen Klar located an ARM with a start rate of 4.25 percent—well below the then-average initial ARM rate of 5.71 percent. During their first year, the Klars made payments on their $450,000 mortgage of around $2,200 a month. The fixed-rate mortgage they were offered at the time carried an interest rate of 8.875 percent and would have required payments of $3,580 a month—which meant a first-year out-of-pocket savings of $16,560 for the ARM.

— 51 —

Even if the Klars had been hit with maximum annual increases in their ARM payments due to rising interest rates, it would have taken nine years for their total ARM payments to catch up with the fixed-rate payment they were alternatively offered. By that time, they may have moved on to another property. Or, with inflation then running at 2.5 percent a year, the chances looked good that fixed rates would fall substantially. The Klars would then refinance. Either way, they were nearly certain to come out ahead with their ARM.

As it turned out, the Klars figured right. When they refinanced several years later, their full savings, relative to their fixed-rate alternative, totaled $58,371.

The Buchleightners Used a Hybrid

Many borrowers choose a hybrid ARM. These ARMs, often referred to as 3/1, 5/1, or 7/1 options, offer a set rate for a period of years, then morph into ARMs that adjust yearly (e.g., a 3/1 means fixed rate for three years, the adjustable each year thereafter).

Walter and Sara Buchleightner found a competitively priced 3/1 ARM. Their $200,000 loan started with an interest rate of 6.37 percent, which held steady for three years. After that, it adjusted once a year for its remaining 27-year term. By choosing a 3/1 hybrid, Walter and Sara cut their mortgage payment from $1,599 a month for the then-proposed 9 percent fixed-rate plan to $1,240 a month for the ARM they selected.

Explaining why they were attracted to this particular ARM, Walter says, "Paying $1,240 a month sounded so good. I shopped the mortgage market and I had people quoting me a full point higher."

Would You Rather Do the Two Steps?

With most ARM hybrids, the mortgage interest rate is fixed for three, five, or seven years and then adjusts annually for the remaining term of the mortgage. In contrast, a two-step (5/25, 7/23/ 10/30) starts with a low interest rate; then after the initial fixed-rate period of, say, 3, 5, 7, or 10 years, the interest rate adjusts to market and then holds constant for its remaining years. However, if the market for fixed rates stands higher at the time of adjustment, you could refinance into another lower cost ARM.

Which Type of ARM Is Best?

No firm conclusions apply to ARMs. They come in all shapes, sizes, and combinations. There are as many models of ARMs as there are models of automobiles. Models change just as quickly, too.

Most experts say, "If you plan to own a property for just a few years, select an ARM and gain from its lower start rate." That advice sounds reasonable, but it doesn't always hold true. Sometimes, the mortgage yield curve flattens or inverts. During these times, short-term loans (ARMs) can actually cost more than longer-term loans. We experienced that situation in the early 1980s, the late 1980s, and throughout 2006–2007.

In most years, ARMs do provide short-term cost savings. The experiences of the Klars and Buchleightners show that if you shop the mortgage market, you may discover a bargain-priced adjustable that lifts your buying power while saving you thousands of dollars in interest expense. Compare a variety of ARM models; then decide which plan can best stretch your buying power, save you money, and, through low annual and lifetime caps, minimize your future risk of payment shock. (*Mortgage Secrets* discusses the various detailed features of ARMs in Chapter 4.)

SECRET # **19**

State and local housing finance agencies offer lower-interest mortgage loans.

Congress enacted legislation that permits states, counties, cities, and various government agencies to offer below-market home loans. Under these programs state and local governments sell tax-free bonds to Wall Street (or European or Asian) investors to raise low-cost mortgage money. The government then uses this bond money to make lower-interest-rate loans available to first-time homebuyers (usually defined as anyone who hasn't owned a home for at least three years, or possibly homebuyers who have recently divorced and now want to buy a home on their own).

To locate a bond program in your area, ask knowledgeable Realtors and mortgage lenders. Closely read mortgage loan and real estate ads. Look for words such as "bond money" or "bond financing." This type of mortgage money might be referred to by the abbreviated letters of the issuing government agency, such as:

+ GRFA (Georgia Residential Finance Agency)
+ THDA (Tennessee Housing Development Agency)
+ CHFA (California Housing Finance Agency)
+ NJH & MFA (New Jersey Housing and Mortgage Finance Agency)
+ MHDC (Missouri Housing Development Commission)
+ MSHA (Maine State Housing Authority)

This list only samples bond finance programs. To investigate further, telephone the community finance, housing, or redevelopment agencies run by your state, county, or local governments. Many of these same government offices offer down-payment assistance to first-time homebuyers (see Chapter 6).

Stay Alert: Bond Money Comes and Goes

Since governments do not offer unlimited amounts of bond money to finance home mortgages, stay on the lookout for this type of financing. It comes and goes. Likewise, interest rates for these programs fluctuate. Bond money typically shaves one-half point off the current market interest rate. Some programs, especially those directed toward low- to moderate-income families, might cut their interest rate by two percentage points or more. Either way, you've boosted your buying power and slashed your interest costs. Check out the low interest mortgage loan programs that your state and local housing finance agencies offer now or plan to offer in the future.

SECRET # **20**

Assume a low-interest-rate mortgage.

When market interest rates climb, escape from those higher rates. Shop for a property that's already financed with a lower-interest-rate assumable loan. Imagine it's three years into the future and you want to invest in a home or rental property. Market interest rates are fluctuating between 8.0 and 9.0 percent. You recall those bygone days when 30-year fixed-rate loans were at 5.5 to 6.0 percent. If you could only step into a time machine and return to the past.

No Time Machine? Then Return to the Past with an Assumable Loan

When you assume a mortgage, you roll back the clock and take over the mortgage of the seller at the same interest rate the seller is paying—even when that rate sits below the current market. Years ago, nearly all sellers could transfer their low-rate mortgages to their buyers. By the early 1980s, however, many lenders had changed their mortgage contracts to include the notorious "due on sale" clause. This clause gives the lender the right to call a loan due if the borrower sells (or lease-options) the property to a new buyer.

Many people erroneously believe that *all* assumption possibilities have died. In fact, loan reps rarely tell borrowers about assumptions because assumptions take place between sellers and buyers. You cannot walk into a lender's office and say, "I'd like one of those low-rate, assumable mortgages that's going to save me tens of thousands of dollars." Before you can assume a real estate loan, you must locate a seller who has one.

What Sellers Can Offer Assumable Financing?

Generally, sellers who finance their properties with FHA, VA, or some types of adjustable rate mortgages can offer an assumption to their buyers. Realtor Roger Rodell described his experience with assumables during a past period of high mortgage rates.

Roger said, "I promote low-interest assumable FHA/VA mortgages. Buyers need to qualify to assume these loans. And some lenders I deal with aren't eager to push through loan assumptions for a few hundred dollars in transfer fees (compared to the several thousand dollars they earn for new loan originations). But the lower rates and monthly payments make qualifying easier, and the cash savings for buyers are tremendous. If a fairly priced home with a low-interest rate assumable hits the market, I tell my buyers to go for it. Don't try to pull the sellers down. When there's a pile of thousand dollar bills sitting in front of you, don't get greedy and demand an even better deal.

"I've worked out the numbers," Roger continued. "Over a period of five years on a $100,000 loan, as compared to a 9 percent new mortgage, a 7 percent assumable will save you $8,400 in interest. Over 10 years, the savings are nearly $17,000; over 25 years, you'll keep an extra $42,000. And those numbers don't include the $2,000 to $4,000 that an assumable might save you in points, origination fees, appraisal, and closing costs.

"Or here's another way to figure it," explained Roger. "Let's say your low-interest assumable saves you $135 a month over the amount you'd pay with new financing. If you bank those savings every month in an IRA or 401(k) plan that earns a return of just 6 percent a year, after 25 years your accumulated savings with interest will amount to $93,200. Now you can see why I refer to a good low-interest assumable as a pile of thousand dollar bills."

Short-Term Strategies

In some situations, you might gain by assuming a mortgage that carries a higher-than-market interest rate. Say, current rates hover around 6.5 percent and you're negotiating with a seller whose assumable mortgage shows a rate of 7.5 percent. Not worth assuming? Don't jump to that conclusion. Assumptions usually cost less in terms of time, effort, and cash-to-close than new mortgage originations; therefore, this higher rate, 7.5 percent assumption could prove profitable under short-term strategies such as the following:

- You plan to own the property for only a year or two.
- Inflation has dropped and interest rates seem sure to fall further. You want to time your new mortgage to coincide with the market bottom that you foresee.
- You plan to improve the property to increase its value. Then, you'd like to get a new loan based on this higher improved value.
- Your borrower profile displays some warts. New financing at the lowest rates available could prove iffy. To qualify for the assumption probably won't require the same exacting standards. One or two years of perfect payments could set you up to then qualify for a refinance as an "A" borrower.

How to Find Assumables

Millions of outstanding FHA/VA loans (fixed-rate and adjustable) permit assumptions. In addition, most conventional (Fannie/Freddie) and portfolio lenders will allow sellers to transfer their adjustable-rate loans to buyers. Also, many investor mortgages on larger apartment, office, and retail properties permit assumptions by buyers. To find assumable loans requires you to ask and investigate. Sellers (or their realty agents) may not know or publicize this fact. On the other hand, when interest rates shoot up, the search for assumables becomes intense. Savvy sellers and agents then tout their assumables to favorably distinguish their properties from others that require buyers to obtain costly new loans.

Lower Rate Assumable ARMs

Nearly all adjustable-rate mortgages include lifetime rate caps. No matter how high market interest rates climb, ARM borrowers know that their loan rate will max out at, say, 8, 9, 10, or 12 percent. Consequently, in periods of extraordinarily high rates, you can find ARMs that are maxed out—or close to maxed out—yet still sit below the going rates for new 30-year, fixed-rate mortgages. In that case, your (assumable) ARM rate can't go up much, but it can go down.

SECRET # **21**

"Assume" a nonassumable mortgage.

Most non-FHA/VA long-term fixed-rate residential mortgages include a so-called "due on sale" clause. This clause reads (in part) as follows:

> ¶ 18. If all or any part of the [mortgaged] property or an interest therein is sold or transferred by the Borrower *without Lender's prior written consent*... *Lender may, at Lender's option, declare* all the sums secured by this Mortgage to be immediately *due and payable*.

Few people read the precise wording of this clause. Yet that wording proves more favorable than commonly believed.

What This Clause Does and Does Not Say

Notice that nothing in this clause prevents owners from selling their properties to buyers without paying off their mortgage. This clause only gives lenders the right to call the mortgage due and payable if such a transfer occurs without "Lender's prior written consent."

You Can Assume a "Nonassumable" Mortgage

Nothing prevents a buyer and seller from asking a lender to give its written consent. Why would the lender agree to accept your request? Here are several reasons:

♦ The sellers owe four months back payments. You agree to bring the mortgage payments current.
♦ The interest rate on the mortgage equals or exceeds the current market rate. Lenders hate "portfolio runoff" of their market or above-market rate loans.
♦ You, the sellers, or both parties give the lender substantial business such as loans, CDs, savings, and checking accounts.
♦ You or the sellers promise to move much of your banking business to the lender.

Will these or other reasons motivate the lender to consent? Sometimes yes, sometimes no, but you won't know until you ask. When you offer persuasive evidence, lenders will approve "nonassumable" assumptions.

When looking at properties, most people ask the wrong question and get the wrong answer. "Is the financing assumable?" they query. If the mortgage includes a "due on sale" clause, the sellers or real estate agent will answer, "No, the mortgage is not assumable." Wrong answer. The correct answer is, "Yes, it's assumable if lender consents. Would you like to assume it? We can submit your proposal to the lender."

Buying Subject to: "Assuming" Without Consent

Again notice that the wording of Paragraph No. 18 does not stop the owners from selling a mortgaged property to anyone they choose to. Nor in such sales does it *require* the sellers or the buyers to pay off the loan. The "due on sale" clause merely gives the lender the right (or option) to call the loan due.

Sometimes when buyers and sellers believe that a lender won't allow an assumption, they complete the sale and never inform the lender that the owner has sold the property. The buyer then makes payments to the lender on the same terms and interest rate that applied to the seller. Contrary to what some people say, this "subject to" technique is neither illegal, immoral, or fattening. Nor does it violate the mortgage contract. Nevertheless, the "subject to" technique may rattle the nerves of buyers and sellers.

Risky Business for Buyers. If the lender learns of the sale, it might mail the seller a nasty letter and demand a very large check. With the loan called due, someone would quickly need to pay off, refinance, or negotiate a settlement with the lender. Weak borrowers who can't come up with the cash, credit, or negotiating power to satisfy the lender face foreclosure. The buyers may lose the cash they've invested in the property. On the other hand, if you are financially strong enough to deal with this "call" potential, your risks are low. You simply refinance (obtain a new loan).

Risks to Sellers. Typically, under a lender-approved mortgage assumption, the lender qualifies the buyers of the property. When the buyers gain approval, the lender releases the sellers from liability on the mortgage note. Whatever happens to that mortgage in the future does not concern the sellers or their credit record.

Not so with "subject to" transfers. In those cases, the seller's credit and finances remain at risk for as long as the mortgage remains outstanding. If the buyer pays the mortgage late, the lender forwards scurrilous remarks about the seller to the credit bureau. If the property goes into foreclosure, the lender will chase down the seller for any money (deficiency) judgments the court awards it.

Is This Technique Worth the Risks? Yes, for creditworthy, financially strong buyers, and for sellers who adequately protect themselves against the buyers' default. I have used "subject to" financing on several occasions. In 1981, for example, market mortgage rates were at 16 percent. I bought a property "subject to" that carried a mortgage rate of 10 percent. Because this property was a "flipper," I resold after 18 months but, during that short period, the "subject to" mortgage saved me $17,000 in interest, points, and closing costs.

Amateurs Beware. Several current authors promote "subject to" purchases to those "no cash, no credit" buyers who probably should not buy until they have strengthened their fiscal fitness. Here's my advice: Amateurs beware! Although this technique can prove appealing in some situations—short-term holding periods, high interest mortgage environment, credit impairment—don't get in over your head or take on risks that you cannot deal with successfully. "Subject to" financing presents rewards *and* risks to sellers and buyers. Measure both.

Will Lenders Really Call the Loan? The gurus say, "Not a problem. Here's a bag of tricks. Use these tricks, and the lender won't find out about the property transfer. Surely, what the lender can't see won't hurt you. Just keep the lender in the dark."

Do these tricks work? Not likely for any extended period of time. After suffering through the high loss 1980s and early 1990s, lenders have become far more watchful. Within a year or two, at most, the lender will probably discover the transfer.

"No worries mate," the gurus say. "Even if the lender discovers the transfer, chances are it won't call the loan due. Most lenders follow a 'don't ask, don't tell' policy. They're not going to advertise their waiver. As long as your monthly checks keep flowing in on time and the property taxes and insurance get paid, your risks are small." On this point (for now at least), I agree, because interest rates on most "subject to" mortgages today do not sit much below market rates. If interest rates spike up, though, lenders may send out their enforcers. So, although you can wisely buy "subject to," prepare to refinance, sell, or renegotiate should the lender demand payment (i.e., accelerate the mortgage note).

Table 3.8 **MHFA's MCC Program**

$100,000 Loan 8.875%	Conventional Monthly Amounts	MCC/American Dream
Principal and interest	$795.64	$795.64
Taxes and insurance (est.)	200	200
MCC value	0	−147.42
Net payment (PITI)	$995.64	$848.22
Housing cost ratio	.28	.33
Required monthly income to qualify for mortgage	$3,500	$2,575

SECRET # **22**

Save $1,000s with a Mortgage Credit Certificate (MCC).

The mortgage credit certificate (MCC) can shave $1,000s off the cost of home financing. This tax credit is available in about 25 states. Although an MCC doesn't directly reduce your interest rate, it does help you qualify for a larger mortgage with lower payments by cutting thousands of dollars off your income tax bill.

State and local housing finance agencies cooperate to sponsor MCC programs with selected mortgage lenders. An ad for the Massachusetts American Dream/MCC first-time buyer mortgage plan, says, "This special Mortgage Credit Certificate will lower your income taxes and increase your buying power." Table 3.8 illustrates the Massachusetts Housing Finance Agency (MHFA) program using an 8.875 percent, 30-year, fixed-rate mortgage of $100,000. (Of course, the MHFA used 8.875 percent only for illustrative purposes. Market or below-market rates typically apply.)

Limiting Features of MCCs

As with many government programs, not everyone qualifies for an MCC. In some cities you must earn less than $50,000 or $60,000 a year and buy a house priced at less than $250,000. (These figures are illustrative only. Each sponsoring government agency sets its own figures.)

Just like mortgage bond loans, MCCs come and go. "The clock is ticking for Chicago's mortgage credit certificate program, which encourages home ownership for working class people by slicing their tax bill to Uncle Sam," advised T.J. Becker in the *Chicago Tribune*. "The current program expires on New Year's Eve." Fortunately for Chicagoans, shortly after that MCC plan ended, the city started a new one. But it, too, will run out. So to save $1,000s and stretch your buying power, act now. If an MCC is available, don't delay. Your area's MCC program may expire shortly. If not available now but as a coming attraction, put your name on the list so you'll stand near the front of the line when these tax credits next become available.

SECRET # **23**

Seek employer assistance, or seek an employer who gives assistance.

In John Grisham's novel, *The Firm* (Random House, 1991), senior law partner Royce McKnight uses employer-sponsored, low-interest-rate home financing to help recruit Mitch McDeere into the law firm.

> "As you know" [Royce tells Mitch], we require you to buy a home. It adds stability and prestige and we're very concerned about these things, especially with our associates. The firm provides a low-interest-rate mortgage loan, 30 years, fixed rate, non-assumable should you decide to sell in a few years. It's a one-shot deal, available for your first home. After that, you're on your own."
>
> "What kind of interest rate?" [asks Mitch].
>
> "As low as possible without running afoul with the IRS. Current market rate is around 10, 10.5. We should be able to get you a rate of 7 to 8 percent. We represent some banks, and they assist us. With the salary we're paying, you should have no trouble qualifying. In fact, the firm will sign on as a guarantor [i.e., cosignor], if necessary."

"That's very generous, Mr. McKnight."

"It's important to us. Once you find a house . . . all you have to do is move in." [Note, too, the references to "non-assumable" and "guarantor."]

Could your employer use its influence with banks or other mortgage lenders to help you and other employees get below-market financing? At Colgate-Palmolive, Robert Berg says, "We came up with a mortgage assistance plan that used the financial muscle of the company to help our employees get the best possible terms. Our program is a very cost-effective fringe benefit . . . it's tax-effective to employees and much more desirable than just giving people a salary increase."

To reduce the costs of homebuying, Fannie Mae has developed an employer-assisted program named Magnet. Participating employers offer their employees homebuyer helper techniques that include lower interest rates, down-payment assistance, second mortgages, loan guarantees, closing cost assistance, and interest rate buydowns. Employers know that homeowners make more stable employees. If your employer values your contribution to the firm, ask how they might help boost your buying power. When bargaining for a new job, include mortgage assistance as part of your requested package of pay and benefits.

Keep an exit strategy in mind. Find out what happens to the mortgage— or other homebuying assistance—if you get fired, laid off, or change jobs voluntarily. The employer could withdraw its contribution, or even declare the loan due, as is the practice with loans secured by an employer 401(k) plan.

SECRET # **24**

Obtain a lower interest rate; pay points.

Nearly all lenders trade off points (fees paid at the time the mortgage money is loaned) and interest rates. Say you're looking at the choices shown in Table 3.9.

Which of these choices will give you the lowest costs? It all depends on how long you keep your mortgage. If you keep your loan for more than

Table 3.9 **Illustration of Different Payback Calculations:**
Interest Rate/Points Trade-Offs

$100,000 Mortgage at 30 Years

Interest Rate (%)	Points/Amount	Monthly Payment ($)	Months to Break Even
8.0	0/0	$733	00
7.75	1/$1,000	716	58 months
7.5	1.5/$1,500	699	44 months
7.25	2.0/$2,000	682	39 months
6.75	3.0/$3,000	648	35 months

three years (36 months), the 6.75 percent/3-point loan will save you the most money. Although you pay an extra $3,000 at closing to get this lower rate, the loan will save you $85 a month over the 8.0 percent/0-points loan. Compared with the 8.0 percent mortgage, you'll earn back your $3,000 in points in just over 35 months ($3,000 ÷ $85 = 35.29). After that, it's all gain.

The figures in Table 3.9 illustrate a simple way to compare costs, although the actual trade-offs you see will differ from these. This calculation works well to select the lowest loan cost *based upon your expected circumstances*. A competent loan rep can work through interest rate/points trade-offs with you to figure out which look best. A greedy loan rep may steer you into an interest rate/point combination that yields the largest sales commission. Don't ask your loan rep, "Which one is best?" Instead, ask him or her to show you the lender's rate sheets that list trade-off choices—often as many as 10 or 12—then work through the numbers together after the loan rep clearly explains the results.

SECRET # **25**

Negotiate a buydown with the sellers.

"When I'm working with investors or homebuyers who want to lower costs and increase affordability," says Realtor Nathan Browne, "I ask the sellers to pay points to reduce my buyers' mortgage interest rate."

To illustrate this technique, say your lender quotes a fixed 8 percent interest rate for a 30-year loan. With a 3-2-1 buydown, your first year's interest rate would drop 3 points to 5 percent. For years two and three, your interest rate would move up to 6 percent and then to 7 percent. For the remaining 27 years of the mortgage, the monthly payments would remain at the 8 percent contract interest rate.

For each $100,000 borrowed, here's what the monthly payments (principal and interest) would look like with a 3-2-1 buydown from that 8 percent loan.

Temporary Buydown	Monthly Payment
Year 1 @ 5%	$537
Year 2 @ 6%	598
Year 3 @ 7%	659
Years 4 thru 30 @ 8%	724

Without a buydown, you'd need a gross income of around $2,750 a month to qualify for this loan (.28 housing cost ratio). With this buydown, you'd qualify for a $100,000 mortgage with a gross income of $2,025 to $2,375 a month, depending on which interest rate the lender uses to qualify you. Easy lenders might use the 5 percent, $537 a month payment. Tougher lenders might not give you the full benefit of the buydown. Instead, they might qualify with an interest rate of 6 or 7 percent. Either way, the temporary buydown lifts your borrowing power as it lowers your qualifying ratios. (For higher loan amounts, use proportionately higher payment and income figures.)

How Much Do Temporary Buydowns Cost?

In the previous example, the 3-2-1 buydown would probably cost around $5,500. As a rough calculation, you can figure this cost by summing the total percentage points you're buying down (such as 3-2-1 equals a total of 6 points) and then multiply that percentage times the mortgage amount. Discount that dollar amount by 5 to 15 percent. (You negotiate the exact cost of your buydown with the lender.)

Buydowns aren't cheap. Nevertheless, if affordability is your goal, then a buydown can work to reduce monthly payments and help you qualify for a larger mortgage. To pay for the buydown, you can contribute some of the money, the sellers can pay part, and for low- to moderate-income homebuyers, government housing finance agencies, or even the lender itself (as part of a first-time homebuyer program), might pay part of the cost.

SECRET # **26**

New homebuilders offer mortgage incentives.

To gain competitive advantage, some homebuilders and condo projects offer low interest and down payment incentives. Special finance packages ebb and flow, but you can often find something. Or, if you don't find what you need, negotiate your own special financing. "If you're hunting for a new home," writes real estate consultant Jim DeBoth, "negotiating a finance package should top your list of priorities."

When you talk buyer incentives with homebuilders, think beyond decorator allowances, landscaping, carpet grades, and lighting fixtures. Add these later. Rather than ask for top-of-the-line appliances or a built-in security system, negotiate a 3-2-1 buydown, a six-month moratorium on monthly payments, or even sweat equity (see *Secret* #53) to help offset your down payment. You can negotiate your best incentives from builders when mortgage market interest rates head up and/or the inventory of unsold new homes begins to pile up.

SECRET # **27**

How to borrow jumbo amounts without paying jumbo rates.

Each year Fannie Mae/Freddie Mac set limits on the maximum-sized, single-family home mortgage that they will buy (now $417,000). Loan amounts that exceed Fannie/Freddie limits are known as jumbos and usually carry an interest rate that's about one-half percent higher than Fannie/Freddie's best rate. When Fannie/Freddie's 30-year fixed rate wandered around 6.0 percent, lenders typically priced jumbos at 6.5 percent. (Shop closely, since competition is forcing jumbo rates lower. Recently I've seen jumbos priced at just .25 percent over the Fannie/Freddie conventional rate. Remember, interest rate spreads for amounts, terms, and default risk fluctuate constantly. No fixed rules apply.

Save Interest with a Second Mortgage (or a Higher Down Payment)

On a loan of $450,000, that extra one-half percent for the jumbo loan would cost $148 per month more ($2,872 as opposed to $2,724).[3] Viewed differently, you pay $2,525 per month to borrow the first $417,000, and $347 per month for the additional $33,000 to bring your total home mortgage up to $450,000. In terms of interest for that extra $35,000, your effective charge is around 12 percent. If you limit your first mortgage to Fannie/Freddie's maximum, therefore, you could borrow the remainder ($33,000) as a second mortgage. As long as your interest rate on this loan falls below 11 percent, you save money.

Alternatively, if you can come up with $33,000 more for your down payment, you would profit—unless the cash or investment source of this down payment was earning a very safe tax-free return of 11 percent or greater (not an easy feat in today's investment climate.)[4] You could pledge collateral to secure this $33,000 (see Chapter 6).

These examples illustrate tiered financing, which can often save you money. This same technique applies to loans with low down payments and mortgage insurance (also in Chapter 6). You need not understand how to make these calculations, but you do need to see the potential of the technique. Then ask a smart loan rep to run the numbers.

Buy a Two- to Four-Unit Income Property

When most loan reps quote Fannie/Freddie's maximum loan amount, they typically recite the figure that applies to houses and condominium units.

---

[3] These numbers are approximate at the time of writing, Fannie has not yet released its maximum loan amounts for the coming year.

[4] Unless you're investing in income properties, that is. See my books, *Investing in Real Estate*, 5th ed. (2006), and *Value Investing in Real Estate* (2002).

Table 3.10 **Two to Four Units: Fannie/Freddie Maximum Loan Amounts (2007)**

Units	Lower 48 States (Loan Limit $)	AK, HI, VI (Loan Limit $)
1	417,000	625,500
2	533,850	800,775
3	645,300	967,950
4	801,950	1,202,925

Because most borrowers prefer this type of housing, loan reps forget to mention that these megaplayers in the mortgage market also give their lowest rate financing to borrowers who own and occupy two- to four-unit properties (see Table 3.10). In addition, Fannie/Freddie establish higher limits for Alaska, Hawaii, and the Virgin Islands.

FHA permits higher loan amounts for two- to four-unit properties, too (see Table 3.11). Even though multi-unit loans can exceed the maximum FHA single-family (and Fannie/Freddie) loan limits, many lenders do not charge a jumbo premium for these mortgages.

Remember that jumbo loans on single-family houses and condos not only charge higher interest, they may require 10 to 30 percent down. You can finance two- to four-unit properties with a 5 to 10 percent down payment. You'll enjoy faster equity buildup, larger amounts of appreciation, and a conventional interest rate. Two to four units make sense.

Table 3.11 **One to Four Units: FHA Maximum Loan Amounts (2007)**

Units	Basic Limits	Highest Cost Areas
1	200,160	362,790
2	256,248	464,449
3	309,744	561,411
4	384,936	697,696

Unlike Fannie/Freddie, FHA designates its maximum loan amounts county by county throughout the United States. For the latest figures, go to hud.gov.

As I have urged before, more homebuyers and investors should profit with these properties.

Your after-tax cost of borrowing may not be as low as you've been told.

Real estate agents and loan reps frequently tell potential borrowers not to focus on the nominal rate of interest that lenders charge. Instead, borrowers should consider only their after-tax costs. Good advice, but their specific figures sometimes err.

The Standard Line

The standard line goes something like this:

> Borrower: "Wow, the loan on this house is going to cost us $2,000 a month. We're only paying $1,350 for rent."
>
> Realty Agent: "Oh, don't worry. Remember, in the early years nearly all of that payment goes to interest. And you can deduct interest from your tax return. If you're in the 30 percent tax bracket, your after-tax monthly cost will total around $1,400 (.7 × 2,000). Considering the great advantages of buying your own home—especially appreciation—owning actually costs you about the same as rent."

Like sales agents, I strongly advocate home ownership and investment in property. But get the numbers right. Agents and loan reps overstate the value of those interest tax deductions. Unless your taxable income exceeds $114,650, you're not in the 30 percent tax bracket. The majority of taxpayers pay effective income tax rates of 15 to 25 percent.

On the other hand, if you're among the fortunate whose taxable household income exceeds $114,650 a year, your combined state and local marginal tax rates will push you above 30 percent; however, you face another problem. Above $100,000 a year, the government thinks you're too rich to deserve the full benefit of the interest deduction. At that income level, the government starts slicing back the amount you can deduct.

How to Really Calculate the After-Tax Cost of Your Monthly Mortgage Payments

To accurately calculate your tax break, first estimate your total monthly payment:

$$\text{Monthly payment} = P + I + HOI + MI + Tx + HOA$$

where: $P = \text{principal}$
$I = \text{interest}$
$HOI = \text{homeowners insurance}$
$MI = \text{mortgage insurance}$
$Tx = \text{property taxes}$
$HOA = \text{homeowner association dues}$

Recall that monthly payments may include items other than principal and interest, such as property insurance, HOA fees, mortgage insurance, and so forth. As a starting point, estimate the amount you will pay for each monthly expense. Next, back out only the amounts for interest and property taxes.[5] For example, if your total monthly payment of $1,600 includes every item in the list, interest and property taxes might give you a deduction of only $1,200 per month, not $1,600 per month. This amount is all you can deduct (12 × $1,200 = $14,400 as opposed to $19,200).

Once you estimate your future interest and property tax figures, pull out your most recent tax returns. Recompute your income taxes with these amounts as deductions. But here's the catch: To deduct property taxes and interest, you must give up the standard deduction of $7,950 for married couples ($4,750 for individuals filing separately).

So, low- to moderate-income (nonitemizing) homebuyers who purchase modestly priced houses (say, under $150,000) will experience a net gain of no more than $2,000 to $4,000—and maybe less. Nonitemizing

---

[5] Here, I just want to show why the tax break for monthly payments isn't as large as you've probably been told. To actually perform this calculation, you need figures for your home and home loan. In contrast to homeowners, remember property investors may deduct all monthly payment expenses except principal.

middle to upper-middle income earners may net a gain in deductions of around $3,000 to $6,000. If you already incur a number of other deductible expenses but do not presently itemize, you will gain more. If you earn over $150,000 (adjusted gross income), mortgage interest will add nothing to your tax deductions—even if you already itemize.

Tax Deductions Exceed Tax Savings. The figures cited in the previous section for tax deductions do not translate directly into tax savings. To compute tax savings, subtract these and other allowable deductions and exemptions from your adjusted gross income; then turn to the tax tables in the back of your 1040 booklet. Figure your new tax liability, and compare it to the taxes you previously paid. How much difference did you find? If you're like most homebuyers, you'll find that the savings amount to less than the tax savings estimates of most real estate agents and loan reps.

Nothing written here intends to discourage you from buying a home. *Mortgage Secrets* strongly advocates property ownership. History and demographic forecasts support the fact that property will rank among your best investments. Nevertheless, before you buy or refinance, calculate how much your proposed purchase or refinance will change your after-tax, monthly cash flows. Correctly estimate the tax benefit of mortgage interest deductions. For most homeowners, this deduction doesn't yield the amount of benefits that is widely promised. Compute the savings, if any, that you can expect; then after you know your monthly costs, ask, "Does this amount fit my comfort zone? Does it leave sufficient funds for saving and investing? Can I manage those out of the ordinary, yet always expected budget-busting surprises?"

Definitely, buy a home.[6] Enjoy your tax savings. But the odds are, you will save less than you might have figured. In contrast, though, to homeowners, investors may deduct 100 percent of the mortgage interest they pay on the rental properties they own—regardless of their income level, and regardless of whether they itemize personal deductions.

---

[6] See, for example, *The 106 Common Mistakes Homebuyers Make (and How to Avoid Them)*, 4th ed. (John Wiley & Sons, 2006). The biggest mistake of all, No. 106, is "Continuing to Rent." Of course, as an investor, I'm glad that many people do choose to rent.

Plan to Close in January or February. If you do not currently itemize income tax deductions, close your financing in January or February. You can use the standard deduction for the preceding year, and you can maximize your mortgage points, interest, and property tax deductions for the year in which you buy.[7] If instead you close in June or July, you may not gain enough interest deductions to make itemizing worthwhile.

Understandably, you won't schedule your home buying simply to get a tax break. But if convenient to do so, plan accordingly. As Robert Bruss, the nationally syndicated real estate advisor, points out, "You often get your best deal on a property during the Thanksgiving-Christmas-New Year's holiday season. Because relatively few buyers home-shop during the Christmas season, motivated sellers may accept your low-end offer." Buy in December, close in January. You will get a discount price and maximum tax savings. Sounds like a good tactic if you can arrange it.

---

[7] Homebuyers may deduct all costs paid to compensate the lender for the borrowed funds. In addition to interest, such amounts include origination fees and loan discount points, but not the appraisal, title insurance, or garbage fees.

CHAPTER 4

The Risks and Rewards of ARMs

Now's the time to slay the misconceptions about adjustable rate mortgages (ARMs) that misguide many borrowers, loan reps, and realty agents. These misconceptions block you from the information you need to choose wisely. As a result, you could bypass ARMs without a second look. Or you might select an ARM for the wrong reasons.

SECRET # **29**

ARMs do not necessarily present more risk than fixed-rate loans.

For many people, ARMs excite fears of potential loss. If interest rates head up, you stand to lose a lot of money as your monthly payments climb above the payments that you would have made with a 30-year, fixed-rate mortgage. Or you view the ARM risk in terms of uncertainty; you wonder if you can afford the higher payments. You fear that rate hikes might wreck your budget—or even force you to quickly sell the property.

You know what? More than likely, you've exaggerated the risks and misinterpreted the facts.

Risks As "Chance of Loss"

Granted, the monthly payment on your ARM could climb above the amount of your fixed-rate monthly payment, but if you follow the advice of *Secret #31*, you can squash that possibility. Still, for the sake of argument, assume that it does. Have you really suffered a loss? Not necessarily; to calculate "loss" in this sense, you would need to total all of your interest paid compared to the amount of interest you would have paid with a fixed-rate loan. Experience shows that throughout most of the past 25 years, borrowers who chose ARMs paid less total interest for the same amounts borrowed than their 30-year fixed-rate peer group.

Regret or Loss

Human nature programs us to feel regret when hindsight reveals that our decision turned out badly. Thoughts of "woulda, coulda, shoulda" run through your mind. But that's not the same thing as loss. That's life. Say you buy a new Saturn in March for $15,000. You tell all your friends about the great deal you negotiated.

In April, General Motors announces a $3,000 rebate program or zero percent financing for three years. Have you suffered a loss? No, at the time you bought, you (presumably) got the best deal available. But do you kick yourself for not waiting? Do you, after the fact, concoct stories about how you felt GM would soon come out with a rebate deal, but immediate gratification overwhelmed your perceptive talents?[1] Probably yes, if you're like most people.

Fixed-Rate Borrowers Should Suffer the Same Types of Regrets

What if you pass up a one-year ARM with a 4.0 percent start rate and a 5.5 percent contract rate, no points, in favor of a 7.0 percent, one-point, 30-year fixed-rate (a trade-off that was available several years ago). Then, within the next 18 months the 30-year fixed-rate falls to 6.0 percent. At the same time, the new rate on the one-year ARM falls to 3.75 percent (T-bill index + 2.5 margin). You're now paying hundreds of dollars more

---

[1] The perceptive talents necessary to forecast interest rates attach to very few mortals. But in *Secret #32* you will learn several clues to look for.

per month than you would have paid with the ARM.[2] Do you feel the same high level of regret? Maybe not. Why?

When your ARM payment goes up, you're cash-out-of-pocket. But if you have chosen a fixed-rate loan and interest rates fall, you do miss a chance to benefit immediately, yet suffer no cash loss. The economic effect, however, remains the same: In either instance, ARM or fixed-rate, when the market moves against your present interest rate (down for fixed-rates, up for ARMs), your monthly payments may stand higher than they otherwise would have been had you chosen differently at the time you originally obtained your mortgage.

Distinguish Regret from Actual Loss

No matter which mortgage you choose, you can't know its true cost until after the fact, but you can forecast likely costs and benefits under a variety of reasonable (or even unreasonable) eventual outcomes. Only after you make these calculations can you decide which choice looks best. Gut reactions like, "We don't want the risk of an ARM" cost you plenty. Run the pertinent numbers, then choose.

All mortgages present risk in an economic sense—either out-of-pocket or opportunity costs. You gain when you vanquish emotions and focus on the figures. You may discover that some type of ARM saves you money and helps you qualify for a larger loan. Or if you're an investor, the ARM might help your property yield a positive cash flow.

Rate Increases and Wrecked Budgets

Sometimes ARMs appeal to the wrong types of borrowers. During periods of high 30-year fixed interest rates, ARMs permit borrowers to obtain larger loans than they otherwise could. A lower qualifying interest rate when combined with higher qualifying ratios (a feature of some ARMs) attracts marginal borrowers. Because they're struggling from the beginning, unexpected payment increases (called "payment shock") push these types of borrowers into financial distress.

---

[2]You could possibly refinance, but that could cost you several thousand dollars—a loss that you would not have incurred had you selected the ARM. Of course, the ARM borrower could also refinance into that new lower rate.

Indeed, in reaction to the recent uptick in ARM defaults, many lenders have decided to qualify ARM borrowers at the fully indexed rate—rather than the teaser rate. Even stricter, some lenders now qualify ARM borrowers at the maximum possible ARM contract rate.

Payment Shock

By the time you agree to accept an ARM, your loan rep should have eliminated the possibility of payment shock. The loan rep should show you a monthly payment schedule outlining the maximum amounts you could ever pay, and the dates when those maximums payments could go into effect. If your payments at some time did reach those levels, you could not justifiably claim to be shocked any more than Claude Rains when he discovered gambling operations in the back room at Rick's cafe in Casablanca.

ARMs versus GPMs

Some borrowers confuse ARMs with graduated payment mortgages (GPMs) because GPM borrowers experience an increase in the payments over time. With a GPM, however, you pay less during the first year so you can qualify for a larger loan; then, during the next four years, your monthly payments increase gradually. Thereafter, your payments remain the same for the next 25 years. Your lower monthly payments during the early years of the mortgage offset the higher payments you'll make during the later years. For an example, see Table 4.1.

Table 4.1 **Monthly Payments (8%, 30-Year, $100,000 Loan) 30-Year Fixed-Rate vs. GPM**

Years	Typical Level Payment ($)	Graduated Payment ($)
1	769	580
2	769	623
3	769	670
4	769	721
5	769	775
6–30	769	883

FHA, VA, and conventional loan programs offer GPMs with a variety of payment schedules. Like an ARM, the GPM will usually help you buy more property. But unlike an ARM, you will know your future payments. An ARM's monthly payments will adjust up or down according to swings in the market interest rates (subject to any floors or caps). Your GPM's monthly payment will steadily go up, unaffected by changes in the market interest rate, until it hits its scheduled plateau. Also, during those early years of lower payments, your mortgage balance may actually go up. Before you accept this type of loan, just as with an ARM, closely review your payment and amortization schedules.

Borrowers Be Aware

Rather than caution "beware of ARMs and GPMs," we should advise "be *aware* of ARMs." As an intelligent borrower, prepare for the ups and enjoy the downs. Do not complain, "Gee, I'm shocked. I never knew rates could go up this much."

Never use an ARM to achieve temporary affordability. Instead, use it when the odds lie in your favor—and you accept the fact that this choice could increase your payments.

The Upside of ARMs in Down Markets

In the late 1980s, the California housing market was booming. Even though interest rates were around 9 to 10 percent, homebuyers, investors, and speculators pushed prices higher and higher. Then the recession of the early 1990s hit California hard. Mid- to upper-price-range homes fell in value by 15 to 30 percent. Unemployment rates approached 10 percent. By 1993 to 1994, mortgage interest rates dropped to as low as 6.0 percent. Great time to refinance, right?

Yes. But falling property prices, layoffs, and job uncertainty blocked many recent buyers from refinancing at lower rates. Some couldn't qualify for a new loan because of job loss or feared cutbacks. And among those who could qualify for a refinance (refi), most couldn't swing the deal. Their property values wouldn't support a new loan—unless they could bring cash to the closing table.

So, who did gain? Property owners who in the late 1980s had chosen ARMs. Their interest rates slid down. Some were able to convert their

ARMs (see *Secret #38*) to a 15-year or 30-year fixed-rate loan at the low rates that prevailed. Although no buyers like to consider down markets, they happen, especially in California and other sometimes volatile urban markets like New York City, Miami, Phoenix, Boston, and Washington, D.C. In those situations, ARMs give owners an advantage over fixed-rate loans, yet this advantage is rarely pointed out.

Few real estate agents or loan reps want to frighten buyers with talk of downturns. Nevertheless, view all outcomes that experience reveals to be possible (or in some cases, quite likely).

SECRET # **30**

For the short term, ARMs *usually* cost less.

Mortgage counselors give this advice: "If you're going to own your property for less than, say, five to seven years, take out an ARM. You can avoid payment shock and save big dollars at the same time." That's good advice for most people, but an exception exists that could prove even better than an ARM.

ARMs for the Short Run

The shorter the length of time you plan to own your property, the more likely you should select an ARM. You can usually find an adjustable that will cost you less than a 30-year fixed-rate loan if you plan to sell within seven years. Take a look at 5/25 or 7/23 (sometimes described as a 30/5 or 30/7) adjustables. (Exceptions to this rule occur when the yield curve inverts.)

These types of ARMs fix your interest rate and monthly payments for the beginning five or seven years of the loan. Then they periodically adjust to keep your rate in line with the market. Even this limited type of adjustable may cut your rate by .5 to 1.5 percent as compared to a fixed-rate mortgage. For instance, at a time when 30-year fixed-rates were at 7.25 percent, I saw several 5/25 ARM plans with start rates as low as 5.75 percent.

For each $100,000 borrowed, payments for a 7.25 percent 30-year fixed-rate loan cost $682 a month. If you could select a 5/25 at 5.75 percent, your payments would drop to $583 a month (per $100,000 borrowed). Although the rate differences between 30-year fixed-rate loans and various types of ARMs change daily, it pays to look. When you plan to sell (or refinance) within seven years, an ARM might limit your risk at the same time it reduces your monthly payments. And, as your income goes up, you should be able to manage any increases in your ARM's monthly payments until rates come back down.

An Assumable Low-Rate, Fixed-Rate Loan Can Boost Resale Value and Lead to a Quick Sale.

ARMs for the short run usually make sense. But before you choose, compare the ARM to the short-term advantages you might achieve with an assumable fixed-rate loan. Say that at the time you buy, interest rates sit near their ebb. Everyone says, "Now's a great time to buy." But you expect your employer will transfer you within three to seven years, or that you will move for some other reason. Should you buy, and if so, should you go for an ARM or a fixed rate?[3] As to buying, that answer is easy. Absolutely. Please permit a digression.

Short-Term Buying Strategy

When I was offering my Stop Renting Now!™ seminars, most attendees I met had thought of themselves throughout life as "temporary" renters—no matter how old they were. It surprised me that most of these renters were in their thirties and forties. They had drifted from temporary personal situation to temporary personal situation. They told themselves, "Well, when I know for sure where I'm going to be and what I'm going to be doing, then I'll buy."

Unfortunately, while indecisive renters drift, housing prices do know where they're going—and that's up. So, if you face an uncertain personal situation, create a short-term buying strategy;[4] then finance it with either

---

[3] As *Mortgage Secrets* reveals, your financing choices extend far beyond this simple comparison, but let's keep these examples manageable.

[4] Such strategies are discussed in Gary W. Eldred, *Make Money with Fixer-Uppers and Renovations* (John Wiley & Sons, 2003, 2008).

an ARM or a new assumable fixed-rate—if you're in a low-interest-rate environment.

Why an Assumable Fixed-Rate?

A low-interest-rate assumable plays into your short-term strategy. This loan will help your property sell quicker and at a higher price. If you've selected the property wisely, you could probably sell without listing the house with a brokerage firm. Because only FHA and VA now offer new assumable fixed-rates, you may pay more closing costs than you would for a conventional (Fannie/Freddie) fixed-rate, but in this short-term situation the FHA/VA loan could prove profitable.

As another possibility, look for a low-rate FHA/VA loan that you can assume. At a time when market rates were at 10 percent, I sold a property with an assumable 8 percent fixed-rate in two days simply by word of mouth. I never hired a sales agent or even ran a newspaper ad. On another occasion when market rates were at 16 percent, I bought a property with an assumable 13.75 percent from a for-sale-by-owner (FSBO) during the first week he had placed the property on the market. Also, the "subject to" property that I bought (see Chapter 3) with a 10 percent (way below the current market rate) interest rate was a word-of-mouth transaction.

When you plan to move within three to seven years, ARMs make good sense. But experience shows low-rate assumable (or subject to) fixed-rates can work as a short-term ownership strategy—either as a new origination or as a loan you take over from your sellers.

SECRET # **31**

ARMs for the long run: How to lower costs and alleviate risk.

An ARM will often save you money if you plan to sell within five to seven years, but you also might save money over the longer term. Here's why.

Imagine you must choose between a 30-year fixed-rate loan at 8 percent and a 7/23 that starts at 6.75 percent. You want to borrow $100,000. With the fixed-rate plan, your payments will cost $733 a month. With the 7/23, you'll pay $648. For at least the first seven years, you'll save $85 a month, for a total of $7,140.

Instead of pocketing this monthly savings of $85, though, add it to your monthly mortgage payments. Even though you're only required to pay $648 a month, you go ahead and pay $733 ($648 + $85 = $733). This tactic causes you to pay down your outstanding mortgage balance much faster. By making extra payments, your mortgage balance after seven years would fall to approximately $83,000. On the other hand, your mortgage balance with the fixed-rate plan at 8 percent would drop to only $92,480. Obviously, if you sell at this point, you're way ahead of the game with the ARM.

But what if you don't sell? As long as your new adjustable rate stays below 9.5 percent, your monthly mortgage payments won't amount to any more than $740—about the same as you've been paying. At 10.5 percent, your payments would just increase to $798 a month. Now, what if interest rates are lower when your loan adjusts after seven years? Not only will you have accumulated an additional $9,480 in equity, but your monthly payments can decrease.

These figures are illustrative only. Because the *relative* costs of ARMs and fixed-rate loans change frequently (recall the discussion of interest rate spreads on p. 45), you must work numbers with your mortgage loan advisor that are current at the time you buy your property.[5] Still, this basic fact holds true: For some buyers, the right ARM can add thousands of dollars in equity as compared to a 30-year fixed-rate mortgage.

SECRET # **32**

You can (sort of) forecast interest rates.

To get some idea how high your ARM interest rate might go up (or down), you need to forecast movements in the interest rates; however, most mortgage pros say that no one can predict interest rates, so why even try.

---

[5] In 1981 and 2006, newly originated ARM interest rates exceeded 30-year fixed-rate loans.

In one sense, the mortgage pros are right. Neither you, I, nor anyone else can know for certain where mortgage rates will sit six months or six years from now. But that fact doesn't mean that reasoned estimates won't prove better than sticking your head in the sand. Mortgage rates don't land where they do for arbitrary reasons. Long-term mortgage interest rates tie into the expected rate of inflation.

The Real (CPI-Adjusted) Rate of Interest

To calculate the inflation-adjusted, real interest rates, subtract the year's increase in the consumer price index (CPI) from the average nominal mortgage rate—that is, the rate lender's quote. When *real* interest rates are relatively high, you can reasonably forecast nominal rates to fall or remain relatively stable.

Nominal Interest Rates

During the mid-2000s, mortgage costs seemed relatively low only because most people don't realize that from the 1940s through 1965, U.S. mortgage rates ranged between 4.0 percent and 6.0 percent. During some periods of U.S. history, mortgage interest rates have dropped as low as 2.5 percent.

The mortgage rates of 8.0 to 14 percent that we experienced during most of the 1970s, 1980s, and early 1990s do not tell us how to judge today's rates. High nominal interest rates prevailed throughout much of the past 40 years because we also experienced (and then came to expect) high rates of inflation.

CPI-Adjusted (Real) Rates

To understand whether current interest rates sit high or low, adjust the nominal (quoted) rates for the annual rate of increase in the CPI.[6] The cost of money is cheap when *real* mortgage rates are low, and expensive when *real* market rates are high.

As you can see from Table 4.2, mortgage borrowers today pay a real rate of around 3.5 percent. Viewed correctly, history suggests that, as long as

---

[6]The nominal mortgage interest rate less the annual percentage increase in the CPI equals what economists call the *real* rate of interest.

Table 4.2 **Comparing Nominal and Real Rates of Interest**

Years	Nominal Rate (%)	CPI Increase (%)	Real Rate (%)
1945	4.0	2.3	1.7
1950	4.5	1.3	3.2
1955	5.0	−0.4	5.6
1960	5.0	1.7	3.3
1965	5.89	1.6	4.29
1970	8.56	5.7	2.86
1975	9.14	9.1	.04
1980	13.95	13.5	.45
1990	10.08	5.4	4.68
1995	7.86	2.8	5.06
2002	6.5	2.05	4.0
2007	6.50 (est.)	3.0 (est.)	3.50 (est.)

the chairman of the Federal Reserve Board, Ben Bernake, keeps inflation low, nominal *and* real interest rates are likely to remain below 7.0—at most 8.0—percent.

No one predicts that ARM rates will push past their annual or lifetime caps within the foreseeable future. In terms of expected inflation, ARMs do not present much risk of payment shock.[7] In contrast, look at the period 1970 to 1980 when inflation leaped up. Real rates fell below their historical norms. In response, mortgage rates skyrocketed. Financial markets came to believe that high inflation was built into the country's economic future.

Disinflationary Trends

At least five major reasons support a forecast of low inflation and correspondingly moderate mortgage interest rates (within the range of 5 to 8 percent).

---

[7] This discussion does not intend to revoke my earlier caveats to marginal borrowers. No one can guarantee that rates won't jump up two or three points, but the Fed's intentions do not support that forecast. Also, as occurred during 2003–2006, at times the Fed raises short-term rates to calm inflation worries. In such instances, short-term interest rate indexes can increase significantly—yet long-term rates remain stable. See *Secret #35.*

1. The Fed's concerted effort to keep inflation in check.
2. Increasing amounts of money flowing into the bond market as skittish investors shy away from stock market volatility.
3. Worldwide overcapacity in major industries, such as computer, telecommunications, steel, auto, textiles, and farm products.
4. The 70-plus million Americans between the ages of 40 and 60 who are shifting from consumption to saving as they prepare to accumulate enough money for retirement.
5. Most labor unions no longer enjoy enough power to push up wages faster than gains in productivity (the opposite of the situation in the late 1960s through the early 1980s). In addition, immigration and outsourcing will subdue inflationary wage increases.

Are there also calamitous scenes that could be painted? Certainly. But like Scarlett O'Hara, let's think about those another day. If the future you see spotlights fear, stock up your cabin hideaway with canned foods and survival gear. For now, *Mortgage Secrets* sees a positive outlook. History, current evidence, and reasonable forecasts support that view.

SECRET # **33**

Low teaser rates: Bait or bargain?

Compare a variety of ARMs, and you might find attractive low rates. Do such rates represent a good deal? Maybe, maybe not. That's what you must watch out for.

Some Teasers Bait the Hook to Catch the Gullible and Desperate

As standard operating procedure, lenders advertise enticing ARM rates (or monthly payments) to make their phones ring. In response to such an ad for a 2.95 percent ARM, I called the lender. As it turned out, the loan did guarantee that I would pay the 2.95 percent interest rate during the first year. However, the mortgage was attached to the following "gotchas."

- *Negative amortization:* If the underlying index for the loan went up during that first year, the extra amounts owed would add to the outstanding principal balance.
- *Prepayment penalty:* If I paid off the loan within the first three years, I would pay a 3, 2, or 1 percent penalty for years one, two, or three, respectively.
- *Qualifying rate:* To calculate the qualifying ratios, the lender would compute P&I payments with a 5.7 percent interest rate.
- *Lifetime cap:* Over the life of the loan, the mortgage rate could increase (theoretically) to as high as 13 percent.
- *Loan size:* Minimum loan amount recommended was $400,000.
- *Loan rep knowledge:* I had to push hard to extract the details of this loan product from the loan rep. Either he did not really understand the loan, or he didn't want me to understand it. He did, though, try to switch my interest to several other products the company was offering that "might better meet my needs."

Most likely, in this case, the lender did not want to make this loan except to a few specialized niche borrowers. The lender used it as a bait-and-switch come-on.

Sometimes, though, lenders do want to hook borrowers with teaser-baited ARMs—especially those borrowers who lack understanding, or who desperately want to finance a property with a *seemingly* affordable loan. It's in those instances when you must inquire closely to learn all features of the product (as *Mortgage Secrets* shows you throughout the remainder of this chapter). When some lender offers loan rates, terms, or monthly payments that look too good to be true, ferret out the gotchas. You'll probably find some. But not always.

Some Teaser Rates or Payments Do Make Good Loans

Recall the Klars from Chapter 3. Their low rate ARM provided a near certain benefit-cost advantage. Why do some lenders overwhelm their competitors with an unbeatable interest rate and/or product? Here are several reasons:

- *Rebalance its portfolio.* Lenders may want to shift their loan portfolios more to ARMs. To rebalance their allocations, these lenders may create some exceptional ARM offerings.
- *Achieve growth targets.* Lenders set growth targets that may require the sacrifice of profit to sales (dollar volume originations).
- *Gain market share.* Likewise, if a lender wants to quickly grow its market share (or stop a slide), it may market attractive ARM products.
- *Make deals.* To win friends and influence referrals, lenders may cut especially good deals for customers of favored Realtors or home builders.
- *Change their image.* Through aggressive offerings, lenders well-known for fixed-rate products may decide to create attention for their ARMs.

Mortgage lenders sell into a competitive market. To attract notice they sometimes place one or more of their loan products "on sale." Shop thoroughly, question closely, and your efforts may turn up an ARM bargain.

SECRET # **34**

Your start (teaser) rate isn't your contract rate.

Some ARM borrowers get hit with payment shock when teaser rates (low payments) end. That's because they fail to distinguish their start (teaser) rate from their initial contract rate. Often, sharpshooting loan reps permit this borrower confusion to continue lest they lose their mark.

Teasers versus Contract Rates

Lenders may lure you into ARMs with a low teaser rate. But to calculate increases or decreases, the lender will use the note rate that's written in the loan paperwork. When this contract rate sits well above the teaser rate, the first rate adjustment could shock you—if you have not anticipated this event.

Contract Shock

For example, the lender in *Mortgage Secret* #33 offered a teaser rate for 12 months at 2.95 percent. The current index (see *Secret* #35) rate for this loan was 1.8 percent. The loan carried a margin of 2.75 percent. Add the index rate (1.8 percent) to the margin (2.75 percent), and you find that the initial contract rate totals 4.55 percent. Therefore, if the index remains unchanged during the first 12 months of the loan, the monthly payment will still jump up by 22 percent.

The payments for a $200,000 loan would figure out as follows:

Teaser rate payment @ 2.95% / 30-year term = $822.

Contract rate payment (assuming no change in the index) @4.55% / 30-year term at end of year 1 = $1,001.[8]

Now, assume this index moves up one point to 2.8 percent. Add the margin of 2.75 percent, and the adjusted contract rate becomes 5.55 percent for a second-year payment amount of $1,135. That's $322 a month more than the first-year teaser payments.

No Real Surprise to the Informed

Critics of ARMs call this huge jump payment shock. But this supposed shock resulted because the naïve borrower didn't read the details of this loan. In fact, in the first edition of this book (2003), I wrote, "given the extremely low yields on short-term maturities during 2002, you should not be surprised to see this index move up to at least 3 or 4 percent during the next several years." And that's what happened. This same index today sits at around 5.0 percent.

With a 2002 inflation rate of, say, 2.0 to 2.5 percent, indexes then based on short-term yields such as the one-year Treasury showed negative real rates of return (see *Secret* #32). Short-term rates were unusually low in 2002 because the Federal Reserve Board slashed interest rates to stimulate the economy. During 2002, mortgage borrowers (especially short-term borrowers) loved these ARMs tied to short-term yields. At that time, the steep yield curve made ARMs the low-cost choice for savvy borrowers who knew how to play the mortgage game.

---

[8] All figures are approximate due to rounding.

SECRET # **35**

There's no one best index.

Every adjustable-rate mortgage links to an index. Some of these indexes move up and down slowly (typically much less than one percentage point per year). Others can rise or fall a point or more within a matter of months. Many mortgage advisors tell would-be borrowers to select a slow-moving index so that they face little risk of payment shock.

Remain wary of financial advisors who obsess that payment on some ARMs can jump quickly. Instead, to avoid payment shock, know exactly how both your interest rate and/or monthly payments might change. Then prepare for the worst as you enjoy the short-term gains which, when calculated over time, may cut the costs of your loan.

What Indexes Can You Choose?

Lenders can confound you with more index choices than Baskin-Robbins has flavors. Listed below are four such ARM indexes.

1. *Treasury Constant Maturities (TCM).* To fund the debts of the United States government, the Treasury issues interest-bearing notes, bills, and bonds with maturities that range from 30 days to 30 years. Most TCM ARMs are linked to the one-year TCM. Three-year, 5-year, and 20-year TCMs also may be available to you. After their start-rate ends, most hybrid ARMs link to the one-year TCM (not the Treasury Bill, as this index is mistakenly called by many).

2. *London Interbank Offered Rate (LIBOR).* This index reflects the interest rate often used by London banks when they lend short-term to other European banks. American lenders may use it for mortgages because they frequently sell such loans (mortgage-backed securities) to European investors.

3. *National Average Contract Mortgage Interest Rate (NACR).* This index averages the mortgage rates charged by lenders on loans for owner-occupied housing (not including new construction). This index adjusts more slowly than either the one-year TCM or the LIBOR.

4. *Eleventh District Cost of Funds (COFI)*. This index averages the interest rates that many Western banks (California, Arizona, Nevada) pay their depositors. Similar to the NACR, this index adjusts slowly.

Many loan advisors recommended the COFI index to ARM borrowers throughout the 1980s and 1990s as interest rates consistently trended downward. These advisors emphasized that slow changes in this index would protect borrowers from bearing the brunt of interest rate spikes.

How to Select an Index

Unfortunately, such advisors still feared 1981-sized interest rates; yet, during the second term of President Ronald Reagan, all economic fundamentals were in place to push interest rates lower. As of the mid-1980s, *real* (inflation-adjusted) rates for mortgage interest had climbed to 6 or 7 percent. Recall that when tamed inflation meets high historical real rates (*Secret* #32), you can safely conclude that nominal rates—the contract rates that lenders quote—will fall.

What This Means for You

To choose the index that will likely cost you less, note where the index sits today relative to its history and relative to the rate of inflation.

As noted, in 2002 the LIBOR and one-year Treasury indexes had fallen to (or near) their 40-year lows. Plus, both of these indexes fell below the rate of inflation. Given these relationships, one could reasonably conclude that the risk of significant increases greatly exceeded the potential for declines. Without tight caps (see *Secret* #37) and a short time frame, say less than three years, such a loan didn't offer many advantages. Increases looked far more probable than decreases.

At that time, three- to five-year ARMs were priced at 4.25 to 4.75 percent as opposed to about 6 percent for a 30-year fixed-rate; such loans looked very attractive because you were guaranteed the low rate during that entire introductory period. Again, though, this advice presumes a relatively short-term holding period, and it also presumes that you don't want the assumable fixed-rate mortgage alternative explained in *Secret* #30.

As to COFI, it also sat so low in 2002 (2.821 percent) that long-term upside moves seemed more likely than further downward drift. In closely comparing rates, ARMs looked especially attractive for the short run but not for periods greater than, say, five years. However, today the mortgage choice favors fixed-rate. The basically flat (and even partially inverted yield curve) makes ARMs look relatively expensive. Nevertheless, if 15- and 30-year fixed-rate loans bounce up to 7.0 to 8.5 percent, while inflation stays at 3.0 percent or less, the relative costs, risks, and benefits could shift back to favor ARMs.

Compare, Compare, Compare

To select the best index you and your loan rep should review your needs and the loan choices with these issues in mind:

- *Time horizon:* Determine your relevant planning horizon (job transfer, trade-up home, refi possibilities, Section 1031 exchange, family size, and so on) that will affect the number of years you might hold your mortgage.
- *Review possibilities:* Look at the ARM and fixed-rate loans that might fit your needs.
- *Historical perspective:* Compare the respective ARM index rates to where they stand now relative to their history.
- *Index versus CPI:* Compare the respective ARM index rates to the current and expected rates of inflation.
- *Payment increases:* Go through period by period to calculate potential payment increases.
- *Qualifying and affordability:* Eliminate loans that would not work because you could not qualify for or afford them.

No one can simplify the process of choosing an ARM product and its corresponding index[9] partly because no permanent rules or relationships

---

[9] Many ARM products do not permit you to choose an index. They're offered as a package of index and features that you choose or reject in total.

exist.[10] You can, however, examine the evidence. Make your calculations and then choose the loan that appears most likely to optimize your total outcome—including wealth building through mortgage paydown.

SECRET # **36**

Don't ignore the margin.

The interest rate you pay for your ARM includes the index rate plus the margin. The margin pays a lender's overhead, operating expenses, and profit, as well as the costs lenders suffer when borrowers default and lenders foreclose.

Often, ARMs include margins that range between 2.0 and 3.0 percent, although I have seen margins as low as 2.125 percent and as high as 6.0 percent. (Margins on loan products that target sub-prime borrowers with stained credit exceed other types of ARMs.) Because the National Average Contract Mortgage Interest Rate Index is calculated from mortgage rates (as opposed to other types of baseline rates), ARM loans tied to this index apply no margins.

When you compare the same ARM product and index among various lenders, ask for the applicable margins. Pay special attention to margins when you compare similar products and indexes with teaser rates that differ from each other. Say you find two lenders who offer COFI ARMs. One lender opens with a teaser rate of 3.95 percent for six months. The other lender gives a 4.5 percent teaser for three months. Superficially (all other features equal), the 3.95 percent teaser looks best. But remember, that teaser could dull your comparison. The lender uses it to distract you from the fact that that lender will be adding to the COFI a high-end

---

[10] During the early 1980s and mid-2000s, some short-term interest rates exceeded long-term rates, which is called an inverted yield curve. This situation can occur when inflation fears arise, but investors believe the Fed will prevent big price jumps over the longer run. Generally, long-term rates exceed short-term rates to protect investors against an unexpected, money-cheapening rise of the CPI. Investors fear that rising consumer prices will erode their buying power (the value of their money) when eventually borrowers pay back the money investors put up today.

margin of perhaps 3 percent. In contrast, if the competing lender offers a 2.5 percent margin, that lender offers you the better deal.

SECRET # **37**

All caps aren't created equal.

ARM caps limit how high the lender can lift your monthly mortgage payment. Many ARMs set their caps at 2/6. With these caps in place, the lender could not increase your loan's interest rate more than two percentage points at a time nor more than six percentage points throughout the life of the loan. However, also investigate:

- *The period of adjustment.* Loan payments may adjust monthly, quarterly, semi-annually, or annually; or payments may stay fixed for 3, 5, or 10 years and then adjust annually or more frequently.
- *Negative amortization (neg-am).* Your ARM's at 5 percent; interest rates shoot up. Your loan's index jumps by 3.5 percent. "Whew!" You think, "Thank goodness for my yearly cap. The lender can raise my loan's interest rate only two points: from 5 to 7 percent." True, but if that loan shackles you with negative amortization, you don't escape the pain of a higher rate—you merely postpone it. The lender adds the interest deficiency (1.5 percent) to your outstanding mortgage balance. Instead of owing less, you owe more.
- *The baseline rate.* Your ARM may actually include two initial rates: the teaser rate (say 4.0 percent), and the contract rate (say 5.5 percent). Which of these rates provides the baseline for adjustments? If your lifetime cap is 6 percent, how high could your rate go: 10.0 percent (6.0 + 4.0) or 11.5 percent (6.0 + 5.0)? A similar question also applies to the loan's periodic adjustments. If your payment caps limit annual increases by two points, what base does the lender stat with? Contract rate, or teaser rate?
- *Can borrowers do better than 2/6 caps?* Yes, they can. Although conventional ARMs (Freddie/Fannie) typically carry 2/6 caps, FHA/VA

ARMs apply 1/5 caps. You may even find periodic caps as low as .5 percent and lifetime caps of 2 or 3 percent.

Nearly all ARMs include caps of one sort or another. But to compare ARMs, calculate just how much protection those caps really give you. All caps are not created equal.

SECRET # **38**

That flashy convertible could prove a clunker.

In their early years, ARMs were selected by marginal borrowers when interest on fixed-rate loans started climbing. "Well," the loan rep tells the disappointed homebuyer, "I can't get you qualified at 9.5 percent for that 30-year fixed-rate loan, but here's what we can do. We can qualify you at 8.0 percent for the ARM. And what's great is that when interest rates come back down, you can convert this ARM into a fixed-rate 30-year loan."

At What Cost and Rate?

Have you found that elusive free lunch? Probably not. On occasion, the convertible option pays off. More often, its chrome dazzles more than its horsepower. Few borrowers ever exercise their option to convert. Here's why:

- *Higher interest rate.* Most borrowers think they can convert at the market rate. Not true. If, for example, at the time of the conversion, fixed-rates have dropped to 7 percent, your converted fixed-rate would probably carry an interest rate premium of .25 to 1.0 percent— or a total rate of somewhere between 7.25 and 8.0 percent.
- *Conversion fee.* Lenders will charge a conversion fee that may range from a low of $100 to as high as 1 percent of the outstanding balance on your loan.

♦ *Up-front cost.* You also typically pay for the conversion privilege at the time you take out the ARM—chiefly through a higher starting interest rate or higher loan origination fees.

When Can You Exercise the Convertible Option?

Anytime you want to? Not necessarily. Most frequently, the option to convert lasts only between the thirteenth and sixtieth months (fifth year) of a 360-month (30-year) loan. Some conversion options terminate earlier than 60 months. While many ARMs do permit you to convert anytime within that four-year window of opportunity, others limit the conversion to the annual anniversary dates of the loan. If interest rates hit rock bottom in June and your anniversary dates in November, you could end up out of luck. To comply with the lender's conversion rules, you will need to provide timely notice as spelled out in the loan agreement.

If a loan rep offers a conversion option completely without charge, take it. But if this feature requires an up-front cost, or if the option stands critical to your decision to accept an ARM, stay focused on the substance. Remember, that flashy convertible that you're admiring could prove to be a clunker.

SECRET # **39**

APRs tell you nothing about ARMs—and very little about fixed-rates.

The Federal Reserve board and the Office of Thrift Supervision have published a booklet called *Consumer Handbook on Adjustable Rate Mortgages*, available online at www.hsh.com. Unfortunately, this *Handbook* reinforces numerous widely held misconceptions about mortgages. Consider this advice given in the handbook:

Because all lenders follow the same rules to ensure the accuracy of the annual percentage rate (APR), it provides consumers with a good basis for comparing the costs of loans.

When you compare the costs of mortgage loans, you will see the term annual percentage rate (APR). To comply with government truth-in-lending laws, mortgage-interest-rate advertising must include this figure. The APR always exceeds the stated interest rate because it supposedly accounts for your total cost of borrowing (interest, fees, points, and certain other expenses). Supposedly, compare APRs among various loan products and lenders and you find the lowest-cost loan.

Real life proves more complex. APRs that apply to ARMs make no sense. Under the law, these APRs are calculated as if the ARM interest rate will not change during the full life of the loan (except for the scheduled boost up from the teaser rate to the initial contract rate). Yet, the very idea of an *adjustable*-rate mortgage means that the interest rate will change. So, APRs for an adjustable-rate mortgage gives us mathematically precise yet irrelevant figures. No one can accurately predict the APR for an ARM.

In an effort to force lenders to tell the truth about the costs of their mortgage loans, the government misleads borrowers. To compare ARMs, you cannot rely on the stated APRs. You may find a COFI ARM with an APR of 7.86 percent and a one-year Treasury ARM at an APR of 7.21 percent. But because no one knows how these respective ARM indexes will change over time, the APR does not tell which one represents the lowest-cost loan.

Contrary to what the Fed's customer booklet says, mortgage lenders do not compute APRs in lockstep with each other. The law remains ambiguous on many types of expenses—and some lenders take advantage of this fact to lowball their APRs. Ignore the ARM's APR. It means nothing to consumers.

Fixed-Rate APRs

Although it might appear that the APR would apply accurately to fixed-rate mortgages, that is true only in the unlikely event you pay off the loan balance precisely according to its schedule over the full life of the loan. If you pay ahead of (or behind) schedule, your actual APR will increase. Similarly, if you sell your house or refinance your mortgage, your actual APR will exceed the APR figure the government requires lenders to calculate. Likewise, as with ARMs, lenders omit some expenses from their APR—even though the lender will require you to pay them.

APR disclosures aim to fulfill a real need: to help consumers compare the total costs of mortgage loans. In practice, you must look beyond the APR. To obtain the best loan at the lowest cost, compare loan products according to your financial situation, your tolerance for risk and the expected period over which you plan to hold your loan (see *Secret #24*).

CHAPTER 5

Perfect Your Credit Profile

Today, if your credit score sits above say, 720, you might whiz through the loan underwriting process. As a borrower you can choose from among the lowest-cost, lowest interest-rate mortgages. The lender may ask for relatively few documents and verifications, it may waive mortgage insurance, and perhaps even loan you the amount you need for a down payment.

If instead your credit profile ranges somewhere between "bottom of the barrel" and "looks decent," lenders have created loan products, interest rates, closing costs, down payments, and documentation to fit you, too. But the more risk the lender sees, the more onerous the terms, fees, costs, and paperwork. For each $100,000 borrowed, higher-risk borrowers (especially when they choose higher-risk loans) might pay interest costs of $5,000 to $10,000 more *per year*, plus an additional $2,000 to $6,000 to cover origination points, fees, and expenses.

That's why it pays to perfect your credit profile. In today's world of mortgage lending, credit profile impacts multiple decisions the lender makes about you and your loan:

- ◆ Size of down payment
- ◆ Qualifying ratios
- ◆ Type and cost of appraisal (e.g., computer generated, drive-by, written form report, or full narrative report)
- ◆ Mortgage insurance premiums

- Quantity and quality of verifications and documentation (e.g., bank statements versus income tax returns)
- Interest rate
- Loan product
- Escrow requirements
- Origination fees and closing costs
- Prepayment penalties

For many borrowers, perfecting a credit profile may require only a few months and minor tweaks. For others, the process may take two years or more, plus a profound restructuring of their spending, borrowing, saving, and investing. The faster you perfect your financial profile, the faster you will grow your wealth—not just through mortgage cost savings, but also through your new attitude toward saving and investing versus destructive spending and borrowing (e.g., credit cards and new car loans).

SECRET # **40**

Emphasize all eight Cs of loan approval.

Want to convince a lender to shower a huge pile of cash on you—a total stranger? Then think about your loan profile the same way a lender does. In fact, not only lenders but sellers and potential investors/partners in your acquisitions evaluate each of the following criteria:

- Consistency: Fast track or flake?
- Character: Can the lender trust you?
- Capacity: Will your income cover the payments?
- Collateral: What loan-to-value ratio applies?
- Credit record: Have you managed credit responsibly?
- Cash reserves: Can you handle financial setbacks?
- Compensating factors: What positives add to your borrower profile?
- Competency: Can you effectively manage the property?

Among these eight Cs, credit score stands most important. Great credit can ease every other underwriting guideline. Without strong credit, mortgage lenders will require you to prove your other Cs more persuasively—or they will severely increase costs and impose less desirable terms. In other words, credit stands tall, but it doesn't stand alone. If you suffer blemishes (or stains), work to enhance the strength of the other Cs. Offset weak credit and you can lower your borrowing costs, increase your borrowing power, and turn a "not likely" into an "approved." So, before we look more closely at credit, let's review several of these other influential standards.

Consistency: Fast Track or Flake

Have you job hopped or job flopped? Have you lived in more places than you can remember? Did you jump through six majors before you finished community college? Do you suffer bouts of binge spending and borrowing? Does your background look more like a tossed salad that's been thrown against a wall than the impeccable dinner presentation of an expensive French restaurant? If so, you've got some explaining to do.

Loan reps and underwriters want to make sense of your life as it's displayed on your mortgage application. They want to evaluate where you've been and where you're headed. To satisfy their penchant for consistency, figure a theme or angle that ties your loose ends together. Give the lender confidence that six months after you've closed your loan, you won't abandon the property to join a Hare Krishna colony. The lender wants to envision your steady path toward job promotions and career advancement. In borderline cases, a captivating story can make the difference.

Character Counts

Remember J.P. Morgan's first rule of lending: "I wouldn't loan money to a man I did not trust on all the bonds of Christendom." Don't you feel the same way? Prove that you're trustworthy, that you'll honor your obligations. Your credit score provides one indicator, but you can bolster this score (if necessary) with other types of written information, such as:

◆ *Employer reference.* If your lender requires a completed verification of employment (VOE) form, ask your supervisor to enclose a letter that commends your dependability, integrity, and responsibility at work.

- *Credit blemishes.* Explain how misplaced bills, your vacation, a move of residence, or other non-character-indicting reasons account for these lapses that you deeply regret. Even better, discuss the new bill-paying systems that you have now put in place to prevent future lapses.
- *Credit wreck.* Explain serious problems as once-in-a-lifetime, beyond-your-control events that you coped with as honorably as possible. If actually due to irresponsibility, emphasize that you've learned your lesson the hard way and have now transformed your life. Provide written objective evidence that supports the "new you" claims.
- *Personal references.* In times past, lenders would loan money to younger borrowers merely on the basis of family character and reputation.[1] "Why, I've known Luke Jr.'s family for 30 years," says the loan rep. "They're good people. Loan approved." In our big-city, automated world, personal references to lenders seldom count for much. Nevertheless, if you've established good rapport with someone who could prove influential, it wouldn't hurt to enlist their help.

Unless you provide alternative documentation, the lender will infer your dependability from the shading provided by your record of credit and consistency. When such evidence paints too dark a picture, add brighter colors to the hue.

Capacity: How Much Mortgage Debt Can You Safely Carry?

As you learned in *Secret #7*, lenders use qualifying and debt coverage ratios to help them determine how much money to loan you. Recall that you can improve these ratios in a variety of ways, such as:

- *Income.* Increase the amount of your qualifying income. Beware: Some loan programs merely require you to state your income (or assets) with no lender verification. These loans are known as "liar's

---

[1] Loan applications used to include spaces for personal references similar to those found on some job applications.

loans." However, if you falsely represent your income (or assets), you commit loan fraud. Contrary to popular belief and practice, stated income loans do not grant you a license to lie.

- *Debt.* Decrease the amount of your *dis*qualifying monthly payments.
- *Interest rate.* Use a loan program or product that offers a lower qualifying interest rate and/or monthly payment (e.g., ARM, GPM, buydown). Two such loan products that gained wide use during the 2001–2006 property boom were interest-only loans that required no principal payments for 5, 10, or even 30 years, and option ARMs with negative amortization. Option ARMs permit (within a wide range) borrowers to select the amount they wish to pay month to month. Although these and similar easy-qualifier loans greatly increase borrowing power, they add greatly to the risk of foreclosure.
- *Compensating factors.* List and explain reasons why the lender's methods of calculation understate your ability to pay back the loan.
- *Decrease PITI (MI) (HOA).* Because principal, interest, homeowners insurance, mortgage insurance, and monthly homeowners association dues all conspire to increase your qualifying ratios, take aim at each of these items. Shop for homes that require low insurance, lower property taxes, lower mortgage insurance premiums, or lower homeowners association fees. You can also reduce your qualifying principal repayment through longer terms (say, 30 or 40 years as opposed to 15 or 20), GPMs (*Secret #29*), and balloon loans (*Secret #69*).

Recall the most important theme of *Mortgage Secrets*: Qualifying and affordability depend on you! You need not become a Sister Carrie blown about by the winds of fate. If, after improving your ratios as best you can and you still don't qualify with one lender, switch to another lender or loan program that might accept higher qualifying ratios (or a lower debt coverage ratio).

Collateral Value: We Don't Want the Property, But We Do Want You to Want It

Except for a few predatory loan sharks (see *Secret #82*), lenders don't want your property. That's why most mortgage loans emphasize *credit*. As a means of last resort, lenders will foreclose, but they rarely expect to get their money back from doing so. Why then do most lenders require an appraisal of a property's value?

Appraisals protect against fraud. The lender checks to see if the property seems to be worth the price you're offering to pay. Without this check, scam artists can bilk mortgage lenders out of billions (as with the savings and loans in the mid- to late 1980s).[2] The lender also wants to verify that you're committed to the property. Thus, the loan-to-value ratio. From the lender's perspective, the more cash you invest in the property, the less likely you'll mail the keys to the lender if times get tough.

Never Tell a Lender that a Foreclosure Will Yield It a Profit

Borrowers with spotty credit err egregiously when they expect their large down payment to substitute for commitment and credit.[3] These borrowers might say something like this to the loan rep: "Why should you care about my credit? I'm putting 30 percent down. If you foreclose, you're going to make money." Do not adopt this approach. You will alienate the lender. Your loan application will get deep-sixed.

You will never persuade reputable lenders to loan you money if you point out how much money they will reap if they foreclose. Lenders don't want to foreclose. They do not want an inventory of real estate owned properties (REOs). And they do not knowingly make loans to would-be borrowers who do not appreciate those facts.

Show Your Commitment

Use a larger down payment to show your *commitment* to the property. Emphasize how much the property means to you. Detail the improvements you plan to make. Relate how much effort you put into finding a property whose features exactly match what you've been trying to find for the past two years.

A higher down payment can to a limited degree offset less-than-perfect credit, but never think of it as a profit incentive for the lender in case you don't pay as agreed. Big down payments signal commitment.

---

[2] This instance of massive widespread fraud included many dishonest loan reps, appraisers, sales agents, developers, loan underwriters, lawyers, and other insiders.

[3] Except when borrowers are dealing with predators or hard money lenders.

Investor Loans, Ditto

This same advice applies to real estate investors. Traditionally, lenders require investors to put more money down to diminish the possibility that the investor will abandon the property if rent collections fail to cover property expenses. Experience proves that homeowners will struggle to keep their properties during economic downturns or personal setbacks. Investors more readily abandon ship. So, investors, show your commitment, too. Lenders do not want your failures.

SECRET # **41**

Credit scores influence, but do not determine, the terms and costs of your loan.

As emphasized, most mortgage lenders assess your creditworthiness through credit scoring. Fannie Mae, Freddie Mac, FHA, VA, and portfolio lenders such as Washington Mutual all follow some form of this so-called "black box" credit evaluation.

If your credit score pops out at, say, 720 or higher, problems are not likely. Just make sure you've not messed up any of the other Cs of credit approval, and you're home free at (or near) the lowest interest rates and costs available (provided that you understand the mortgage process and don't let some sharpshooting loan rep get you in his sights). If your score totals between 660 and 720, however, you may not get the best terms with the least amount of hassle. And if your score falls below, say, 620, some lenders will push you into subprime (much more expensive) mortgages unless your other Cs tell a persuasive story. Below 600 or so, watch out for predators or try for protection with FHA or VA.

What Is Credit Scoring?

Through credit scoring, lenders try to push personal judgment away from credit evaluation. Credit scoring data from auto loans, department store accounts, and credit cards prove that computer statistical programs can distinguish platinum, gold, copper, lead, and plastic far better than back-office loan clerks or front-office loan reps.

To create these credit-scoring programs, math whizzes study the credit profiles, borrowing habits, and payback records for millions of people. Then they search for statistically significant correlations that tend to rate borrowers along a continuum from walk-on-water (say, 800 or higher) to neck-deep (say, 550 or lower). Credit scores range from 350 to 850, but more than 80 percent of Americans score between 600 and 800.

Credit Scoring Is Spreading

If you've received a preapproved credit card in the mail or obtained instant credit at Sears, Home Depot, or Best Buy, you've been run through a credit-scoring program. That's why the store could quickly decide with only slight information from you (social security number, name, address). Even insurance companies (especially auto) now turn to credit scores to decide whether to insure you and, if so, at what price. Employers, too, have started running credit scores on job applicants and, in some cases, current employees.

You must do all you can to bolster your score. And if your score now shines platinum keep it there. In the United States of tomorrow, Mensa will become old hat. It's far more prestigious and practical to get invited into the FICO 800 club. (Fair, Isaac and Company—FICO—is the leading supplier of credit scoring software programs.)

SECRET # **42**

Your credit score doesn't necessarily represent your credit strength.

Contrary to what increasing numbers of loan reps (and others) believe, your credit score doesn't necessarily represent your credit strength. You may never have paid a bill late in your life and still earn a credit score of less than 600.

Credit Scoring Doesn't Rate You Personally

The credit scorers select certain characteristics that you share with others who have (or have not) paid their bills as scheduled; then, based on these selected characteristics, the scorer's mathematical formula assigns you a number. Supposedly, this assessment accurately gauges the risks you present to the lender—but it doesn't. Why? Because you are a unique individual. Although you share some similarities with this computer sample of borrowers, you also differ in many ways of which the credit scoring programs know nothing. These unaccounted-for differences may give you more (or less) borrowing credibility than your credit score indicates.

Credit scores parallel SAT scores and other college admissions tests. If you fail to register a top score, you can kiss Stanford good-bye—unless, that is, you write a superlative admissions essay and bolster your application with distinguishing achievements (and, of course, a big donation from your rich uncle wouldn't hurt your chances).

I'm Not a Number

Remember the Bob Seger rock classic, "I'm Not a Number"? When you apply for mortgage credit, make that song your anthem. Certainly, do all that you can to boost your credit score, but never deal with a lender who confuses the total *you* with your credit score.[4] By the same token, never assume that your astute loan rep and underwriter will intuitively recognize your worthwhile qualities. Just as the aspiring Stanford applicant must document why she deserves admission, you, too, must persuasively document why the lender can trust you to pay back that $750,000 you're asking to borrow.

SECRET # **43**

Discover your credit scores.

In the late 1990s, when mortgage lenders began widespread use of credit scores, the credit score providers told lenders to keep the scores secret from the borrowers. The score providers would otherwise cut off the lender. This secrecy created a howl of protest.

[4] Unless, perhaps, your credit score makes you look better than you deserve.

Nevertheless, eloan.com braved the storm and began releasing scores to its customers. True to their word, the credit score providers threatened to throw eloan.com out of the fraternity. Not only did eloan.com refuse to buckle under, the California legislature entered the fray and mandated release of credit scores to all Californians. Shortly thereafter, Fair, Isaac (FICO) set up its web site, myfico.com. Now, for around $50, anyone can learn their FICO scores as created from credit data held by the three major credit repositories (Equifax, Experian, and Trans Union).

Not All You Need

You can't rely on myfico.com numbers alone. When a lender or its auto-mated underwriting system runs your credit, it uses a tri-merged credit report from all three credit repositories. The lender will receive three credit scores for each person who applies or co-applies for a mortgage (six scores will be generated for a couple, nine scores for three investment partners, and so forth).

The three separate scores provided for each individual sometimes vary by 80 points or more. That's because Equifax, Experian, and Trans Union do not necessarily use the same credit data. Different data yield different scores. Big differences in credit data may yield big differences in credit scores.

Save Money on Your Credit Reports

If you don't want to pay for your credit information, you have several alternatives.

- *Consumerinfo.com.* This web site operated by Experian will give you a free credit report, but it also will automatically enroll you in a $79.95 credit-monitoring service. Cancel this service within 30 days and you owe nothing.
- *Free reports.* Various states require credit bureaus to provide reports for free, or at nominal cost. Also, under federal law, you may receive free reports from each of the repositories if you're unemployed and looking for work, you're on welfare, or you've been turned down for credit during the past 30 days.

◆ *General commentary.* For the latest (usually critical) commentary about credit scoring and credit reporting, go to www. creditscoring.com and www.creditaccuracy.com. Also, the Federal Trade Commission maintains consumer information on all types of credit issues at www.ftc.gov.

SECRET # **44**

Improve your credit scores.

When credit scoring caught the public's eye, credit score providers not only refused to tell borrowers how they rated in the system, they also refused to tell precisely how the system itself operates. Today, that refusal still stands. Until Congress or state legislators force the issue, credit scoring remains a black box operation.

Credit scorers enter your credit data into their programs and out pops a number, but they won't reveal how or why they calculated that figure. You're left in the dark. (Credit scorers defend their secrecy for two reasons: (1) They don't want you to game the system; and (2) they don't want to tip off their competitors as to the techniques they are using.)

Turning Up the Lights

Fortunately, even though the credit scorers have not shined much light into their black boxes, mortgage loan reps and underwriters who see everyday results are beginning to develop some keen insights. In addition, while still cloaking their systems in secrecy, credit scorers have reluctantly released some clues over which borrowers can puzzle.

Indeed, myfico.com will give you pointers on how to improve your FICO scores. To learn how much your scores actually do improve (if any) over the next 12 months, you will need to pay another $40 or so. For that price, you get four FICO reports. Turns out that turning up the lights a little will prove to be a real moneymaker for Fair, Isaac. Millions of Americans must now go to myfico.com and *pay* to glimpse their credit destiny.

I say "glimpse" because the info provided doesn't go far enough. It's more like "try this and pay us to see what happens." You really can't tell ahead of time the specific score boost that their suggested changes might bring about. Nevertheless, piecing together clues from myfico.com and experienced loan reps, here are the best tips currently available. (However, FICO and other credit scoring companies periodically revise their scoring systems. So, pointers that applied yesterday may not apply in the same way tomorrow.)

- *Number of open credit accounts.* You can have too few or too many. The optimum number probably ranges between four and 10. One highly paid, credit-perfect (no lates) executive I know scored 640. After closing 6 of her 12 credit card accounts, her score went to 780, but it took six months before her score climbed up to that level. Some observers now say that closing accounts has been overrated as a credit boosting technique. So, do not close old accounts in favor of newer ones. Longevity counts. Nevertheless, over the long run, fewer accounts should help you maintain better credit discipline—thus, a higher credit score.
- *Balances.* Open accounts that carry balances reduce your score more than open accounts per se.
- *Balances/limits.* Numerous accounts with balances close to the limit will lower your score.
- *Credit inquiries.* Whenever a potential creditor checks your credit file, it counts against your score; however, multiple checks within two weeks or so may not hurt much if it appears that you're merely shopping different lenders for one loan. Your personal inquiries don't affect your score. Nor do insurer or employer inquiries.
- *Payment record.* Obviously, late payments hurt your score, but supposedly FICO doesn't distinguish between late mortgage payments and late payments on your Visa or student loan. (Mortgage lenders, though, most certainly do care. Always pay your mortgage or rent first.)
- *Recency counts.* Late payments recorded two years ago don't hurt as much as those that occurred two months ago.
- *Black marks.* Multiple lates on multiple accounts, collections, unpaid judgments, and tax liens devastate your score.

◆ *Kiss of death (but not always fatal).* Go straight to credit scoring purgatory if you're within two years of a past bankruptcy discharge or a foreclosure sale. Chapter 13 bankruptcy plans and credit counseling debt management plans also count negatively. Nevertheless, some lenders (e.g., FHA loan programs) will originate a mortgage for people who are successfully carrying out a debt repayment plan including a Chapter 13 bankruptcy.

Myfico.com also shows that some categories weigh more heavily than others. These are:

◆ Age of credit (15%)
◆ Mix of credit (10%)
◆ Amount of balances (30%)
◆ Payment history (35%)
◆ Recent credit inquiries (10%)

These clues shed some light on the credit scoring process. Most importantly, they display why perfect payments do not necessarily generate a high FICO score. To improve your score, you must not only pay your bills on time, every time, you must also manage your credit according to the likes and dislikes of the FICO (or other) credit-scoring program.

SECRET # **45**

Garbage in, garbage out (GIGO).

Researchers everywhere know of GIGO (garbage in, garbage out). Clearly, this rule applies to credit scoring. These programs pull in raw data from the files of Equifax, Trans Union, or Experian. If your credit file data include errors, as do more than 50 percent of all files, your credit scores will also err; of course, some errors might work to your benefit (e.g., unrecorded lates, understated balances, and missing liens and judgments).

Examine Your Credit Reports Now

Seventy-five percent or more of mortgage loan applications require tri-merged credit reports and, correspondingly, three credit scores per borrower. Because each credit repository has set up more than 200 million files for individuals and registers billions of computer-generated entries every year, you are unlikely to find three flawless, perfectly matched reports. Yet, inconsistencies and mistakes can slow down or derail your mortgage approval.

What to Look For

You're looking for errors, but what kinds of errors? There are more kinds than you might imagine, such as:

- *Inconsistency.* Do the reports differ significantly from each other? Does each report accurately show your credit accounts along with an appropriate "open" or "closed"?
- *Late payments.* Make sure that all late payments shown were in fact late. Also, check the category of lates—30, 60, 90 days or over. Sometimes creditors overstate the number of days payments have been late. Watch for rolling lates; you miss a payment, then get back on schedule. Every subsequent payment may show up as late.
- *Balances.* Verify that the outstanding balances and credit limits don't adversely misstate your credit position. When balances push against limits, your credit score goes down.
- *Disputed claims.* Have you justifiably refused to pay any creditor's bills? Health clubs and other service contract providers often continue to bill, and report as unpaid, fees for membership that customers canceled long ago.
- *Credit experience counts.* Do the reports accurately indicate the length of time each account has remained open?
- *Omissions.* Have you established excellent credit with a credit card, landlord, or retail merchant that does not show up in your credit files? Some creditors fail to report excellent payment records and balance information. Why? If your credit score goes up, that lender's

competitors will mail you offers to switch to their better terms or higher limits.

- *Tax liens.* Typically, before your loan closes, you must pay liens.
- *Judgments.* Ditto for judgments unless the statute of limitations has passed.
- *Collections/write-offs.* Ditto for collections and write-offs, subject to the statute of limitations.
- *Time limits.* Does any derogatory information violate these legal time limits? The limits are: credit inquiries (two years); foreclosure (seven years); lates, collections, write-offs (seven years); judgments and tax liens (usually until statute of limitations runs out). To calculate time limits, work back from the date of last activity on the debt. (In some cases, the time limits for reporting begin to run 180 days after your last payment.) Also, creditors often sell their bad debts to credit collection vultures. These outfits may improperly report debts beyond their lawful date of removal. Beware: You can trigger a new time limit by partial payment or settlement. The bankruptcy reporting clock starts on the date of discharge, not the date of filing.
- *Other information.* Verify all other information, such as names, addresses, employment, date of birth, and so on.
- *Consistency with application.* Remember, your loan underwriter will compare the data in your credit files with the liabilities and other information you list on your mortgage applications. Do they match up? Can you credibly explain variances?

What to Do Next

Should you discover errors, omissions, or inconsistencies that bear negatively on your credit score, immediately start the correction process. If you wait until a loan rep asks about these items, you could lose your loan and the property you have agreed to buy. Some problems can disappear in a matter of days, but others may take months to clear up.

Contact the Credit Source and the Repository Simultaneously

Most credit advisors tell you to notify the credit repository, point out the change you deserve, and formally, in writing, seek compliance with your request. This is good advice except for one critical fact: Credit repositories primarily report only that information given to them by your creditors. Unless the repository has botched the data it's been given (quite possible), the repository must contact the (mis)reporting creditor. If the creditor does not respond within 30 days, the repository must remove the disputed item.

However, if the creditor says, "Sorry, no mistake on our part," the record remains as is. The problem is back in your lap—but now 30 days may have passed by. To head off this potential delay, contact the original source of the (mis)information at the same time as you contact the creditor. Ask the original source to give new, corrected data to the repository. Upon request, some creditors will reverse derogatory entries for customers they do not want to lose—or as a perk to encourage payment or settlement.

On the other hand, if you deal with a hostile or indifferent creditor, you could face a prolonged battle. In that case, the loan underwriter will either waive the black mark upon suitable explanation from you; offer you a higher-cost, less-desirable loan; or decline approval until you obtain the creditor's correction or release.

To close their mortgage in a timely fashion, many borrowers have had to pay disputed claims. Act early and you prevent forced settlements on eat-crow terms. Carefully review your credit report now. Avoid last-minute pleas under deadline conditions.

Credit Scores May Adjust Slowly

Your credit score may take 30 to 60 days to incorporate new or changed credit file data. In the meantime, if your loan program requires a 660 score and your uncorrected score stands at 648, you could be out of luck. (Some mortgage lenders use the lowest middle score of all loan applicants. Most lenders do not merely average credit scores. So, ask your loan rep in what precise way the lender weighs the individual scores of a single borrower as well as the multiple scores of two or more co-applicants.)

Some loan reps can correct the negative effect of reporting errors within a matter of hours through a "rapid rescoring" process. But here's the catch: To gain rapid rescoring, you must provide the loan rep a document from a creditor who confesses error. This technique won't work for disputes. It won't work when the creditor fails to respond in a timely manner; and it doesn't work to achieve the score boosts you could achieve through savvy credit management.

Credit Scores Adjust Like Molasses to Changes in Credit Management

To improve your long-term credit score, change your credit profile. Pay your bills conscientiously; close excessive accounts; reduce the amount of your outstanding balances—but total payoffs of all accounts may hurt because you want to maintain an active credit experience—and resolve disputes, liens, judgments, and write-offs. No one can quickly overcome the stains that soil a credit report when they lawfully belong there. Just clean them up as best you can. At the same time, manage your credit as if the FICO folks were looking over your shoulder—because they are.

SECRET # **46**

Most credit repair firms (or deceptive tactics) can't fix your credit or boost your credit scores.

"Erase bad credit" the credit repair ads say. The Federal Trade Commission (FTC) says something quite different. "Don't be misled by credit repair ads. . . . Promises to repair or clean up a bad credit file can almost never be kept." How do these firms get away with making false promises? They just operate until the government shuts them down; then they open shop again under a new name.

Even worse, many tactics these firms promote could land you in jail. For example, one trick they pull is to get you a new credit file under a different (false) social security number or business tax number. If caught (and you will likely get caught in our ever-more-automated, no-privacy world), the Feds can prosecute you for identity fraud or obtaining credit through fraudulent misrepresentations. Anytime you fib, deceive, mislead, omit, overstate, or understate to obtain credit from a federal- or state-regulated financial institution, you commit criminal fraud.

You can improve your credit record and scores when you follow the steps outlined in *Mortgage Secrets* or other books by reputable authors and publishers. Countrywide Funding, the huge mortgage banking firm, publishes an excellent (and free) credit repair manual. Also see *Your Credit Score*, by Liz Pulliam Weston (2nd ed., FT Press, 2007). This book provides many good credit repair tips and tactics. (Credit repairs in this sense doesn't mean jettisoning lawful negative entries from your credit file. It means correcting wrongful entries, adding legitimate entries, and careful credit management that complies with the rules manufactured by Fair, Isaac and other credit scoring systems.)[5]

SECRET # **47**

Bogus credit counselors can scam you, too.

As sham credit repair firms finally begin to get the tar and feathers they deserve, many similar scam operations now do business as credit counselors, debt consolidators, and "get out of debt for dimes on the dollar" firms. Similar to their credit repair brethren, these firms typically over-promise, overcharge, and under-deliver.

Rather than detail all of their seedy practices, let me pass along the recommendations of Clark Howard, one of the best consumer intelligence experts in the country. For credit counseling and debt repayment plans, Clark recommends the not-for-profit Myvesta (located at myvesta.com) or Consumer Credit Counseling Service (CCCS).[6] CCCS charges its clients a nominal fee of less than $50.

---

[5] Although FICO currently dominates the field of mortgage lending, numerous other scoring systems will soon challenge Fair, Isaac. Such systems will be forthcoming from Fannie Mae, Freddie Mac, FHA, and the Vantage system developed by the three large credit repositories.

[6] Formerly known as Debt Counselors of America (DCA). Myvesta's web site offers a cornucopia of credit advice and information.

If you select some other counseling or debt management advisor, get all promises *in writing*. Do not accept glowing hype. Read your written contract carefully in the comfort of your home. Federal law (the Credit Repair Organization Act) gives you three days to rescind. Do not pay any fees, costs, or debt installments until after you thoroughly investigate the organization.

SECRET # **48**

Credit counselors and debt management firms do not improve your credit record or boost your credit scores.

Why go to a credit counseling-debt management service? Three reasons: To get help with budgeting; to seek legal advice about bankruptcy and creditor collection practices; and to prevent or stop creditor collection efforts. If you've got good credit, budgeting assistance can help you retain it. If you've bruised or busted your credit, however, debt management or consolidation plans will not redeem you anytime soon. To most creditors, you either pay your bills on time or you don't.

They may agree to accept less money than you owe on revised terms as the best outcome for a bad situation, but your credit file will still get hit with a write-off unless you negotiate otherwise. If in collection, that, too, will remain. In general, neither Fannie Mae's nor Freddie Mac's underwriting will accept mortgage applicants who currently participate in debt workout plans (including Chapter 13 bankruptcy). Conventional loans have generally required two years of nearly clean payments *after* completing debt rehab.

FHA and VA lenders, though, do take a case-by-case approach. If you've got a good story to explain your past credit problems, neither FHA nor VA will reject you arbitrarily. After at least one year of paying as agreed, flexible government program lenders may approve your application. Essentially, these lenders (and most others) like to hear how your credit problems arose from a run of misfortune, not perpetual irresponsibility.

SECRET # **49**

Bankruptcy (Chapter 7) doesn't necessarily ruin your credit.

Many hapless borrowers are talked into ill-fated debt management repayment plans including Chapter 13 bankruptcy. They are told that bankruptcy (Chapter 7 liquidation) will ruin their credit. It stays in the credit file for 10 years. In response, these troubled debtors quake with the fear of stigma and the thought of becoming a credit leper.

While it is true that both Chapter 13 (debt repayment) and Chapter 7 (liquidation) show up in your credit report for 10 years, it does not follow that Chapter 7 bankruptcy ruins your credit for 10 years, or even 2 years.

What's the Best Outcome?

If your bills get out of control, consider a debt repayment plan only when you own substantial assets that you would lose in a Chapter 7 filing. Experience shows that more than 50 percent of the people who enter debt management plans fail to successfully complete them. Consequently, they continue to botch up their credit and merely postpone their day of reckoning.

On the other hand, if you want to rebuild your credit as quickly and securely as possible, Chapter 7 can make sense. After you obtain a Chapter 7 discharge, you're debt free, except possibly for past-due taxes, student loans, and some types of judgments. Instead of plugging $300 to $3,000 a month into paying off debt, you can put that money into savings. Within a year or two, you'll be much further ahead financially than if you were still stuck in a payoff plan. As to credit profile, cash in the bank and no (or very limited) debt give you a better credit profile. Fannie and Freddie will each consider Chapter 7 bankrupts two years after discharge. FHA/VA will consider such persons after one year. In other words, when you're really drowning in debt, Chapter 7 can put you on the path to mortgage approval and financial stability faster and more effectively than a debt repayment plan.

Won't We Lose Everything?

Every state exempts some of your valuable assets from loss in a Chapter 7 bankruptcy. You may emerge from Chapter 7 with your home equity, retirement plans, automobile, life insurance cash values, and the tools of your trade. But even if you lose everything, wouldn't your new debt-free, anxiety-free net worth feel better than dodging the collection agencies?

No Endorsement for Bankruptcy

My tentative advocacy of Chapter 7 (in hopeless cases) does not stand as a billboard for bankruptcy lawyers. My intent is to warn against the ill-fated, debt-repayment schedules that entrap so many people. Such folks continue to struggle financially for years, yet see no light at the end of the tunnel.

Remember, most reputable not-for-profit credit counseling agencies are funded by banks. Although these organizations employ dedicated people who would like to help you, their jobs depend on encouraging borrowers to elect partial debt repayment rather than Chapter 7. As to the disreputable for-profit and ersatz not-for-profit debt management companies, they reap credit repair fees by taking a slice of your monthly debt management payments. The debt counseling industry does not gain when debtors file Chapter 7.

If you are (or become) overwhelmed by debt, weigh your choices and select the one that advances you to where you want to go most quickly and surely.

Changes to the Bankruptcy Law

In 2005, Congress finally yielded to the bank lobby. As a result, consumers now face a revised bankruptcy law that forces some households into debt repayment plans—even when they prefer to file under Chapter 7 (debt liquidation). In general, this law requires filers who earn more than the median income in their area to pass a means test. If the bankruptcy court finds that debtors can pay at least part of what they owe, they will not receive a full discharge. They must continue to pay what the court says they can afford. (A bankruptcy specialist can work through your income, bills, and expenses to tell you how you might fare in bankruptcy court.)

SECRET # **50**

Your ex-spouse can ruin your credit (and other tales of double counting).

Are you divorced, married, or planning a wedding? Might you buy a property with a partner or significant other? Then you're going to face the multiple scores and multiple-person problems of credit scoring and mortgage approval.

The Ex-Spouse Dilemma

If a sharp lawyer handled your divorce, you cut up all joint credit cards and closed all joint accounts. If you and your ex owned a home with a joint mortgage, one spouse bought the other spouse out and refinanced solely in his or her own name. Without these precautions, you're still on the hook for such debts; they will figure in your qualifying ratios when you apply for a mortgage. If you haven't yet eliminated this potential debt overload, work out something now.

Even worse than debt overload (for purposes of qualifying), your ex-spouse's poor repayment habits on joint debts will show up to bruise your credit. Similar problems can also confront married couples who separate either legally or by informal agreement. When you end your lives together, abolish all joint credit accounts. In some instances, a lender will permit you to explain away poor credit where full responsibility actually falls on your ex, but the lender will not overlook joint credit obligations that remain open. If the law imposes eventual liability on you for the debt, as far as the lender's concerned, it's your debt, or it's your credit line for as long as it remains open or unpaid.

One Borrower, Multiple Credit Scores

Earlier, *Mortgage Secrets* discussed the fact that any given borrower will receive a credit score from each credit repository. Should the credit data in these files materially differ, the corresponding credit scores will differ. This fact brings up the question: Which score will the lender choose to use if one or two of your scores fall below program minimums? To a certain extent, it will depend on the persuasive story you tell. In most instances the lender selects the lowest middle score of all applicants. If you and your co-borrower (spouse, relative, partner), respectively, show these scores, 580, 610, 655 and 720, 730, 760, the lender might very well use 610 as the relevant credit score for underwriting.

Multiple Borrowers, Multiple Scores

Even when you and your spouse (co-borrower) show more than adequate income to buy and finance a property, both borrowers often need credit scores or explanations that surpass lender standards. Without meeting this requirement, the lower-score borrower might have to withdraw as a co-borrower. The lender will then limit the loan amount to the qualifying capacity of the higher-score borrower.

You can work around this problem. Buy a two- or four-unit property, or a home with an accessory apartment, and use lease income from the rental units to lift the higher-credit scorer's qualifying income. Also, you could bring in another strong credit person (parent, sibling, friend) to serve as cosigner or co-borrower; however, the amount and repayment performance for that mortgage will impact that person's future credit record and borrowing power.

If you are asked to help someone qualify for a loan, be wary. Likewise, if you ask someone to sign for you, pay the loan diligently. Otherwise, you risk the other person's credit score as well as your own.

CHAPTER 6

The Lowdown on Low Downs

If you think that you lack money for a down payment, think again. In this chapter, *Mortgage Secrets* explores many ways to get over, under, or around the problem of too little cash. But it also reveals how little- or nothing-down mortgages can seriously increase the costs of your financing. Fortunately, *Mortgage Secrets* suggests techniques that can alleviate or even eliminate these costs.

Of course, just because you can buy with little or nothing down doesn't mean it's wise for you to buy. Financial discipline must precede property investment. If your lack of cash results from a spend and borrow, no need to worry attitude, shape up your finances before taking on more debt—even if it's constructive debt. Little or nothing down works best for people who manage their money well and/or those who want to consciously use leverage to maximize their wealth building. If you fit either of those descriptions, here's the good news.

SECRET # **51**

You can buy with little or nothing down.

No matter where you live, there's a low- or no-down-payment property finance plan waiting for you. Without a doubt, if you shape up your fiscal fitness you can become a property owner without a large down payment.

What's more amazing, the down payment, small as it may be, need not come from your own pocket. Some property finance plans allow you to raise all or part of your down payment through loan, gift, grant, rent credits, investment partners, or do-it-yourself (sweat) equity.

Nevertheless, even though you can buy a property with little or nothing down, first realistically (even pessimistically) critique your patterns of spending, borrowing, and saving. "No cash, no credit, no problem" may get you the financing you want, but it won't keep you out of foreclosure. Prudence dictates cash reserves.

Have you taken control of your finances? Or might "nothing down" deepen your failure to manage your money diligently? During the past year or two, record numbers of marginal borrowers (homebuyers and investors) have defaulted on their mortgages. *Mortgage Secrets* definitely encourages you to acquire a portfolio of properties. For most people, property represents the best route to wealth. Definitely, read this chapter to learn the techniques of little or nothing down. But also, put *Secret #4 (Shape up your borrower profile)* into practice.

Do not merely buy a property; you want to own it until you sell—on your own schedule. Unfortunately, experience shows that "little or nothing down" borrowers suffer foreclosure at rates 4 to 10 times higher than borrowers who make a down payment of at least 20 percent. Play it safe. Budget carefully. Allow for the unexpected.

SECRET # **52**

No matter how much you earn, FHA may hold the key to your financing needs.

The most popular low-down-payment home finance plan is offered by the United States Department of Housing and Urban Development/Federal Housing Administration (HUD/FHA). Yet, contrary to popular belief, FHA does not limit its loans to people of low or moderate incomes. Perpetuating this fallacy, one of Florida's largest newspapers continues to describe FHA as a program for low-income homebuyers. Not true. No matter how much you earn, FHA may provide the key to your home financing. (FHA does not finance property investors per se. But you can use FHA to acquire a two- to four-unit rental property—if you intend to live in one of its units for at least a year. However, if after moving in, your plans change, you can move before the full year passes.)

What Is FHA?

When Realtors and mortgage lenders talk about an FHA loan, they typically refer to the FHA 203(b) mortgage. With hundreds of thousands of new FHA 203(b) loans made last year alone, this program is the largest low-down-payment loan available throughout the United States.

You can get into an FHA mortgage for just 3 to 5 percent out-of-pocket cash—sometimes a little more, sometimes less. On an $85,000 property, you would pay around $3,250; to finance a $125,000 property, you'd pay approximately $6,000; a property priced at $175,000 would require cash of around $8,250.

How Much Will FHA Finance?

If you would like to buy a low- to mid-priced home, carefully consider the FHA 203(b) program. In this context, the meaning of "mid-priced" depends on where you live because FHA sets specific loan limits for each locale around the country. In high-priced cities such as Los Angeles, San Diego, Washington, D.C., and Boston, the FHA maximum loan currently tops out (for single-family houses, condos, and town homes) at $362,790. In the lowest-priced areas of the country, the maximum FHA home loan comes in at $200,160. Because FHA limits vary, consult with a mortgage loan advisor in the area where you would like to own. Compare these limits to home prices to see if the FHA 203(b) can work for you. (You also can check limits by locale at www.hud.gov.)

Reconsider Rental Properties

As another choice, buy a duplex, triplex, or fourplex. As noted, live in one of the units and you still can take advantage of a relatively low down payment. Again, here are examples of maximum FHA loan figures for these properties.

	Lowest Cost Areas	Highest Cost Areas
Duplex	$256,248	$464,449
Triplex	$309,744	$561,411
Fourplex	$384,936	$697,696

If you buy a two- to four-unit property, you won't have to qualify for the loan using just your monthly earnings. The rents that you collect from the property also count. Because the first home I bought was a fourplex with an additional detached carriage house, I enthusiastically endorse this multiple-unit approach to property ownership. You gain both a home and an investment. You build wealth faster.

Other Advantages of FHA

Besides a low down payment, FHA borrowers enjoy many other advantages, such as:

♦ You can roll many of your closing expenses and mortgage insurance premiums into your loan. This cuts the out-of-pocket cash you'll need at closing.
♦ You may choose from either fixed-rate or adjustable-rate FHA plans. (Note that FHA ARMs give you lower annual and lifetime caps— 1/5—than most other ARM programs; that is, your interest rate will not increase by more than one percentage point a year, nor more than five percentage points throughout the life of the loan.)
♦ FHA authorizes banks and other lenders to use higher qualifying ratios and easier underwriting guidelines. After you've shaped up your finances, FHA will do all it can to approve your loan.
♦ If interest rates drop, and as long as you have maintained a clean mortgage payment record for the previous 12 months, you can do a "streamline" refinancing of your FHA loan at lower interest rates without a new property appraisal and without having to requalify.
♦ If you can persuade your parents or other close relatives to offer the down payment to you as a gift, you won't need to come up with any closing-table cash from your own pocket.

- FHA also indirectly permits sellers to fund your down payment. I recently sold a property to a young single man (age 23). As part of the deal, I donated several thousand dollars to an FHA-approved, not-for-profit housing organization. This housing group then gave the young man the money I had donated—which in turn served as his down payment. (Yes, this technique is currently legal—but under attack from some critics. In many cases, sellers merely raise their price to accommodate the "gift" of the down payment money.)
- Unlike most nongovernmental loans, FHA mortgages are assumable. Someone who later agrees to buy your property need not apply for a new mortgage. When mortgage interest rates are high, a low-rate assumable FHA mortgage will give you a great selling advantage.

FHA Drawbacks

FHA mortgages display two drawbacks. First, you'll pay FHA mortgage insurance premiums (MIP) to protect the lender should you fail to make your mortgage payments. This mortgage insurance initially will cost around 1.5 percent of the amount you borrow, such as $1,500 on a $100,000 mortgage. (Remember though, if you don't have the cash, you can add this premium onto your mortgage loan balance.) As another drawback, your loan interest rate will be boosted by one-half percent to cover additional mortgage insurance premiums that you'll make along with your monthly mortgage payments.

The Verdict on FHA 203(b)

What's the verdict? FHA 203(b) loans can generate costly settlement expenses and mortgage insurance premiums. Granted, too, FHA paperwork can sometimes make you tear your hair out as you hassle with bureaucratic detail. But if you rely on a specially skilled FHA lender (called a direct endorsement [DE] underwriter), your hassles can probably be alleviated. As to higher loan costs, don't forget you'll also gain offsetting benefits such as a mortgage your future buyers may assume; a streamlined refinance when interest rates fall; low down payments with little or no cash from your own pock; and easier underwriting.

In full view of these costs and benefits, anyone who wants to become a homeowner (or an investor in a two- to four-unit owner-occupied apartment building) should definitely consider FHA 203(b). The Department of Housing and Urban Development (the parent of FHA) is pushing for favorable changes in the 203(b) program. Lower costs, higher limits, and faster closings set three major goals. The FHA plays a starring role in the national strategy to make home ownership a reality for every American who is willing to make a conscientious personal and financial commitment. Take a look at this possibility. Its benefits often prove superior to any other home finance plan.

SECRET # **53**

Discover FHA's best-kept secret: The 203(k) program.

Like many renters, Quentlin Henderson of Orlando, Florida, hoped to own his own home someday. Yet, with little savings, Quentlin thought he wouldn't realize his hopes for at least three to four years. He never dreamed that within six months he would actually own a completely renovated, three-bedroom, two-bath home of 2,288 square feet—more than two-and-a-half times as large as his 900-square-foot apartment.

How did Quentlin manage this feat? He discovered the little-known, but increasingly available, FHA 203(k) mortgage loan program. FHA 203(k) allows buyers to acquire and improve a run-down property with a low- or no-down-payment loan. "The house needed a new roof, new paint, new carpeting, and a bad pet odor needed to be removed," says Quentlin. "There was no way I could have paid for the house plus the repairs at the same time. And there was no way I could have otherwise afforded a house this size."

Locate an FHA 203(k) Specialist

To use a 203(k) plan, first locate a mortgage loan advisor who understands the current FHA 203(k) purchase and improvement process. In the past, FHA often stuck borrowers in red tape for months without end. Now, however, with recent FHA streamlining and special computer software, Robert Arrowwood of California Financial Corporation reports that up-to-date, direct endorsement (DE) firms like his can "close 203(k) loans in four to six weeks instead of four to six months."

Search for Good Value

After you've located 203(k) advisors who know what they're doing, search for a property that offers good value for the money. In Quentlin Henderson's case, his Realtor found him a bargain-priced, six-year-old house that was in a sorry state because its former owners had abandoned it as a result of foreclosure. "The good news for people who buy such houses," says HUD/FHA's office in Orlando, "is that purchase prices are generally low so that after repairs are made, the home's new value often produces instant equity."

Not surprisingly, the term "instant equity" was also used by John Evianiak, a 203(k) homebuyer in Baltimore. "Not only can you buy a property and fix it the way you like," John says, "but you can buy a home for much below its market value, put some money into it, and create instant equity. There were a lot of other houses we checked out, but we were going by the profit margin."

Wanda Stokes, a 203(k) loan specialist in Indiana, says her typical loan is with buyers who spend $50,000 to $100,000 for a home, add $20,000 to $25,000 in improvements, and then end up with a home appraised at $100,000 to $150,000. But Wanda adds that she recalls one customer who borrowed $147,000 to pay $98,000 for a house and cover $50,000 in renovations. Upon completion that property appraised at $188,000. (In higher priced areas, larger amounts apply.)

Inspect, Design, Appraise

After you locate a property that you can buy and rehab profitably, you next agree with the owners on price and other conditions of sale. With agreement in hand, the property is inspected, a formal plan of repair and renovation is designed, and it is appraised according to its value as if your improvements had been completed. The amount of your loan is based upon your purchase price plus your rehab expenses up to 110 percent of the property's future renovated value.

Eligible Properties and Improvements

As long as you pay more than $5,000 in rehab expenses, you can use a 203(k) mortgage to acquire and improve nearly any one- to four-family property. In fact, using 203(k) money, you can convert a single-family home into a two-, three-, or four-unit property; or you can convert a multifamily property into, say, a duplex or single-family home. As long as you create value, you can adapt the property as you like.

For the repairs and renovations, the 203(k) mortgage permits an endless list of possibilities. Stay away from luxuries such as saunas and hot tubs—although you can spend to repair these items if they're already installed—and you can do about anything you want. Here are some examples:

- Install skylights, fireplaces, energy-efficient items such as thermopane windows and heavier insulation, or new appliances such as a stove, refrigerator, washer, dryer, trash compactor, and dishwasher.
- Finish off an attic or basement.
- Eliminate pollution or safety hazards such as lead paint, asbestos, and underground storage tanks.
- Add living units such as an accessory apartment or mother-in-law suite.
- Recondition or replace plumbing, roof, or HVAC systems.
- Improve aesthetic appeal with paint, carpet, tile, and exterior siding.
- Install or replace a well or septic system.
- Landscape and fence the yard.

"This program doesn't restrict the niceties," says Michael Noel of Pinnacle Financial. "If you want to install upgraded kitchen cabinets, you can do that. If you want to add crown moldings, you can do that. You can't borrow the money to install a swimming pool, but you can use the money—up to $1,500—to fix up a swimming pool."

Buy with Little or Nothing Down

Down payment requirements for 203(k) loans generally match the same rules that apply to FHA 203(b) mortgages; however, the 203(k) plan gives first-time buyers a pure no-down-payment possibility. Here's how this works.

You locate a house that shows promise. The house can be bought for, say, $180,000; after rehab, its market value appraisal will increase to $240,000. Next, you or your Realtor could locate an investor or contractor who will buy the house and take responsibility for the improvements. If this investor or contractor will pledge to sell the rehabbed home to a qualified first-time buyer, FHA will loan approximately $230,000 against this property. Upon completion of repairs, you then buy the property from the investor and assume the $230,000 FHA 203(k) mortgage. FHA calls this first-time buyer plan Escrow Commitment Procedure.

You achieve a no-down-payment purchase. The investor or contractor gains because he or she has paid $180,000 for the house plus, say, $17,500 for the value-creating improvements—a total investment of $197,500. That leaves a profit for the investor of $32,500. Of course, the exact numbers vary according to each property, but the process remains the same.

Some investors, in fact, enter the FHA 203(k) program and locate properties on their own for repair and resale to first-time buyers. "Investors love the program," says Jackie Carlisle of Malone Mortgage in Oakland, California. "Most of them can do their own work and get paid for it. It's the best game in town for rehab money."

Of course, if you do buy from an investor, he or she is the person who will profit from the rehab work, not you. Make this choice for only two reasons: You can't come up with the small cash-to-close that FHA requires; or you want a freshly renovated property, but can't take the time or risk to perform (or arrange) the work yourself.

SECRET # **54**

Too many vets pass up VA loans.

The VA mortgage is truly one of the best benefits offered to those who have worn our country's uniform. Millions of veterans have benefited from this loan program. Here are several reasons to use a VA mortgage.

- *No down payment.* With a VA loan, you can finance up to $417,000 with no money down. If you want to buy a higher-priced home, the law has now changed. To buy a property at a price that exceeds $417,000, you will typically need to pay the excess in cash. For instance, if the property you buy is priced at $450,000, you'll need a down payment of around $33,000 ($450,000 less $417,000).
- *Easier qualifying.* Similar to FHA, VA loans offer liberal qualifying guidelines. Many (but not all) VA lenders will forgive properly explained credit blemishes. The VA loan also permits higher qualifying ratios. I've seen veterans with good compensating factors close loans with a .48 total debt ratio.
- *Closing costs paid.* New home builders and cooperative sellers will often pay all of the veteran's settlement expenses. In fact, builders sometimes advertise that veterans can buy homes in their developments for just $1 total move-in costs.
- *Assumable.* Similar to FHA, a nonveteran buyer may assume your VA mortgage when you sell. Also like FHA, if interest rates fall, you can streamline a no-appraisal, no-qualifying refinance.
- *No mortgage insurance.* Unlike FHA, you won't buy mortgage insurance when you use a VA loan. You will, however, pay a one-time "funding fee" ranging between 1.25 to 2.14 percent of the amount you borrow. If you don't pay this fee in cash at closing, the lender can add it to your mortgage loan balance. (Reserves/National Guard members pay up to 2.4 percent.)

As with many types of mortgages, VA loans require mountains of paperwork as well as compliance with various guidelines that look into job history; property condition; home value report, called a Certified Residential Value (CRV); and seller prepaids. That's why you should work with a mortgage loan rep who is skilled in getting VA loans approved. "The devil is in the details," says loan consultant Abe Padoka. "Make sure you work with professionals who know the ins and outs of the VA home buying and loan approval process."

SECRET # **55**

The USDA offers a prime choice for low- to moderate-income homebuyers.

"I'd like to write to the president about expanding this program," says Tom Dixon of Catawba County, North Carolina. In referring to the United States Department of Agriculture's Rural Development Administration mortgage, Tom enthuses that, "It's a great program...this loan can get people into their own houses. This loan makes a tremendous difference to their lives. Under this program, anyone who has a steady job and good credit can afford a house. That's the wonderful thing about this loan."

Although you have heard of FHA financing, do you know its cousin, the Rural Development Administration (RDA, formerly known as the Farmers Home Administration (FmHA)? If you can live in a small city or rural area outside a Metropolitan Statistical Area (MSA), the Rural Development Administration could provide your easiest route into home ownership. RDA offers several low- or no-down loan programs. In addition, if you earn less than 80 percent of a rural county's median income, RDA will subsidize your mortgage payments.

Funding amounts and specific eligibility requirements for RDA mortgages change frequently. To learn what's currently available in your area, call a mortgage lender who is familiar with RDA loans. Look in the yellow page mortgage ads for FmHA or Rural Development Administration loans. For great financing on low- to moderate-priced houses, it's tough to beat RDA.

SECRET # **56**

Community lending goes mainstream.

When nationally syndicated (*Nation's Housing*) columnist Kenneth Harney wrote, "Mortgage lenders devise more ways to say yes," he was publicizing various community loan products. "If you don't own a home because you believe that your income, cash savings, or job history rule you out, think again," Harney advises. "Banks, thrifts (same as savings and loans), and other mortgage lenders are actually rewriting their rulebooks to get you into home ownership."

Basic Community Homebuyers' Programs

The most widely available community lending initiative is sponsored by the Federal National Mortgage Association (Fannie Mae), and is offered by hundreds of mortgage lenders throughout the country. Several features of this program are as follows:

- For loans up to $417,000, you may put down 5 percent of your purchase price; but only 3 of this 5 percent needs to come from your own savings or other available assets. If you can raise the other 2 percent as a gift from your parents, or maybe a grant or loan from a government housing agency or not-for-profit housing group, that's okay with Fannie Mae.
- Some, but not all, lenders judge your credit on a case-by-case basis. You'll need good-to-excellent credit at the time you buy, but past blemishes and setbacks may be forgiven if you've since proven you can manage your finances responsibly.
- This program is designed for households that earn less than 120 percent of an area's median annual income. In larger cities, this figure typically falls somewhere between $50,000 and $80,000. If you earn "too much," you still might use this or a similar program; you can buy a home in an area that's targeted for revitalization or gentrification.
- Depending on the strength of your credit score and compensating factors, your total debt ratio can go up to .40—or maybe higher. In addition, this type of loan doesn't require cash reserves after settlement; however, that's still a good idea, if you can figure out how to do it. Also, any cash reserves you can put aside will count as a compensating factor.
- Under the community-lending program sponsored by Fannie, you'll buy private mortgage insurance. Depending on the loan amount,

your premium for mortgage insurance could add $500 to $1,000 (or more) to your closing costs, and perhaps $50 to $150 (or more) to your monthly mortgage payments. If you're cash short, your lender may permit you to pay these and other closing costs with a gift, grant, or borrowed funds.

♦ To participate in this program, you must complete four to six hours of homebuyer education. You can meet this requirement by attending qualified home buying seminars that are regularly sponsored by participating mortgage lenders and Realtors. As an alternative, you can schedule a one-on-one homebuyer counseling session offered by mortgage lenders or not-for-profit counseling centers.

To finance a home through the community homebuyer's plan by Fannie Mae, call a Realtor to learn which lenders in your area participate in this program. Alternatively, watch your newspaper for announcements of lender and Realtor home buying seminars (offered weekly or monthly) and homebuyer fairs (usually offered in the spring of each year). Fannie's web site includes valuable information that describes a variety of community homebuyer programs and initiatives.

Other Community Lending Programs

In addition to the previous suggestions, call banks, savings institutions, and various mortgage companies in your area. Ask to speak to a loan officer or assistant vice president who has knowledge of that lender's community lending or Community Reinvestment Act (CRA) loan programs. Some lenders refer to these or similar easier qualifying loans as "first-time buyer" programs.

Community lending has grown quickly. To locate the right program, take your fingers for a walk through the Yellow Pages. "We are making money, and we are in the risk management business," says Tobias Washington, a senior executive with Washington Federal Savings and Loan. "We thought we needed to step out of the box a little more. People are basically honest and they need homes." So they did step out of the box. Washington federal introduced a 1 percent down payment program for first-time buyers for homes priced up to $200,000.

Although your area lenders may not offer a 1 percent down payment community lending or first-time buyer program, you're certain to find relaxed qualifying, 3 to 5 percent down finance plans. Leave no stone unturned. Ask Realtors, loan officers, and friends who have recently bought properties. Closely read the mortgage loan ads in your local newspapers. Ask your Realtor to look through the monthly or quarterly magazines published by your state's Realtors association. Often, these publications include articles and ads that describe easier qualifying, first-time buyer finance plans.

SECRET # **57**

Not-for-profit housing groups help moderate-income people own their own homes.

If you earn less than the average income for your area, another type of community effort can help you over the down payment hurdle. In nearly every city in the country, not-for-profit housing groups are helping low- to moderate-income families become homeowners.

One of the best not-for-profit groups is Habitat for Humanity. Its most famous volunteer worker has been former president Jimmy Carter. As a Christian service organization, Habitat's literature champions the fact that "thousands of volunteers around the world eagerly open their hearts [and checkbooks] and pick up their hammers to build houses in partnerships with God's people in need."

Similar to most not-for-profit housing groups, Habitat accepts applications from hopeful homebuyers. It then chooses those families whose character and sense of responsibility well suit them for home ownership. If selected, you'll buy a Habitat home with a $500 to $1,000 cash down payment, and 300 to 500 hours of work helping the volunteers build your home.

Other Not-for-Profit Efforts

Habitat is just one of hundreds of local and national not-for-profit groups who help low- to moderate-income families buy and finance homes. In addition, Catholic, Christian, and Jewish groups work to help low- to moderate-income families become homeowners. Nationwide, the five largest black religious denominations, representing 43,000 churches, have joined with a variety of corporations to form the Revelation Corporation of America. Revelation plans to finance thousands of homes in minority neighborhoods. Ask a minister for more information.

Susan Cook and Family

"Originally I went out to rent a house but they wanted $600 or $700 a month for something much smaller than this," says Susan Cook, a 36-year-old divorced mother of four, as she surveys the home she bought with the financial help of the not-for-profit Portland Housing Center in Portland, Oregon. "I just fell in love with it," Susan continues. "It was big enough, and I had some friends who had bought a house in the area so I was real comfortable with this neighborhood. I wanted to have something of my own so I wouldn't be under the thumb of some landlord. I couldn't see paying someone else rent.... Now, I can do things to my house and always know it's going to be mine."

Although Susan earned just $1,800 a month and had little or no savings, Realtors Peggy and Alan Glickenhouse and Peg Malley at the Portland Housing Center worked up a home-buying plan that could get Susan and her family into the home they wanted. After Susan got her credit cleaned up, the Portland Housing Center's down-payment assistance program contributed $3,000 toward her home buying cause. Susan borrowed another $1,000 from her parents.

Susan got her 30-year mortgage through an FHA 203(b) loan. Her payments (PITI) came in at just $490 a month—much less than she would have paid to rent. In praise of not-for-profit assistance programs, Portland Realtor Board vice president John Gronewold says, "It's not just a business thing. The more people who own their own homes and improve their neighborhoods and communities, the better it is for all of us."

Anything in Your Area?

What are the not-for-profits doing in your area? In every city in the country, groups similar to the Portland Housing Center, Habitat for Humanity,

Neighbor Works, and others are working with mortgage lenders, Realtors, community organizations, church groups, and neighborhood associations to convert renters into homeowners. Could you benefit from their help? Ask around. If you're willing and able to meet your housing and other credit obligations, a not-for-profit group might offer the financial and homebuyer counseling assistance that will move you into home ownership.

SECRET # **58**

Local governments assist with down payments.

In Oakland, California, several years back, Lynne Jerome and her husband Brian Conan had for years wanted to become homeowners. But they could never put together enough for a down payment.[1] "We tried," says Lynne, "but it was always out of our reach." With Lynne studying for a graduate degree and Brian's work as a truck driver, their family income didn't go far in the expensive California housing market.

"We always paid a lot of money for rent each month," says Lynne, "probably comparable to a mortgage payment, but instead of a mortgage we took out student loans to cover school expense. We hated throwing money down the drain for rent and couldn't see any long-term benefits of paying rent. We always took as much care of the property we rented as we would have our own home. Every time we would go outside and work in the yard or paint a room, it made us cringe because we could have been doing these things to our own place instead."

Fortuitously, Lynne and Brian no longer rent. Thanks to Fannie Mae's HomeOakland Initiative, this couple and their one-year-old daughter have now become homeowners. To buy their Craftsmen bungalow, they received a 2 percent down payment grant from the city of Oakland and a $35,000 mortgage assistance grant. "Without the HomeOakland

---

[1] If the lender can enforce a "due on sale" clause, this technique does bring about that risk. In that situation, a wraparound works better as a short-term financing strategy. If the lender calls, there may be no long term.

Initiative," says Lynne, "we would probably be working close to retirement before we could have afforded to buy."

In explaining Fannie's efforts, Larry Dale explains that, "Working together, cities and Fannie Mae can harness the expertise of nonprofits, Realtors, government agencies, mortgage lenders, and private developers. This combination of resources and combination of efforts is expected to have a far more positive impact on the community than previous, relatively uncoordinated efforts have had." In following through with its central Cities Initiative and Opening Doors Outreach Campaign, Fannie has put together partnership agreements with mayors and local lenders in the country's 25 largest cities.

Down-Payment Assistance Is Available Throughout the United States

Mortgage Secrets has emphasized various Fannie's initiatives only because Fannie provides the largest and most widely publicized effort to encourage local governments to offer financial assistance to first-time homebuyers. Yet, many large and small cities and counties haven't waited for Fannie to lead the way. They offer their own down payment and assistance programs.

In Cobb County, Georgia, for example, Donna White and her two children bought in the Parkside at Village on the Park new home development. To help swing the deal, Donna enlisted sales agent Jeannie Tucker to come up with some creative finance options. "We'll work with a buyer any way we can," says Jeannie, who prides herself on keeping up with all the special mortgage programs in the Atlanta area. "Many people have good credit and can manage house payments, but they just don't have that down payment."

To help Donna raise down-payment money, Jeannie put her in touch with Max Stone, a loan officer at Traditional Mortgage Corporation. With Max handling the paperwork, Donna was approved for down-payment assistance offered by Cobb Housing Inc.'s First HOME program. "Most of my business is first-time buyers," reports Max. "These creative financing options involve extra paperwork and take more time. But because of these programs, some borrowers get in a home who wouldn't have otherwise."

SECRET # **59**

Even Fannie and Freddie accept little- or nothing-down loans.

In the mid 1990s, both Freddie Mac (see www.homesteps.com) and Fannie Mae (www.fanniemae.com) began to create little- or nothing-down loan programs. Since then, in addition to their widely available 5 percent down product, they have pioneered community homebuyer programs, 3 percent down loans, and even 103 percent loan-to-value (LTV) loans, so that qualified borrowers can go through closing with almost no cash out of pocket. To view current programs, visit these companies' web sites.

Tougher Credit Standards and Lower Cost PMI

These Fannie and Freddie low-down-payment loans do apply tougher credit standards than either FHA or VA, but their loan limits reach substantially higher. Also, borrowers whose credit scores reach 680 (possibly as low as 620) will probably pay less for private mortgage insurance with Fannie and Freddie loan programs than they would with FHA.

On the other hand, borrowers with FICO scores of less than 620 may find that FHA's mortgage insurance premiums (MIP) now fall below the premiums of the private insurers who guarantee Fannie and Freddie's low-down-payment mortgages (i.e., LTVs greater than 80 percent). You'll need to compare costs based on your specific situation. No firm conclusions apply because competition perpetually shifts the pricing landscape. Plus, your full range of underwriting Cs (*Secret #40*) can influence loan terms and costs.

SECRET # **60**

Cut the cost of PMI by learning where rates break.

Private mortgage insurance can add other costs to your monthly payment when you finance with little or nothing down. Mortgage insurers, however, do not charge all borrowers the same amount of premium. Instead, they use risk-adjusted pricing. In a manner similar to the way lenders risk-adjust interest rates, conditions, and terms, mortgage insurers vary their premiums according to risk factors such as:

- Loan-to-value (LTV)
- Borrowers' credit scores
- Amount of the mortgage
- Debt ratios
- Borrowers' financial profile such as net worth, cash reserves, job stability, and so on

For example, if your total debt ratio goes above, say, .38, the mortgage insurer boosts your monthly MI premium. Likewise, rates may break, respectively, at 5 percent down or less (95 percent LTV); 10 percent down or less (90 percent LTV); 15 percent down or less (85 percent LTV), or less than 20 percent down (greater than 880 percent LTV).

Should it turn out that your total debt ratio went to .40, and you were putting $29,700 down on a property priced at $301,500 (90.15 percent LTV), you could save considerably by tweaking your numbers. Place just a little more down, figure a way to reduce your monthly payments, and you will slip into a lower MI rate category. The same principle applies to your credit scores. Your credit score of 617 sets a higher mortgage premium than a score of 630. Learn where the PMI rates break, and with a little financial juggling, you might save $60 to $100 a month (more or less depending on the amount of your loan).

SECRET # **61**

Before you obtain a PMI little- or nothing-down loan, understand the cost you'll pay.

Many buyers (especially first-timers) get so enthused about buying with less than 20 percent down that they fail to notice the cost of

Table 6.1 **Mortgage Insurance Cost Expressed as a Percentage of the Amount Borrowed**

	Yearly Costs
Mortgage interest (6.5% @ $15,000)	$ 975
PMI premium yearly	1,500
Total cost	2,475
Cost as a percentage of extra $15,000 borrowed =	$2,475
	$15,000
=	16.5%

low-down-payment PMI mortgages. To keep the numbers simple, imagine you buy a $100,000 property and borrow $95,000. In that case, most lenders will require you to purchase PMI. If instead of putting $5,000 down, you put $20,000 down, you pay no PMI.

The True Cost of Low Down Payments

To obtain that low-down-payment loan, you'll pay the lender yearly interest on that extra $15,000 ($95,000 less $80,000), plus you'll pay the annual premium for the PMI. Recall (*Secret #60*), mortgage insurers risk-adjust their premiums according to your credit profile and other Cs. In addition, rate and premium schedules change as insurer loss experience hits peaks and valleys. Consequently, you can't apply the results shown in Table 6.1 to your situation. You can, though, apply this *technique* to calculate the real cost of your low down payment.

For that extra $15,000 (i.e., 5 percent down versus 20 percent down), your interest and mortgage insurance costs total $2,475, or 16.5 percent. In today's market, that's a high cost of funds. But I've seen low-down loans where the effective cost goes above 20 percent. Before you jump for a low-down-payment loan with PMI (FHA's MIP) calculate the cost of that marginal amount of money you're borrowing in excess of an 80 percent LTV; then compare the cost (the effective rate) to the cost of raising money through a second mortgage or family loan. Even more costly, some lenders charge low down payment borrowers a higher interest rate and *higher* fees.

Without a doubt, PMI has helped millions of homebuyers. Just remember, that help comes at a pretty stiff cost.

SECRET # **62**

Reduce the higher cost of low down payments with a second mortgage (piggyback loan).

Piggyback financing refers to 80-10-10, 80-15-5, or even 75-15-10 loans. The first figure represents the LTV of the first mortgage; the second figure shows the added LTV of the second mortgage; and the third figure is the percentage of cash you put down. Sellers sometimes agree to carry back this second mortgage. Given the cost of PMI, you may be able to pay the sellers an interest rate of 8 percent (or more) and still come out ahead. As long as you keep the first mortgage LTV at or below 80 percent, your lender may not require mortgage insurance.

(Note: Some homebuyer loan programs do not permit *sellers* to carry back financing. Such lenders believe this type of transaction increases the potential for LTV fraud, i.e., no seller second mortgage actually exists. The buyer/seller have merely colluded to increase the stated price of the property to gain a larger first mortgage LTV without the lender's knowledge. Also, real seller seconds may cause lenders to question whether you've paid the seller too high a price in exchange for the favorable seller financing. Investment property deals, though, often include seller second mortgages and other types of seller financing.)

Second Mortgage Specialists

When possible, get sellers to carry back financing. But if the sellers cannot (or will not) assist with seller financing, turn to a lender who offers second mortgages. Here's what Eagle Mortgage says in a promotional brochure that this company mails to Realtors:

> If you knew how to lower the monthly payments on a property purchase for your "A" credit buyers, while helping them build equity

faster—would you be interested enough to listen ... what if you could help your marginal "B" and "C" credit customers close the gap between their 60% to 70% loans and the funds they actually have available for their down payment? Our purchase-money seconds offer alternative financing that can provide your buyers with up to a 90% total loan-to-value (LTV) financing. ... With No PMI!

Eagle Mortgage, like hundreds of other lenders, can help reduce the down payment gap and drop your first mortgage balance low enough so that you can avoid buying private mortgage insurance. Sometimes second mortgage lenders will charge you larger loan fees and a higher interest rate than most sellers, but if seller-assisted financing isn't available, locate a reputable mortgage lender who knows how to structure an 80-10-10 or similar piggyback loan (tiered financing). As with other types of financing, the costs and terms of second mortgages adjust along with interest rates, market conditions, and your risk/credit profile. Sometimes such financing looks better than PMI and other times it looks worse. Also, when your mortgage balance decreases and property value increases, lenders permit you to cancel your PMI (*Secret #103*). But you will pay interest on your second mortgage for as long as it exists. Never follow rate rules. Question and calculate.

SECRET # **63**

Use pledged collateral to eliminate PMI.

If you don't have enough money for a big down payment, and you can't (or don't want to) buy mortgage insurance or obtain a second mortgage, you've got another possibility. It's called pledged collateral. "We don't care where the collateral comes from," says Elmer Frank of First American Savings. "As long as we feel secure, we'll consider the loan. We've taken stocks, bonds, mortgages, retirement accounts, and once a Mercedes 300 SL Gullwing. We did, though, refuse to accept a racehorse."

Pledged Retirement Accounts

In terms of popularity, Elmer Frank adds, "Retirement accounts have become one of the most frequent sources of pledged collateral for our first-time buyers. We don't even require that the account belong to the buyers. We'll accept funds from any close family member. On no-down-payment mortgages, we usually like to see 30 percent, but for good customers, we've gone as low as 20 percent."

"In other words," Elmer continues, "we'll give buyers a no-down-payment, 100 percent loan, if, say, those buyers (or close relatives) move enough of their 401(k) funds to our bank to offset 20 or 30 percent of the property's purchase price. Last week, we closed a loan for a young couple in their thirties who bought a $365,000 duplex. Between them, they had good credit and earned $90,000 a year, but little savings because they're rapidly paying off student loans. We financed their full purchase price without PMI, and the wife's mother deposited $85,000 of her 401(k) monies with us.

"As long as the couple keeps their loan current, we won't touch the pledged collateral. As soon as the couple's mortgage balance falls below an 80 percent LTV and as long as they've kept a clean payment record, we'll release our lien against the 401(k) certificates of deposit."

Other Types of Pledged Collateral

Retirement funds aren't the only source of pledged collateral. As Elmer Frank says, his bank (like many lenders) will accept assets such as savings accounts, stocks, bonds, even a valuable antique automobile. If friends, relatives, or partners have built up equity in another property, many lenders will accept that equity as pledged collateral.

Blanket Mortgage

Sometimes you might use a blanket mortgage. This type of financing covers two or more properties under the same lending agreement. For example, say you (or someone else close to you) owns a $800,000 property. Its mortgage balance stands at $300,000. You want to buy a $400,000 property.

If you (and/or others involved) would pledge both properties, a lender could offer a new first mortgage that covers (blankets) both properties for

$700,000—a total LTV of less than 60 percent. This loan would not require PMI or a second mortgage. It could save you money and at the same time provide a "no down payment" purchase. Given this jumbo's low LTV, it should not carry an interest rate much (if any) higher than smaller loans.

SECRET # **64**

Search for sellers with low-equity assumables loans.

You've already seen (*Secret #20*) that in periods of relatively high interest rates, you can slash your costs of financing by assuming a mortgage that carries a below-market interest rate. In addition, assumables sometimes require little or nothing down. Just locate a seller who has bought (or refinanced) recently with a low-down, high-LTV, FHA/VA (or otherwise assumable) mortgage. Within the past three or four years, FHA and VA have originated more than a million low- and nothing-down mortgages.

Because the original loan balances often include closing costs and fees, many such buyers (now sellers) have built little equity. You can probably assume their loan for less than 10 percent cash out of pocket. In cases where sellers have accumulated substantial equity, ask for a seller second, or arrange a second mortgage through a mortgage lender (*Secret #68*). You might also create a wraparound loan (*Secret #73*).

SECRET # **65**

Avoid PMI with a higher interest rate mortgage.

Fannie and Freddie require PMI on all home loans they buy with LTVs greater than 80 percent (less than 20 percent down); however, lenders who do not sell into the secondary mortgage market can make low-down-payment loans without PMI. These portfolio lenders frequently use that advantage to create a competitive edge over Fannie/Freddie affiliated lenders. Here's the catch: The "no PMI" lenders typically price their loans as much as .5 percent higher than the Fannie/Freddie interest rate.

Does this pricing make for a good deal? Maybe. It depends on the amount you are otherwise required to pay for mortgage insurance. But other factors play a role. From a tax angle, the higher-interest, no-PMI loan probably proves advantageous. Although you may not be able to legally deduct PMI premiums, you can deduct all amounts you pay for interest.[2]

This next point tips toward PMI, under certain conditions (*Secret #103*), you can cancel your PMI; therefore, you shouldn't pay the PMI premium for the full term of your loan, though you will pay the higher interest rate until the date you pay off the loan (by property sale, refinance, or full payoff through amortization).

As with many loan decisions, someone must run the numbers for each specific PMI premium and the applicable tax law; next, compare the results to the interest rate alternative. Ask a trusted loan rep. You could save yourself several thousand dollars or more.

---

[2] Subject to the high-income, $1,000,000 loan tax rules.

CHAPTER 7

Win Big Savings with Seller Financing, Foreclosures, or REOs

Robert Bruss, a nationally syndicated columnist, real estate attorney, and investor, was recently asked, "Where's the best place to get a mortgage? At a bank, savings and loan, or credit union?" Bob Bruss answered, "None of these is the best. The best source of financing for your home is the seller." If you can persuade the sellers to help with your financing, you can often get easier qualifying and lower costs. Likewise, here's what realtor Robert Deimel says about seller financing in an issue of *Real Estate Today*:

"In today's complex marketplace, sellers and buyers don't always see the opportunity. That's why innovative sales people need to bring owner-will-carry (OWC) into the mix of financing possibilities. You make sales happen when you know how to encourage sellers to offer the carrot of seller financing."

What benefits does seller-assisted financing offer? Here are several:

- *Easier qualifying*. Although lending institutions apply easier qualifying standards today than 10 years ago, most are still tougher (or more costly) than many sellers.
- *Flexibility*. Mutual agreement sets the price, interest rate, monthly payments, and other terms. You and the sellers can put together a financing package in any way that works for both of you. No bureaucratic underwriting rules apply.

- *Lower closing costs*. Sellers do not require points, junk fees, and loan application costs. Unlike lending institutions, sellers don't pay office overhead or loan rep commissions.
- *Less paperwork*. Although sellers may ask for a credit report, they won't require a stack of forms, documents, and verifications piled higher and deeper.
- *Quicker sale*. Seller financing can help sellers get their property sold more quickly. Plus, for properties that require extensive repairs or renovations, or otherwise fail to meet lender underwriting standards, seller financing can make the difference between a sale and no sale.

The types of seller-assisted financing that you might use to buy a property vary according to the needs, wants, creativity, and knowledge of the parties involved. But realize, many owners who will accept OWC financing do not advertise that fact. Indeed, Robert Bruss says, "I've bought many houses with seller financing, but can't recall a single one that was advertised 'seller financing.' Until they saw my offer, none of the sellers had informed their agent that they would help finance the sale."

Regardless of whether sellers have advertised OWC, keep this possibility in mind. You won't know for sure until you've put the idea up for discussion. The following classified ads illustrate common types of seller-assisted financing:

Lease With Option to Buy $850/mo. 1 year rent toward down payment on purchase price of $156,000.

315 DOVER—MUST SEE. Completely Remodeled Brick bungalow, foyer, 2+ BR, large kitchen and living room, oak cabinets, dishwasher,

range, recessed lighting, gas frplc, part. Fin. LL, big yard w/privacy fence. CALL 460-0020 Broker

$6950 DOWN on this 3 Bdrm ranch with ceiling fans, fncd yrd. Just redone in pale grays with new carpet, paint, etc. Paid off in full in 25 yrs! $1,695.09 per mo.

OWNER CONTRACT! $284,950. 7.75% APR. NO BALLOON! 768-5350. R.E. Lic./owner.

QUALIFY EASY 5+ Bdrm, 4 Ba. $495K. Owner Financing, only 48K dn. 4118 Catalina Pl. Call 291-1810/224-6806.

Loan reps will never tell you about seller financing or assumptions or "subject to" because they don't originate these loans. Nor can loan reps tell you about foreclosures or REOs (foreclosed Real Estate Owned by lenders, mortgage insurers, or government agencies). Yet, these properties can combine bargain prices with bargain financing. How about the Realtor ad for HUD homes? (See Figure 7.1.)

Can you find a super deal similar to those described in this ad? Maybe. Remember that typically HUD/FHA finances owner occupants, not investors. However, if tough times hit and foreclosures pile up, HUD/FHA may relax its rules against investors. Government and lender rules change to meet the needs of the day.

Granted, super buys aren't always available. In strong housing markets, foreclosures dwindle and multiple bidders give sellers/lenders the upper hand in bargaining power. During the blazing real estate markets of the early 2000s, homebuyers and investors often had to search diligently for great deals with foreclosures and REOs. But times are changing. Delinquencies and foreclosures have doubled during the past two years. Soft property markets conspire with previously easy-qualifying, low-down-payment finance plans to push weak swimmers adrift in deep water.

◆

CALL THE HUD SPECIALIST
COMMITTED TO SERVE

I have the **knowledge and experience** to provide the best service!
Why Rent When You Can Own!

Specializing in first-time homebuyers   **No Closing Costs**
Quick Closing within 14 days   **Low Interest Rates**

♦ **All you need to purchase**   ♦ **Let HUD pay you**
  your Dream Home   **to own a home**
♦ Steady Employment   ♦ $300 to 3% Down Payment
♦ Previous Slow Credit   ♦ $1,000 Renter's Bonus
  & Bankruptcies OK   ♦ Purchase Below Market Value
♦ $500 to $1000 Down

Figure 7.1 Realtor Ad for HUD Homes

If the past forecasts the future, the next several years will produce a strong need for rescuers. To build equity wealth fast, or perhaps to increase your affordability, ask foreclosure specialists whether borrower defaults, foreclosures, and REOs are piling up in your area.

Although you can save big with seller financing, foreclosures, and REOs in all times and places—soft markets spell buyer's delight.[1] Yet, as high tide rolls in, many would-be buyers fear to even dip their toes in the water; but if you're willing to take the plunge when others shiver in a blanket of worry, you will earn a gold medal.[2] Now let's look at these lesser-known property finance possibilities in more detail.

---

[1] No one likes the personal hardships created by tough times, but when sellers, borrowers, and lenders need relief, someone else stands to profit. This someone could be you.

[2] During the previous high tide of foreclosures and tough times in California (1993–1996), my books of that day went firmly against the accepted opinion that "homes were no longer a good investment." I strongly urged homebuyers and investors to take advantage of the amazing buying and financing opportunities then available. Those who acted upon my advice earned extraordinary profits.

SECRET # **66**

Sellers can nearly always beat the banks at their own game, but you must do more than ask.

Mortgage lenders operate by bureaucratic rules. Sellers can listen to any deal that provides worthwhile benefits. For you to obtain their best terms and lowest costs, lenders require piles of qualifications, paperwork, documents, and verifications, whereas sellers can agree to as few documents and qualifying standards as reasonable in a specific situation. Lenders pay huge costs for fancy buildings, office overhead, loan rep commissions, and executive perks. Sellers incur none of these expenses. Lenders charge thousands in fees, closing costs, and mortgage insurance. Sellers charge only interest and maybe a few other costs.

Lenders pay their depositors much less than they charge for mortgage interest.[3] Sellers can match or beat the lender's mortgage rate and still earn a higher net return than placing their funds in bank CDs or savings accounts.

Search for Mutual Advantage

All of these advantages give sellers generous opportunity to offer buyers a more appealing property finance plan than institutional lenders. But often, sellers who are well-situated to provide or assist with financing don't realize the possibilities and benefits that lie in front of them. Like Bob Bruss, I've entered many OWC transactions even though the sellers had not previously considered this choice.

How to Get the Sellers Interested

When out-of-the-blue you ask a seller to carry back financing, you could hear a quick "No." But write your proposal into an offer to buy the property and you gain a more favorable hearing. Don't expect agreement on this

---

[3] For borrowers with low to moderate credit scores, this difference can reach 4 to 10 percent, or more.

issue right away. (Prior to writing an offer, however, I pose feeler questions such as, "Have you given any thought to helping with financing on the property?")[4] Most importantly, learn the seller's needs and selling motives, such as:

- Do the sellers want or need a quick sale?
- Do they have a pressing need for cash?
- Would a 6 to 8 percent (more or less) return seem attractive to them?
- If an investor-owned property, what kind of capital gains tax liability will the sellers incur from an all-cash sale? Would an IRS-approved installment sale save the sellers taxes?
- What do the sellers plan to do with the proceeds of sale?
- How do other pressures such as time, money, family, or work bear on the sale?

These questions merely suggest lines of inquiry. Overall, tactfully discover as much about the sellers as you can and then draft your written offer to play into their most pressing needs. Explain point by point how your offer alleviates their concerns without giving rise to new ones. Are you a credible buyer? Does your offer create too much risk? A skilled Realtor should help you achieve this end. Remember, a confused mind always says no. Eliminate seller doubts with clear and compelling reasons. Emphasize your strongest Cs.

What Type of Seller Financing?

Use any type of seller financing that meets the needs of buyers and sellers without imposing undue risks or benefits on one party or the other. The sellers could offer a first mortgage or trust deed similar to those available at banks. In addition, seller-finance might include any or some combination of the following: assumption (*Secret #20*), "subject to" (*Secret #21*), or perhaps a refinance blend, second mortgage, balloon mortgage,

---

[4] For more on negotiation, see pp. 150–175 of Gary W. Eldred, *The 106 Common Mistakes Homebuyers Make*, 4th ed. (John Wiley & Sons, 2006); and pp. 150–175 of, *Investing in Real Estate*, 5th ed. (John Wiley & Sons, 2006).

contract-for-deed (installment sale), lease option, lease purchase, or wraparound. We will now cover each of these techniques.

SECRET # **67**

Ask the seller and lender to cooperate with a refi blend.

Some years back, Patrick O'Brien had his home up for sale. His listing price was $110,000. He owed around $72,300 on his old mortgage, which carried an interest rate of 7 percent. Mortgage interest rates at that time were 12.5 percent. These high market rates discouraged buyers who would have liked to buy Patrick's home but couldn't qualify for new financing. To solve this problem, Patrick talked to his mortgage lender. He persuaded the firm to refinance his home with an assumable fixed-rate mortgage of $88,000 at an interest rate of 10 percent. In effect, this 10 percent rate blended the seller's existing interest rate of 7 percent with the then-current market rate of 12.5 percent.

The mortgage lender profited because it got the old money-losing 7 percent mortgage off its books. Patrick (the seller) gained because he could now offer his property to prospective buyers with attractive (relatively speaking) financing. At 12.5 percent, an $88,000 mortgage requires a payment of $939 per month. At a rate of 10 percent, an $88,000 mortgage requires a payment of $772 per month. Three weeks after his blended refinance, Patrick sold his property for $112,000. With their income of $35,000 a year, the buyers easily qualified to assume Patrick's mortgage. At the then-current rate of 12.5 percent, the buyers would have needed an income of $40,000 or more in order to qualify.

In some future climate of high interest rates, find a seller like Patrick who has a low-interest mortgage that's nonassumable; approach the lender and try to negotiate a refi blend. It's another way to beat the affordability problem in times when mortgage interest rates have risen. Or switch perspectives—if in some future period of high interest rates when you're the seller who holds a below-market mortgage, you could approach your lender as did Patrick. This technique works best with portfolio lenders.

Lenders (or mortgage servicing companies) who have sold their mortgages into the secondary market may not be able to modify rate or terms–depending upon the security agreements that apply to the relevant securitized mortgage pool. Still, you can inquire.

SECRET # **68**

Bridge the assumable gap with a seller second.

Let's return to the preceding example. Say that Patrick's pre-blend $72,300 mortgage could be assumed. Qualified buyers could take advantage of that low 7 percent interest rate, but with a price of around $110,000 the buyers would have needed close to $40,000 cash to pay Patrick enough to cover his high amount of equity. Many buyers would find it tough to raise $40,000.

As another possibility, Patrick (or a mortgage lender) could finance some or all of that $40,000 as a second mortgage. For instance, if the buyers had $20,000 cash, they could offer Patrick a price of $110,000 to be paid as follows: $72,300 mortgage assumption; $20,000 in cash; and a seller-second mortgage of $17,700.

The question becomes, "What interest rate and repayment schedule will apply to this $17,700 second mortgage?" The answer: whatever terms the buyer and seller negotiate. No hard and fast rules. I have seen second mortgages with interest rates as low as 6 percent and others as high as 16 percent. Sometimes a second mortgage is paid back in monthly payments over a period of three years or less. Sometimes it is structured over a term of 15 to 20 years. The terms of a second mortgage typically evolve according to what you can afford and what the sellers can be persuaded to accept.

Just remember, a second mortgage can move you closer to affordability. Or if you are an investor, it increases leverage and ideally magnifies your return on the cash you have invested in the property. Use it when you need to cover the gap between the available first-mortgage financing (assumed or newly originated) and your property's purchase price. Recall, too, that it sometimes pays to use a second mortgage along with new financing to keep the loan-to-value ratio of your first mortgage at or below 80 percent. With a less than 80 percent loan-to-value ratio, the lender isn't likely to require private mortgage insurance.

SECRET # **69**

Avoid the bang of a bursting balloon.

Sellers who agree to carry back a second mortgage frequently insist on a payoff term of seven years or less. Some sellers want their money—the sooner the better. From your view, a short-term second mortgage usually won't make much sense. The short term sends the monthly payments too high. But here's how to solve this problem. It's called a balloon mortgage.

When you use a balloon mortgage, you make monthly payments and then pay the outstanding balance after maybe five or seven years. Say the sellers have agreed to carry back a five-year second mortgage for $25,000 at 10 percent interest. You want monthly payments as low as you can get them. The sellers want to receive as much money as fast as they can. Here are five possible payback schedules:

- *Fully amortizing.* Under this schedule you amortize (pay off completely) the $25,000 second mortgage with 60 equal installments (principal and interest) of $531 per month. The sellers might like this schedule, but you might find it tough to pay $531 a month on top of the payments for your first mortgage. So, a balloon might solve your problem.
- *Partially amortizing (15-year term/5-year balloon).* Under this schedule, you pay $268 per month. After five years, you pay the balance of $20,280.
- *Partially amortizing (30-year term/5-year balloon).* Under this schedule, you pay $219; then after 60 months, you pay a balloon of $24,100.
- *Interest only.* Under this schedule, you do not pay down principal. You pay interest only of $208 for 60 months, then the entire $25,000.

◆ *No monthly payments.* This type of balloon requires no monthly payments. Instead, interest builds and is added to the original balance of $25,000. At the end of five years, the accumulated interest and principal due equals $41,133. Although this type of no-monthly-payments-plan for the second mortgage can increase affordability, few sellers are willing to accept it.

Flexibility reigns. You can tailor a payment schedule to reasonably fit the needs of both you and the sellers. Just one caveat: *Be careful!* Most buyers pay their balloon balances through a refinance or the sale of their property. If not structured with a pessimistic view of the future, however, balloons hoist up a skull and crossbones flag.

Allow yourself plenty of time (at least five years) and plenty of breathing room. Don't base your plan for repayment of the balloon on wild rates of property appreciation or speculative salary increases. Inflated expectations can create a balloon that bursts.

SECRET # **70**

Buy on the installment plan.

Among the most famous lines in American film history is Oil Can Harry's repeated warnings to Pauline, "If you don't give me the deed to your ranch, I'm going to tie you to the railroad tracks." Oil Can Harry knew that if Pauline signed over the deed to her ranch, that deed would transfer the property's title to Harry. Oil Can Harry's no-money-down approach to property ownership was somewhat unorthodox (not to mention illegal). But Harry believed that if he wrangled the deed, he would immediately become the owner of Pauline's ranch.

In some transactions, however, sellers do not deliver a deed at the time of sale. Instead, buyers pay for the property on the installment plan. In this type of purchase, buyers usually pay sellers a small down payment and then promise to pay monthly installments. In return, the sellers give the buyers possession of the property, and promise to deliver a deed to the buyers after they have completed their scheduled payments. This type of purchase agreement is known by various names such as *contract-for-deed*, *installment sale*, or *land contract*. For buyers (or properties) that don't meet the qualifying criteria of a lending institution, an installment contract might prove a good choice. I know from experience.

Why Sellers Are Willing

When I turned age 21, I wanted to build wealth and financial freedom as quickly as possible. At the time I was an undergraduate college student. I had little cash, no full-time job, and no credit record. I knew that back then (unlike today) no bank would approve me for a mortgage. But this small fact didn't crash my goals. No self-defeating self-talk for me. So, I searched for properties that I could purchase from sellers on an installment contract. By the time I completed my PhD, I had bought more than 30 houses and small apartment units. The cash flow from those properties paid many of my college living expenses.

Why are property owners willing to sell on an installment contract? Shouldn't they just deal with buyers who have the cash and credit necessary to get a loan from the bank? In my experience, I found sellers willing to sell on a contract for some combination of seven different reasons:

1. *No bank financing available.* A property may not qualify for bank financing. The property might stand in poor condition, be located in a declining neighborhood, or stand functionally out-of-date (rooming house, apartment units with shared bathrooms, irregular floor plan, and so on). Also, many lending institutions won't write mortgages on condominiums where more than 30 or 40 percent of the units in the complex are occupied by renters instead of owners.
2. *Quick sale.* One of the best ways for an owner to sell a property quickly is to offer easy terms of financing. The contract-for-deed is the easiest and quickest type of home finance plan available.
3. *Higher price.* Property owners who offer easy financing can often sell at a higher price than they otherwise could expect to receive. Many buyers will trade off price for terms. However, if you choose this tradeoff, include a balance discount for early payoff. Or alternatively, include a clause in the contract that permits you to

assign the financing to your future buyer. Otherwise, you've paid a price premium for favorable financing that you did not completely use.

4. *High interest on savings*. Sellers who plan to deposit the cash they receive from a sale in certificates of deposit or money market accounts can get a higher return on their money by financing a buyer's purchase of their property. A 7- to 10-percent return from a real estate installment sale certainly beats a 4 or 5 percent return from a certificate of deposit.

5. *Low closing costs*. With a contract-for-deed, sellers and buyers pay far less in closing costs. You avoid nearly all the expenses that a mortgage lender would charge.

6. *Tax savings*. When the seller is an investor, an installment sale of a property produces a smaller income tax bite than does a cash sale.

7. *Repossession*. Should the buyers default, the installment contract may provide the sellers a relatively quick and inexpensive right to repossess the property. Some states have enacted laws that make repossession more difficult than it used to be. That's one reason why many investors now prefer to "sell" their OWC properties via a lease option agreements. In my view, lease options shift risk from the sellers to the buyers. As a buyer, I would prefer a contract-for-deed.

Follow These Guidelines

When you and the property meet the underwriting standards of a lending institution, favor that alternative unless the seller's terms look too good to pass up. If banks won't finance the deal, by all means consider using a contract-for-deed. Cash-short buyers can also win with this strategy: Buy a rundown property on contract. Then create value through improvements. Next, refinance based on the now-higher value of the property. If you use a contract-for-deed purchase, follow these guidelines:

- *Buy the property, not the financing*. Don't let easy credit lure you into buying an overpriced property. When circumstances warrant, you might in good judgment pay a price slightly higher than market value. But would you pay $6,000 for a 2000 Ford Escort from Easy

Ed's "buy here, pay here" used car lot just because Easy Ed will sell it to you with nothing down and low monthly payments? This same principle applies to property. Be wary of "You name the price; I'll name the terms." Verify value through an appraisal, comparable neighborhood sales, or other professional opinion.

◆ *Beware of hidden defects.* A property that seems priced right might suffer hidden defects. Obtain knowledgeable estimates for repairs or renovations that you plan. Never ballpark or casually figure the costs necessary to bring a property up to the condition you want it. Get accurate property inspections and cost estimates before you buy.

◆ *Law regulates and governs installment contracts.* A contract-for-deed places you and the seller in a relationship that is governed not only by the contract language, but by state laws and court decisions. Under an installment sale, your rights and responsibilities differ from those you acquire when you finance a property via a mortgage or trust deed.

Before you sign an installment sale agreement, consult a real estate attorney who is experienced in reviewing these contracts. Absent knowledge of this specialty, too many lawyers warn against buying a property on the installment plan. (Using similar logic, such lawyers would advise against marriage because divorce can cause such pain.) This type of lawyer fears risks apart from opportunities. Get a lawyer who understands both; then negotiate a contract that can work for you and the sellers. Over the years, millions of buyers and investors (especially those with low- to moderate-incomes or transient jobs) have successfully bought houses, farms, and small rental properties on the installment plan.

SECRET # **71**

Try it before you buy it.

The "try it before you buy it" technique is called the lease option. It combines a lease agreement for a home, a townhouse, or apartment with an option (a contractual right) to buy that property at a later date. In the early 1980s, Robert Bruss called lease options "the most overlooked and underused" property finance possibility. At that time, most homebuyers, home sellers, and real estate agents remained clueless about this technique.

Times have changed. Wherever I travel throughout the United States, I always check through the local real estate classifieds. In most cities, real estate agents regularly handle lease options and other low-down-payment property finance plans. I have also seen lease options promoted by home builders and developers of new condominiums and townhouses. In San Francisco, one ad from Bay Crest Condominiums boldly announced, "If You Can Afford to Rent, You Can Now Afford to Own: Exciting New Lease/Purchase Option." No question, lease options can bring ownership closer to reality in several ways, such as:

- *Easier qualifying.* Qualifying for a lease option may be no more difficult than qualifying for a lease—sometimes easier. Generally, your credit and employment record need meet only minimum standards. Most property owners (sellers or lessors) will not place your financial life under a magnifying glass as would a mortgage lender.
- *Low initial investment.* Your initial investment to get into a lease-option agreement can be as little as one month's rent and a security deposit of a similar amount. At the outside, move-in cash rarely exceeds $5,000 to $10,000, although I did see a home lease-optioned at a price of $1.5 million that asked for $50,000 up front.
- *Forced savings.* The lease-option contract typically forces you to save for the down payment required when you exercise your option to buy. Lease options often charge above-market rental rates and then credit perhaps 50 percent of the rent toward a down payment. You negotiate the exact amount. After you commit to buying, you should find it easier to cut other spending and place more money toward your "house account."
- *100 percent financing possible.* Here's how to reduce the amount of cash you will need to close a purchase. Lease-option a property that you can profitably improve through repairs, renovation, or cosmetics. At the increased value, you may be able to borrow nearly all

the money you need to exercise your option to buy. For example, assume your lease-option purchase price is $375,000. Say by the end of one year, your rent credits equal $20,000. You now owe the sellers $355,000. Through repairs, fix-up work, and redecorating, you increase the property's value by $60,000. The property now boasts a value of $435,000. If you have paid your bills on time during the previous year, you can finance your purchase with the full $355,000 you need to pay off the sellers. As another possibility, you could sell the property, pay the sellers $355,000, and use your cash from the sale as a down payment on another property.

◆ *Reestablish credit*. A lease option can help people who need time to build a higher credit score. The option locks in your price. Pay all bills on time. Avoid all destructive debt. Your score can jump 100 points. (Remember, credit scoring programs weight recent credit history more heavily than the experience of years past.)

SECRET # **72**

Buy and lease simultaneously.

In south suburban Chicago, the not-for-profit New Cities Development Corporation sold 200 of its rehabbed homes via a lease-purchase agreement. "The buyer profile for this method of financing," says Jim De-Both of Mortgage Market Information Services, "covers a wide range of people—from the moderate-income buyer to someone who earns a good income, but who has saved little." Cooperating with New Cities Development in these house sales was Suburban Federal Savings.

How Does the Lease-Purchase Work?

New Cities found buyers for its homes, yet they lacked money for a down payment. These buyers were counseled about home ownership. Next, Suburban Federal qualified them for a mortgage. The buyers then signed a lease-purchase agreement for their homes, moved in, and began making rental payments large enough to cover their future PITI plus $100 to $200 a month extra. After these extra payments (called rent credits) had built up enough to fund a 5 percent down payment, Suburban Federal closed the homebuyers' loans and New Cities Development conveyed title. These families moved smoothly from leasing to owning.

Lease-Purchase Agreements versus Lease Purchase-Options

Although some people use these two terms interchangeably, technically they differ. A lease-purchase agreement commits you to buy the property. Your lease period provides time to build up cash or rent credits for a down payment, or perhaps time to shape up your financial fitness. With a lease purchase-*option*, more frequently called a lease option, you can walk away from the property at the end of the lease. You forfeit the option money or rent credits you have paid, but the sellers cannot require you to buy the property if you choose not to.

Several Key Issues

To buy or sell a property through a lease-purchase or lease-option agreement, you and your lawyer need to negotiate and resolve several issues:

- *Purchase price*. Verify that the price you're offering lines up with other comparable properties that have recently sold in the neighborhood. When you apply for a bank mortgage at some future date, the property must appraise at a value high enough to support the LTV ratio. Some lease-to-own sellers price hamburger as if it were filet mignon.
- *Move-in cash*. Whether you lease-purchase or lease-option a property, you'll negotiate the amount of your move-in money. This cash will be credited toward your purchase price if and when you buy. If you choose not to buy, the sellers will keep all or part of this money.
- *Lease period*. How much time will you need before you buy? Sellers often want to close quickly—sometimes within 6 to 12 months. Make sure you give yourself enough time. If you can't come up with your lender financing at the end of your lease period, you may lose your move-in cash. If you can close sooner than the date in your agreement, most sellers would accommodate you.

♦ *Rent credits.* Many lease-purchase/lease-option sellers apply rent credits to reduce the amount you owe. These monthly credits also can count as part or all of your down payment; but remember, lenders won't count rent credits without question. They count only lease amounts paid in excess of market rent levels. You pay $2,000 a month, the market's at $1,800, the lender will allow a rent credit of $200 per month. If you plan to use rent credits as part of your cash to close, make sure you understand your lender's policy.

(Note: Even though lenders may not count all of your rent credits toward the cash required to close, you still deduct the full amount from the balance you owe the sellers. The larger your rent credit, the less the balance you owe the sellers.)

♦ *Right to assign.* Include a "right to assign" clause in your agreement. If you don't complete your purchase, you can sell (assign for a payment) your right to buy the property at your contract price. That way you won't forfeit all of your rent credits and move-in cash. In fact, if the property has appreciated, you can sell your option to purchase and pocket a nice profit.

That's the technique that flippers use to profit with new construction. They sign a purchase contract with a builder, hope for appreciation during the building process, then sell out before they close on their loan and take possession of the property.

♦ *Inspections and title check.* Get your property inspected by a specialist who knows maintenance and construction. Unless you buy at a steep discount, reduce the risk of unexpected major repairs. Likewise, pay a title insurance company to check the seller's rights of ownership. Many lease-option/lease-purchase buyers skip these precautions and put themselves at risk. Or they wait until they apply for a mortgage—and then discover problems of title, property condition, or appraised value. Play it safe. Negotiate these issues with the seller before you sign the lease-option/lease-purchase agreement.

Although lease-purchase and lease-option agreements can work well for buyers, sellers, and investors, both techniques raise questions that differ from straight purchase offers. So, seek legal counsel. When done right, a lease-purchase or lease-option agreement could move you along the route to property ownership. As a seller and as a buyer, I have used these techniques on numerous occasions and never run into any difficulties.

SECRET #

Beat high interest rates with wraparound financing.

Wraparound financing yields big savings for buyers at the same time as it pays a good return to the seller. Here's a simple example to illustrate how a wraparound works:

> **Financial Facts**
>
> | | |
> |---|---|
> | Asking price | $200,000 |
> | Existing mortgage balance | 100,000 |
> | Existing mortgage interest rate | 6% |
> | Term remaining (years) | 20 |
> | Monthly payment | 716 |
> | Current market interest rate | 9% |

You offer to buy a property for $200,000 if the seller agrees to finance $180,000 at 7.5 percent fully amortized over 20 years. Your payment (P&I) equals $1,450 per month.[5] The existing mortgage remains, and the seller will continue to make payments on this loan. To complete the purchase, you sign a land contract, alternatively known as a contract-for-deed or installment note.

Each month the seller collects $1,450 from you and then pays the bank his monthly mortgage payment of $716 for a net gain of $734 ($1,450 less $716). Because the seller has actually financed only $80,000 ($180,000 less

---

[5] You also pay for the property insurance, property taxes, maintenance, and upkeep.

the 100,000 he still owes the bank), he achieves an attractive rate of return on his loan of 11.1 percent.

$$\text{Seller ROI} = \frac{\$8,808(12 \times \$734)}{\$80,000}$$
$$= 11.1\%$$

But you gain from this deal, too. Had you financed $180,000 with a bank at the market rate of 9 percent amortized over 20 years, you would pay $1,619 per month instead of the $1,450 that you'll pay to the seller.

In one of my property transactions, I wrapped a 10 percent mortgage with a 13.5 percent note. My yield on the money I left in the property exceeded 18 percent. At the time, current mortgage rates were at 16 percent. So, with a note rate of 13.5 percent, my buyer also got a great deal. This example shows how a wraparound can benefit buyers and sellers—true win-win financing.[6]

SECRET # **74**

Don't dillydally with due diligence.

Mortgage Secrets encourages you to ask sellers to provide all or part of your property financing. With some exceptions, you'll find sellers easier to work with than lenders. Plus, you may swing better terms, lower costs, and quicker closings. But this album of advantages plays a different tune on its flip side. Though sellers do make OWC transactions quick and easy, many buyers sign before they investigate.

Only later do they learn that the sellers, the property, or both have failed to meet the buyers' expectations. Troubles brew. Costs mount. The buyers' once-joyful spirit morphs into regret, anger, accusations, and/or litigation. So, yes, eagerly search out seller financing, but don't dillydally

---

[6] If the lender can enforce a "due on sale" clause, this technique does bring about that risk. In that situation, a wraparound works better as a short-term financing strategy. If the lender calls, there may be no long term.

with due diligence. As with all property purchase and finance plans, temper your enthusiastic eagerness with cool calculation. Answer these questions:[7]

- *Can you trust the sellers?* Nearly all real estate experts urge sellers to assess the character and credit strength of their borrowers, but so must buyers assess the integrity of their sellers. Some con artist sellers know they can line up buyers around the block with promises of easy terms and no credit check. Be wary of sellers who come on too glib, or sellers who raise your suspicious instincts. Cheats and scammers can turn up on either side of a real estate transaction.

- *Can you afford the price and terms?* Banker underwriters match your repayment capacity against their approval formulas and qualifying ratios. Sellers may let you slide by. So, it's up to you to realistically (nay, pessimistically) appraise your finances. Some sellers lure hopeful but unprepared buyers into transactions they aren't likely to complete successfully. Why? To keep their buyers' front-end money, kick them out of the property, and repeat the process with the next wide-eyed innocents who bite the "no cash, no credit, no problem" bait the sellers dangle in front of them. Several books written for investors actually promote this unethical seller tactic.

- *How much will you spend to maintain and operate the property?* Experts warn you to "Get the house professionally inspected." Good advice, but it doesn't go far enough. Get the facts on the cost to maintain the property, yard, and operating systems (HVAC, plumbing, water, waste disposal, electrical, and so on). Put actual numbers down on paper. Forget ballparking. Determine precisely: Money trap or wise investment?

- *Have you actually researched the market to determine achievable rent levels and occupancy rates?* Novice investors all too frequently overestimate the rents they will collect from their properties and underestimate the vacancy rates the property might experience. If you plan to pay expenses and monthly payments with revenue from

---

[7] *The 106 Common Mistakes Homebuyers Make (and How to Avoid Them)*, 4th ed. (John Wiley & Sons, 2006), details these topics with examples from real homebuyers.

tenants, carefully research other rental units. Prepare a realistic pro forma that's backed up by actual market results.

- *At what price would the property sell without OWC terms?* You can sometimes sensibly trade off a higher price for great terms or easy credit. But know what trade-off you're making. It's tough to sell or refinance a property when your debt load tosses you upside down.

- *How do you protect your title interest in the property?* If you give the sellers more than a few thousand dollars up front, run, don't walk, to a trustworthy and competent real estate attorney. At very least employ a title company to okay the legal paperwork. I confess that I have violated this rule on a number of occasions and suffered no harm, but *Mortgage Secrets* cannot recommend this approach to those without experience—unless you carry a guardian angel on your shoulder.

- *How much will you pay for property insurance?* During the 1990s property insurers paid more claims than in any other period in history. Fortunately, they made those losses back and more through their investments. The 2000s have not proved so kind. High losses are still mounting (9/11, mold, hurricanes, floods), but investment gains have fallen. That means (if you haven't already noticed) insurance premiums are going up and insurers are cutting back on coverages—especially in high-loss, high-loss-exposure locales. (During the past two years, insurance premiums on my Florida properties have jumped 50 percent—and they're not even located near the coast.) Before you commit to buy, verify the availability of all needed coverages at a price you are willing and able to pay.

- *How much will you pay for property taxes and assessments?* Look to the future, not the past. The amount the sellers paid last year could fall far short of the amounts that the tax authorities will bill you next year. (If you itemize, however, you will be able to deduct those taxes. That's at least some consolation.)

- *Is the property governed by a homeowners association (HOA)?* Homeowners associations add another layer of costs (and benefits) to a property. How much will the HOA require you to pay each month? Is the HOA fiscally strong with cash reserves, or is it looking at deficits that you and other owners will have to pay? How will the HOA's covenants, conditions, and restrictions (CCRs) and "house rules" crimp your actions? Pets, parking, kids, basketball courts, tree houses, exterior color schemes, home offices, fencing, landscaping, yard care? What, if any, restrictions on rentals apply? You name it. The HOA probably regulates it. Just ignore the HOA? Bad idea. HOAs hold the legal power to assess, fine, and even foreclose when amounts levied remain unpaid.

When you knowledgeably plan your finances and your financing, you can almost always afford to buy a home or investment property. But please, before you sign on that dotted line, verify that you can afford to own the property you buy. Don't dillydally with due diligence.

SECRET # **75**

Negotiate a preforeclosure workout.[8]

Each year in every city, hundreds (sometimes thousands) of property owners skid into a financial wreck. Divorce, job loss, accident, illness, business failure, binge spending, destructive borrowing, and other setbacks render people unable to make their mortgage payments.

But rather than effectively deal with their mortgage problem as soon as trouble hits, most owners hang on too long hoping for a miraculous rescue. Because miraculous rescues rarely occur, most of these people end up facing foreclosure.

At that point, you may be able to help these potential sellers salvage their credit score and part of their equity and at the same time secure a bargain for yourself. Faced with pressures of time and money, these property owners may accept a quick sale at a price below market value. The sellers' lender may even let you assume their existing mortgage on favorable terms. Because lenders lose money on foreclosures, the lender will review offers that *credibly* promise to improve its current doomed position.

---

[8] *Secret #s 75–81* address foreclosures and REOs. My book, *Investing in Real Estate*, 5th ed. (John Wiley & Sons, 2006), explains their profit potential more thoroughly. Also, you might listen to my audio book, *Goldmining in Foreclosures*, Trump University, 2006.

Approach Owners with Empathy

No magic system succeeds with owners who face foreclosure. Such owners contend with financial troubles, personal anguish, and indecisiveness. In addition, they probably have been attacked by innumerable foreclosure sharks, speculators, bank lawyers, and recent attendees of get-rich-quick foreclosure seminars. These owners are living with the public shame of failure. For these reasons and more, they are not easy people with whom to craft a deal.

Yet, if you develop a sensitive, empathetic, problem-solving approach with someone suffering foreclosure, you may strike a win-win agreement—but play fair. Other potential buyers will pay them a visit. A "Here's my offer—take it or leave it" approach will anger the owners. It will not distinguish you from the dozen foreclosure sharks who try that ploy.

Negotiate to preserve the owner's dignity. Share personal information about setbacks you have lived through—and how you recovered. Help the owners envision a better future. Illustrate how your offer will free them to gain from other opportunities. Hacksaw that ball and chain that anchors them to their current misery. Offer them freedom and a better life.

Find Owners in Distress

When a lender forecloses, the county clerk files that suit in the public records. Local newspapers or specialty newsletters often publish the borrowers' names and addresses. Web sites also list foreclosures. (Beware, most of these sites require a fee before you can gain access. Verify the integrity of the sites and their data before you pay.)

You can go to the local county courthouse or visit the clerk of court's web site. Some counties make it easy to find pending foreclosures; others make you search. Either way, the information is always available to the public. You also can locate distressed owners with the following techniques:

- *Advertise.* You've probably seen some of the flyers and billboards that announce, "We Buy Houses." Make your ads different and empathetic.
- *Network.* Pay attention to which employers are laying off. What are realty agents and loan reps saying? Who do you know who knows the people experiencing financial difficulty?

- *Contact debt counseling agencies*. Let them know that you're looking to help someone. You could even hang out around an agency and watch who's coming in and out; then talk with them, and learn their names and addresses.

County records, apart from getting inside data from mortgage servicers, represent the surest way to find owners with loan difficulties. If you can discover who these people are before the lender files foreclosure, you're more likely to meet with the owners before the sharks begin to circle.

Work with Lenders

Mortgage defaults, payments in arrears, and foreclosures don't look good to a lender's regulators, mortgage insurers, stock investors, or its general reputation in the community. That's why most lenders with troubled borrowers want to resolve their mortgage delinquencies sooner rather than later. To succeed in negotiations with a lender, emphasize your desire and ability to provide it a permanent relief. In return, the lender may agree to offer you:

- *Additional financing*. In high owner equity deals, the lender could advance you funds to buy out the owner.
- *Below-market interest rate*. Below-market rates permit you to assume the owner's low rate, or knock the existing interest rate down a point or two as an incentive.
- *Reduced closing and origination costs*. These minimize transaction fees by waiving or reducing typical loan costs.
- *Short-sale*. If the owners are upside down (owe more than their property is worth), the lender may slice off part of the loan balance.
- *No catch-up for past-due payments*. To reduce out-of-pocket transaction costs, the lender could add all amounts owed (past due payments, legal expenses, escrow shortfalls) to the mortgage balance, rather than require a cash payment. However, to enhance the appeal of their workouts, REO buyers should bring the loan current with ready cash.

As with all negotiations, results will evolve from current market realities as well as from the needs, wants, motives, and negotiating skills of the parties. But one constant applies. Lenders want to turn around a loan that's going downhill. If you can hit the brakes and maneuver the loan onto a safe route, the lender will reward you for your steering ability.

SECRET # **76**

Buy (carefully) at a foreclosure sale.

When a lender fails to work out a loan in default, the property ends up on the courthouse auction block. Typically, experienced foreclosure specialists who accurately calculate risks win at this game. Yet, it's true—you must start somewhere. If you get to know the condition and value of a property by talking with its owners in preforeclosure workout discussions that eventually failed to secure a deal, consider bidding at the public auction.

Bidders who thoroughly prepare can walk away with great bargains, but not great financing. Most foreclosure sales require cash. To buy, you'll need wealth, a ready line of credit, or a money partner. As it turns out, the foreclosing lender often wins the auction because no investor stepped forward with a bid high enough to pay off the lender's lien.

The property then ends up as an REO in the (unwanted) real estate owned portfolio of HUD, VA, Fannie Mae, Freddie Mac, or the lender itself. In these cases, the owners of the REOs face no choice. The properties have to get sold. This fact gives you another chance to negotiate a good deal on price, terms, or sometimes both.

SECRET # **77**

Locate a foreclosure pro.

Most mortgage lenders do not sell directly to REO buyers: They don't like the unfavorable publicity; and they want to promote good relations with Realtors. Because mortgage lenders expect Realtors to bring them new loan business, these same lenders can't then turn around and become FSBO (for sale by owner) dealers. In business, reciprocity rules.

To find REOs, cultivate relationships with realtors who specialize in this market. To identify REO specialists, look through classified real estate ads such as that shown on page 149.

When you identify several advertised foreclosure specialists, give each one a call. Learn their backgrounds. Do they only dabble in the field of REOs and foreclosures, or do they make this field their full-time business? When I telephoned an REO specialist in Orlando, he talked with me for an hour and a half about property availability, financing, purchase procedures, hot areas of town, rehab potential, estimating repair costs, portfolio lenders, strategies for buying and managing properties, selecting tenants, and a dozen other related topics.

At one point during our conversation, he asked, "I'll bet you haven't talked to any other agents who know as much as I do about REOs and foreclosures, have you? I've been doing this 23 years. Last year, I sold 90 houses and rehabbed 16 others for my own account." Pretty impressive!

Knowledge Counts

This agent represents the kind of pro you want to find. Although many agents claim expertise in REOs and foreclosures—"Sure, I can do that for you"—only a few actively work in the field, day in and day out, year after year. When you work with an agent who's in the know, you won't have to do your own legwork. This agent will screen properties as soon as—if not before—they come onto the market. He will then notify you immediately.

Plus, these specialized agents will stay on top of the finance plans that portfolio, government, and conventional lenders are offering to homebuyers and investors. For example, my REO pro told of portfolio lenders doing 100 percent LTV homebuyer and investor loans for acquisition and rehab. (FHA 203(k) might prove best for this type of financing—but FHA rules may stack up more foot-dragging paperwork than programs run by portfolio lenders.)

HUD, VA, Fannie, and Freddie Won't Sell Direct to Buyers

No matter what approach to REOs and foreclosures you choose to follow, talk with realty pros who make the business a career. If you buy an REO from HUD, VA, Fannie Mae, or Freddie Mac, you *must* process your offer through a licensed real estate agent. Only in exceptional circumstances would any of these organizations deal directly with a potential buyer. Moreover, each of these organizations follows its own procedures.

SECRET # **78**

HUD may hold the keys to your home or investment property.

Each year, FHA insures hundreds of thousands of new mortgage loans. (The total number of these outstanding FHA mortgages runs into the millions.) When FHA borrowers fail to repay their lenders as scheduled (absent a successful workout), the owner of the mortgage will force the property into a foreclosure sale. Then (speaking generally) the lender turns in a claim to HUD (FHA's parent). HUD pays the lender the amount due under its mortgage insurance coverage and acquires the foreclosed property. HUD puts the property, along with all the others it has acquired, up for bid to the public.

In cities such as Atlanta, HUD may sell as many as 1,000 properties a year. In the San Francisco Bay area, HUD's annual sales may total fewer than 150 homes. Depending on the strength of the housing market and the local economy, the number and selection of HUD properties vary widely. Still, every area offers at least some HUD homes. To locate HUD properties, go to www.hud.gov and then click on HUD homes. Go to the state and county that interests you.

Like all sources of bargain prices, HUD homes don't present a sure thing. You can't bid blindly and expect to land a great buy. You first must research neighborhoods and property values. Only then can you confidently buy properties for substantially less than their market value after fix-up work.

Although HUD is best known for single-family houses, it also sells these types of REO properties:

+ Vacant lot
+ Duplex
+ Triplex
+ Fourplex

- PUD, a Planned Unit Development
- Condominium
- Apartment buildings (financed by HUD-insured loans for investors who operate low- to moderate-income rental housing)

To buy a HUD property, submit a bid package to HUD according to set procedures. Violate a rule, and your bid package is tossed out. That's why you need a foreclosure pro. After HUD opens the bid package, it accepts the bid that nets HUD the most money—except that homebuyers receive priority over investors—even when the investor submits a bid that HUD thinks superior. HUD sets bid deadlines that give homebuyer first chance. If no sale results, HUD opens the bid process (but not HUD financing) to investors. HUD also uses a bid package and set bidding procedure to sell its REO apartment buildings.

Financing Programs and Incentives

Ordinarily, homebuyers can finance HUD homes with FHA-insured financing and pay 3 to 5 percent cash out of pocket. Although these cash payments are typical, HUD sometimes runs low- or no-down-payment "specials." Several years ago, HUD-owned, FHA-insurable properties throughout the state of Georgia were offered with just $300 down. Check with HUD-approved real estate sales agents in your area to see what deals HUD may be brewing. If the coming years bring forth the increased number of foreclosures that forecasters predict, HUD may enhance its deals and buyer incentives.

Other Incentives

In addition to low- or no-down-payment specials, local HUD offices may run other types of incentive programs for buyers of HUD properties. To encourage quick closings during a market surplus in Indianapolis, HUD offered a $2,000 early closing bonus (less than thirty days) to investors and homebuyers. In Chicago, HUD offered a rebate up to $1,000 to renters who buy a HUD home for owner occupancy. In Boston, HUD offered a 5 percent purchase price credit on certain designated properties, a $250 bonus to buyers who had arranged a lender's *preapproval*, and a $675 early closing bonus (less than 45 days). In Baltimore, the early closing bonus was $900, but settlement had to take place within 15 days of contract acceptance. On occasion, to reduce its inventory of unsold homes, HUD offers clearance sales at deep discounts. Some years back in Houston, HUD ran a huge "Turkey Day" sale on Thanksgiving.

Local Options

HUD can permit its regional local offices to loosen HUD's requirements. If HUD homes in Chicago do not sell fast enough, HUD will likely increase buyer incentives for its Chicago area properties. When sales boom in a given city and HUD has relatively few properties available, HUD not only refuses to offer incentives, but it may refuse to accept bids at less than a property's list price. You can pull the best deal on HUD properties in down markets. But regardless of the market, it's worth your time to stay abreast of HUD offerings in areas where you may have an interest.

SECRET # **79**

VA offers REO deals (with financing) to veterans and nonveterans.

The U.S. Department of Veterans Affairs (VA) guarantees the payment of home loans for eligible veterans. The guarantee permits veterans to finance their homes with 100 percent (zero down payment) loans. As with any mortgage, lenders foreclose when VA borrowers fail to make their payments *and* fail to enter a workout/VA financial counseling program. In exchange for a loan payoff from VA, lenders return the foreclosed homes to VA, which then tries to sell them as quickly as possible.

VA's Similarities to HUD

To sell its foreclosed properties, VA follows many rules similar to those of HUD. For example, here are twelve ways the programs resemble each other:

1. VA sells through a sealed bid process. As either a potential home-owner or investor, you may submit multiple bids during the same bid period.

2. You cannot *directly* negotiate with or submit a bid to VA. You must submit your bid through a VA-approved real estate agent (your foreclosure pro).

3. VA sells its properties on an as-is basis. Even though it may disclose a property's defects, VA warrants nothing. Buyer be aware.

4. VA does guarantee title and permits buyers to obtain a title policy.

5. VA accepts bids that yield it the highest net proceeds (not the highest price). If your bid reduces VA's closing expenses or realty commission, you can win the bid over others who offer higher prices.

6. Just as HUD/FHA charges FHA buyers an insurance fee, VA charges buyers (who finance via VA) a guarantee fee (currently 2.25 percent, but subject to change). For borrowers who put more of their own cash into a deal, VA charges a lower fee.

7. VA accepts bids only on VA forms. Errors in completing the forms may kill the bid.

8. VA may publicize its properties through newspaper ads, broker lists, and Internet postings. Follow the links from hud.gov.

9. Local VA offices report to regional directors who may issue procedures that differ from other regions throughout the country.

10. VA may choose to keep your earnest money deposit if you fail to close your winning bid for any reason—other than inability to obtain financing.

11. As with HUD contracts, VA does not permit a bid contingency for property inspections. You may, however, inspect a property before you bid.

12. When necessary, VA evicts holdover tenants or homeowners before it markets its REOs. At closing, you will receive a vacant property.

Big Advantages for Investors

Although VA follows rules similar to HUD, it differs in two important ways that work to the advantage of investors:

1. VA does not give homebuyers preferred treatment. VA accepts the highest net proceeds offered by any credible buyer—homeowner or investor.

2. VA offers investors favorable terms of financing. In my area, for example, investors can close financing on a VA home with total cash out of pocket of less than 6 percent of a property's purchase price. In addition, VA typically applies relaxed qualifying standards. VA buyers (who need not be veterans) must show *acceptable*, not perfect, credit records. For REO listings and procedures, talk with a foreclosure pro or follow the link to VA REOs from the hud.gov web site.

With attractive terms of financing, VA homes in good (and even not so good) repair frequently sell at market prices; however, many homebuyers and investors still like the VA program for three reasons:

- *High leverage* permits you to accelerate your wealth-building re- turns.
- Even at market prices and high LTV, many VA properties pull in rents high enough to provide a *positive cash flow* from day one of ownership.
- The VA allows future buyers to assume your VA financing. For buyers who want to "fix and flip," an *assumable loan* makes a great benefit. Plus, in periods of high interest rates, a lower assumable VA rate gives your sales efforts a competitive edge over other properties.

VA provides an excellent source of properties and financing for home-buyers and investors alike. If you're looking for a great deal, regularly scroll through the listings of VA REOs.

SECRET # **80**

Let Fannie or Freddie treat you to below-market financing.

Fannie Mae and Freddie Mac, two large players in the nation's secondary mortgage market, usually don't loan directly to investors or homebuyers; but they buy mortgages that are made by banks, credit unions, and other mortgage lenders. Sometimes when a loan Fannie or Freddie owns goes bad, Fannie or Freddie requires the originating lender to buy back the mortgage. The lender then adds another foreclosed property to its REO portfolio. But, when lenders follow all of Fannie's or Freddie's underwriting guidelines, Fannie/Freddie cannot demand a mortgage repurchase. Fannie or Freddie takes ownership of the foreclosed properties.

Agent Listings

Rather than use a sealed bid procedure, Fannie/Freddie list their REOs for sale with a real estate agency who then places the REOs into MLS. The agent who handles the foreclosed property inspects it and then figures out how to fix it up to sell quickly at a near market price.

Seldom a Bargain Purchase Price

Because Fannie and Freddie may invest thousands of dollars to put their REOs in good condition, you won't find many bargain-priced buys among their REOs. In fact, only in out-of-the-ordinary circumstances will Fannie and Freddie consider lowball or wheeling-and-dealing types of offers. They even try to price their as-is—no repairs—properties as high as the market will bear.

First-Time Homebuyers—Special Financing

Fannie and Freddie aim to attract credit-qualified homebuyers—especially first-time homebuyers. Rather than use the bargain price appeal, these companies lure buyers with well-presented homes and special financing.

Freddie even permits homebuyers to "customize your Homesteps [the name Freddie gives to its foreclosures] home." Under Its Homesteps REO option, Freddie invites buyers (for a price, of course) to upgrade a property's carpets, padding, appliances, and window blinds. Freddie also sells most of its REOs with 5 percent down, no private mortgage insurance (which typically saves buyers $75 to $150 per month), lower closing costs, and a slightly below market interest rate.

All Properties Sold "As Is"

Even though Fannie and Freddie fix up most of their properties, neither warrants the condition of a property. Unlike HUD or VA, as a Fannie/Freddie buyer, you may submit a contract that includes an inspection contingency. If the property qualifies, you can purchase a home warranty plan just as you might with other properties.

Investors Accepted

Both Fannie and Freddie accept offers from investors and offer special financing for credit-qualified investors that requires a 15 percent down payment, rather than the conventional down payment of 20 to 30 percent for investor-owned properties. Closing costs may come in a little lower, too. Investor interest rates usually sit on the low side of market. Locate Freddie and Fannie properties at www.homesteps.com and www.fanniemae.com/homes. (Note: During the go-go years of the early-to-mid-2000s, many lenders offered investors 90, 95, and even 100 percent financing. However, as is nearly always the case, these loans usually came with more fine print, higher costs, and higher interest rates. With the recent steep increase in foreclosures on these easy-money loans—as well as regulatory critique—lenders have tightened underwriting standards. Such high LTV loans will get tougher to find and require stronger borrower profiles than they have in the recent past. Typically, though, when lenders tighten underwriting standards, sellers become more receptive to owner will carry financing.)

SECRET # **81**

Buy and finance directly with a lender.

When a mortgage lender wins the bid at a foreclosure auction, the foreclosed property ends up as an REO. If the lender can't turn the property over to HUD, VA, or other guarantor, it will sell to a homebuyer or investor. As stated a few pages back, most lenders list their REOs with a Realtor, but some will negotiate directly with homebuyers and investors.

The Benefits of Buying Directly from a Mortgage Lender

You can say one thing for certain about an REO: The lender prefers to sell it as quickly as possible. Mortgage lenders loan money and collect payments. They do not want to own vacant houses or rental properties.

As a result, they may provide their REO buyers favorable terms such as low or no closing costs, below-market interest rates, and low down payments.

If the property needs fix-up work, the lender may accept offers at deep discounts from market value. Just as important, prior to closing the sale of their REOs, lenders normally clean up title problems, evict unauthorized occupants, and bring past-due property tax payments and assessments up to date. Some lenders permit buyers to write offers subject to appraisal and professional inspection.

Safer Than Buying at the Foreclosure Sale

To buy direct from a lender typically presents no more risk than buying direct from any other property's owner.[9] You can buy an REO much more safely than you could have bought the same property at its foreclosure sale. Depending on the lender's motivation, its internal policies and procedures, and the property LTV at the time of the foreclosure sale, you might buy below market price.

Why a Lower Price?

Let's say the market value of a property at the time of its foreclosure sale was $585,000. The lender's liens against the property totaled $560,000. To win the property away from the lender at the foreclosure sale, you probably would have had to bid more than $560,000—a price that's too high to yield a good buy.

After the lender owns the property and adds up its expected holding costs, Realtor's commission, and the risks of seeing the (probably) vacant property vandalized, it may decide to cut its losses. It might accept an offer within the range of $500,000 to $550,000—especially if you offer cash. (You can borrow this money from some other mortgage lender.)

---

[9] Several exceptions might include: states where the foreclosed owners may have a right of redemption; if the foreclosed owners still retain some legal right to challenge the validity of the foreclosure sale; or if a bankruptcy trustee or the Internal Revenue Service (tax lien) is entitled to bring the property within their powers. Rarely would any of these potential claims be worth losing sleep over; however, prior to closing an REO purchase, you might run these issues by legal counsel.

Finding Lender REOs

In desperate times REO lenders turn to mass marketing and advertised public auctions to unload their REOs. In stable to strong markets, they generally (but not always) play it low key. No lender likes to publicize the fact that it's throwing down-on-their-luck families out of their homes. Absent tough times and mass advertising, you can find REOs in three different ways: Follow up after a foreclosure sale; cold call lender REO personnel; locate Realtors who typically list REO properties.

Follow Up after Foreclosure

Attend foreclosure auctions and you can easily learn of lender REOs. When a bank rep wins the bid for a property, buttonhole that bidder and start talking business. Or, schedule an appointment to see the officer who manages REOs (usually called loss mitigation). Show the lender how your bargain offer will actually save or make money for the bank. Then you'll be on your way to closing a deal.

Beware of the stall. Financial institutions are run by standard operating procedures, management committees, and other precautionary rules that can work against sensible decisions. If you crash into a bureaucratic stone wall, persevere. Persistence pays off in two ways: (1) You eventually make the deal; and/or (2) you build personal relationships that will open the bank's doors for you in future transactions.

Cold Call REO Personnel (Loss Mitigation Departments)

Every mortgage lender experiences at least a few defaults. No underwriting system can perfectly weed out every loan applicant who might fail to pay. So, all mortgage lenders end up with REOs—even if eventually they pass them along to HUD, VA, or some other guarantor.

Sometimes, too, lenders accumulate REOs without foreclosure. During the last major real estate downturn, lenders would open their mail to find the keys to a house, a signed deed, and a personal note from the distressed owners, "We're out of here. It's your problem now."

To find REOs that lenders have acquired through foreclosure or deed-in-lieu transfers, cold call mortgage lenders. Ask for a list of their REOs. However, this technique seldom turns up much. For various reasons, lenders may keep a tight hold on this information.[10] Nevertheless, you should still ask. Remember to show evidence of your buying capacity and credibility.

Until you establish relationships with REO personnel, the following approach might help: Rather than ask for a full list of REOs, focus. Describe what you're looking for in terms of neighborhood, property size, price range, floor plan, condition, or other features. In that way, a lender can answer your request without disclosing all of the properties within its inventory of REOs.

✿ ✿ ✿ ✿ ✿

As you see from the discussions in this chapter, you can acquire and finance properties without ever applying and qualifying for a loan in the traditional way. I have put together many deals using the techniques presented in this chapter. With perseverance (and some luck), you, too, can succeed as a homebuyer or investor with one or more of these approaches.

When someone advises you, "Go down and get prequalified for a loan so you will know exactly how much you can borrow," you must realize that such advice omits many other possibilities. Indeed, you now understand that even when you choose to buy and finance in a traditional manner—if the word traditional still has any meaning when it comes to mortgages—no one can tell you any "exact amount." To a much greater degree than most borrowers realize, it is you—not any given lender or loan program—who determines the amount of property that you are able and willing to buy.

---

[10] Most lenders don't want to waste time with those investor "wannabes" who have just read a "nothing down" book or "graduated" from a foreclosure guru's "no cash, no credit, no problem" seminar.

CHAPTER 8

Beware of Those Fine Print "Gotchas"

The following question and answer were posted on a large mortgage lender's web site.

Q. "Do I need to know anything about the mortgage loan process before I apply?"

A. "No. Not only is our process very simple, but our web site is full of useful information to help guide you through it. And you can always call our toll-free number to seek further assistance along the way."

Now, compare that statement with a *Wall Street Journal* article (September 6, 2002) headlined "Citigroup May Pay $200 Million in Fines for Predatory Mortgage Practices." The *Journal* further reported, "Federal Trade Commission (FTC) allegations have been hanging over the company and have provided ammunition for critics of Citigroup's practices. . . . Indeed it isn't likely that this record settlement will cool off the consumer advocates who continue to complain that Citigroup's practices haven't improved to adequately protect borrowers."

Eventually, Citigroup did pay—but the fine levied was $400 million, not $200 million. You might think that fines of that size would jolt mortgage lenders into walking the straight and narrow. But it hasn't happened yet. Since 2002 (when I wrote the first edition of *Mortgage Secrets*), deceptive loan practices, overcharging, and mortgage fraud have multiplied far beyond my warnings and expectations. Without a doubt—good credit or bad credit—the creditors are stalking you.

SECRET # **82**

It's a jungle out there.

As the above cited mortgage web site question and answer shows, some mortgage lenders mistakenly lead borrowers to believe that obtaining a mortgage is like buying a ticket on a Greyhound bus. Remember the ad jingle, "Ride the bus and leave the driving to us." Well, if you think you can leave the driving to your lender, one thing is true: You may get taken for a ride—but not on a scenic highway. Instead, you may end up in a jungle of predatory loan reps and/or predatory loan products.

In fact, FTC investigations, HUD studies, and congressional hearings throughout 2007 continued to expose the wild side of mortgage lending. The attorneys general of no fewer than 13 states have opened investigations of the anti-consumer practices that run rampant among banks, their mortgage loan subsidiaries, and mortgage brokers.

What Is Predatory Lending?

When journalists write about predatory lending, they tend to focus on the sub-prime mortgage market (say, unsophisticated borrowers with credit scores below 620). In this ruthless world, unsavory loan reps prey on widows, the elderly, the mathematically challenged, and other innocents. These hapless souls often get stuck with mortgage points and interest rates that more than double the going rate for smart, credit-strong borrowers. Often these prey lose nearly everything. To try to keep up with their impossibly high mortgage payments, they deplete their cash, run up their credit card balances, borrow from friends and family—and yet still lose their properties.

Unfortunately, journalists slight the other half of this story. Some lenders gouge borrowers at the prime and super prime levels of wealth, income, and credit scoring. Without keen senses, even you can get shaved by sharp practices that may include:

- Garbage fees, over charges
- Bad faith estimates of closing costs
- Undisclosed prepayment penalties
- Misleading assumption clauses
- High cost, "no cost" loans
- Lowball rate quotes
- Oversized yield-spread premiums
- Flimsy rate locks
- Lowball/highball appraisals
- Deceptive advertising
- Conspiracy to commit fraud

You might ask, "How can loan reps and lenders get away with these predatory tactics?" As the Citigroup fine shows, some attacks do get punished—especially when they leave claw marks on their victims. Yet, in many cases, such practices don't violate the law in provable ways. When you close your loan, you sign, see, or initial dozens of documents, forms, and disclosures. How much time will you take to carefully read, review, and question this paperwork? Not much, right? The papers will come fast and furious. "Sign here, sign here, sign here, sign here ..."

Written Trumps Oral

Later, when you discover an above-market interest rate, an $8,000 (or more) loan rep sales commission, an onerous prepayment clause, a $400 fee you don't understand, an impotent right of assumption, or a credit life insurance policy you never knew you ordered, your complaint will fall on deaf ears. Why? Somewhere in the file a document will establish your knowledge and consent. You then respond, "But the loan rep told me ..." So there it is, a written document with your signature that conflicts with your recollection of oral discussions. Which will prevail in a regulatory hearing or court challenge?

Nine times out of 10, the paper trail trumps mistaken understandings. Generally, the paper trail loses only when the language of the documents shocks the conscience of the court. Given that lenders employ crafty lawyers to draft their documents, you will find that few judges ever respond with shock. Moreover, in some cases, government itself mandates the use of deceptive forms and disclosures. To name three: the supposedly "Good Faith" Estimate of settlement charges; the APR disclosure (see *Secret* #39); and the FHA appraisal and property condition disclosure form. Many borrowers believe that this form assures them that FHA certifies the property's good condition. In fact, the form actually states that FHA certifies nothing about the property's state of repair. (However, to FHA's credit, it is trying to improve borrower understanding to reduce this confusion.)

No, Most Lenders and Loan Reps Aren't Crooks

Okay, let's talk context and perspective. Nothing in *Mortgage Secrets* intends to imply that all loan reps lie awake nights thinking up ways to cheat their customers. But from Babbitt to Willie Loman, salespeople (like lawyers) have enjoyed far more ethical slack than other occupations. Whether we call it puffing, salesmanship, competitive spirit (or legal argument) salespeople (and lawyers) all too easily slip into partial truths, nondisclosures, and deceptively clever explanations.

Never forget: A loan rep wants you to buy a product that he or she is selling at the highest price he can persuade you to pay. A loan rep earns a commission, salary, or bonus based on his or her ability to sell. Loan reps prosper when they convince you that they offer a better deal than you can obtain elsewhere. Because it's mathematically impossible for a majority of lenders and loan reps to actually offer the best deal—although most promise to do so—it remains your responsibility to identify and negotiate the deal points that get you the loan you need on the best terms available.

Ask questions, probe for detailed answers, run the numbers, compare alternative lenders, compare alternative loan products, search out nontraditional possibilities, shape up your borrower profile, explore a variety of property types and locations. Your reward could easily total $10,000 (or more, much more).

SECRET # **83**

Tell your loan rep to take out the garbage.

In a display of law over fair dealing, the Fourth Circuit Federal Court has told mortgage lenders that they can continue to bilk their borrowers for garbage fees. The court could find no legal authority to stamp out this practice. What are these so-called garbage or junk fees? For the most part, they refer to settlement charges that sometimes grossly overstate, magnify, or duplicate the actual amount of expenses incurred by the lender. Here are several examples:

- $350 for an electronic appraisal that costs $3.
- $65 for an electronic credit check that costs $9.
- $75 for document delivery that cost $16.
- $500 for administrative expenses that already are covered by a 1 percent mortgage origination fee.

Many consumer critics condemned the court ruling that okayed these and similar charges. But rather than impose its own idea of fair play, the court applied the law as it is literally written. If you want your lender to play fair, it is you who must tell the loan rep to take out the garbage. Closely examine every fee and expense listed on the good faith and settlement statements. Ask questions such as: "What amount did the lender actually pay for this service? Is the service actually necessary? Why am I being asked to pay these excessive charges?" Question every item. Negotiate their removal or reduction.

Garbage Fees Vary Widely among Lenders

To show how garbage fees vary, one study surveyed 28 mortgage lenders and found these results:

4 @ $100 or less

10 @ $100 to $1,000

9 @ $1,000 to $3,000

4 @ $3,000 to $5,000

1 @ $7,500

Although you can't judge a lender solely by the amount of its junk fees, you can appeal for their reduction—especially if you show a strong borrower profile. As Jack Guttentag (known as the Mortgage Professor), one of the nation's leading mortgage experts, advises, "This is a 'sloppy' market in which borrowers must stay on guard." (See Table 8.1.) Some

Table 8.1 **Loan Fees and Costs Vary Widely**

	Highest ($)	Lowest ($)	Average ($)
Lender/Broker Fees			
Administration fee	725	45	413.46
Application fee	410	100	266.40
Commitment fee	450	100	268.00
Document preparation	350	50	162.22
Funding fee	300	40	125.57
Mortgage broker fee	895	100	344.17
Processing	850	99	302.71
Tax service	110	10	72.09
Underwriting	595	25	279.93
Wire transfer	335	10	55.27
Third-Party Fees			
Appraisal	375	175.00	269.31
Attorney or settlement fees	820	50.00	373.71
Credit report	65	8.50	36.53
Flood certification	65	8.75	22.21
Pest inspection	400	30.00	86.07
Postage/courier	90	20.00	44.73
Survey	525	25.00	226.59
Title insurance	1,157	161.00	460.23

Based on a $125,000 mortgage from a survey of lenders. This list omits many fees that some lenders charge. None of these fees necessarily represent a "fair" amount for your area. The figures illustrate variance, not appropriateness.

lenders quote relatively low interest rates, then through fees and costs, they make this money back and more.

SECRET # **84**

Don't place blind faith in the good faith estimate.

Within three days after you apply for a loan, your lender must provide a completed form called Good Faith Estimate. This estimate supposedly itemizes the fees and costs you will pay to close your mortgage loan.

Place no faith in these figures. Only place faith in the verified integrity of your loan rep. Generally, loan reps who prepare bad faith estimates face little risk of penalty. Technically, bad faith estimates violate sections 3 and 4 of the Real Estate Settlement and Procedures Act (RESPA), but only recently has HUD been patrolling for abuses. And even when found, HUD's complaint must allege intent to deceive. No law or regulation prohibits "honest mistakes."

On Your Own

Thoroughly review the Good Faith Estimate to immediately question garbage fees, charges, and markups. Check it precisely against the final accounting of charges billed at closing. You should find it no surprise that in the flurry of paperwork at closing, some lenders slip in costs and charges that they previously omitted or understated.

Ideally, lenders should quote a guaranteed lump sum for closing costs and origination fees.[1] You then could easily shop among lenders to compare the total package of (fixed) closing costs, interest rates, origination fees, and discount points. However, lenders know that most borrowers mostly inquire about interest rates and discount points. They less frequently mention other costs that—as you have seen—can run into thousands of

---

[1] HUD is pushing reform in this direction. To do so, HUD must revoke its rules under RESPA that mandate the itemized, good faith approach.

dollars. Thus, until consumers wise up, lenders can still have their way with them.

Closing Costs Aren't Captured by Truth in Lending (APR Disclosures)

Newspaper and magazine articles frequently tell borrowers to compare loans according to their annual percentage rate (APR). Truth in lending mandates this calculation and disclosure. But as revealed in *Secret #39*, the APR errs because it incorrectly assumes that you will hold the loan to the end of its term—a quite unrealistic assumption.

APR also errs because it omits many closing costs that do not count as a cost of credit. The APR you see in the mortgage ads does not, for example, include private mortgage insurance, most garbage fees, cost of title or title insurance, or appraisal fees. Yet, as Table 8.1 shows, the amounts of these and other costs vary widely among lenders.

Naturally, this practice (as authorized by law) loads up profit-maximizing lenders with the ammunition they need to bamboozle you. They focus your attention on their low government-sanctioned APR disclosures and remain silent about their higher fees and costs. Remember, the lender need not give you a Good Faith Estimate until three days after you have applied for your loan and perhaps paid a nonrefundable application fee.

Don't fall for this trick. Ask the loan rep to accurately and comprehensively disclose all costs that you will pay. If the loan rep says he doesn't know for sure, ask for a high-low range. Ask precisely what factors create the uncertainty and when you can expect resolution.

Note: *Mortgage Secrets* advises you not to pay a nonrefundable mortgage application fee unless: (1) You're 99 percent certain that you know all loan terms and closing costs (within tolerable limits); (2) you trust the loan rep without question; (3) your loan closing does not depend on any contingencies other than the title search and property appraisal; and (4) the amount of the application fee does not exceed the customary charge in your area.

In fact, as a general rule, I urge you to negotiate out of paying any application fee. Primarily, lenders use this fee to deter you from changing lenders during the loan processing. No loan rep (or underwriter) wants to spend hours on your file only to see you jump ship before reaching port and thus eliminate the expected payday (for the rep).

SECRET # **85**

What's the real cost of a no-cost mortgage?

Mortgage lenders know that garbage fees and excessive closing costs rankle many borrowers. They also know that cash-short borrowers would really grab the chance to avoid this heavy burden of fees that add to the amounts already set aside for reserve funds, escrow deposits, and down payment. Thus was born the so-called no-cost (or no fee) mortgage (or refinance). With the no-cost loan, you pay a higher interest rate. For many borrowers, this trade-off sounds pretty attractive. But before you take the bait, run the numbers.

Does No-Cost Save You Money?

Of course no-cost doesn't really mean zero closing costs. Instead, it means "pay me later" rather than "pay me now." Given the fact that you're going to pay one way or another, you must determine which turns out better— paying now or paying later.

How Lenders Price No-Cost Loans

As you know (*Secret #24*), lenders typically give borrowers a range of discount point/interest rate trade-offs such as those shown in Table 8.2.

Although you may not see it, the loan rep's 30-year fixed-rate sheet may also show a no-cost loan as follows:

Rate (%)	Discount Points
8.0	−2.50

If you're quick with numbers, you can instantly spot the way the lenders have stacked the no-cost numbers in their own favor. At interest rates between 6.25 and 7.0 percent, you pay closing costs plus one point for each .25 percent that your rate drops. Because lenders know that some

Table 8.2 **30-Year Fixed**	
Rate (%)	*Discount Points*
7.0	0
6.75	1
6.50	2
6.25	3

borrowers can't resist immediate gain (no closing costs) in return for long-term pain (an 8 percent interest rate), they sometimes price the no-cost loan to extract more money from borrowers who choose this option.

For example, if to buy the interest rate down by .25 percent, you pay a full point, "buying up" the interest rate means the lender should credit you 1.0 point for each .25 percent increase in rate—or, in this example, 4.0 points as opposed to only 2.5 points.

Perhaps you agree to an 8.0 percent, no closing cost $300,000 loan. The lender priced the discount points at a negative 2.50 (−2.50). At settlement, the lender waives all fees up to $7,500 (2.5% × 300,000). The final accounting shows that your fees for this loan (had you paid them in cash) would have totaled $5,250.

Do you receive that $2,250 difference ($7,500 − $5,250) as a cash back credit at closing? Not likely. Instead, the loan rep and lender (in some agreed proportion) will split this overage. Your zero-cost loan gives you a money-losing trade-off.

The Potential High Cost of No-Cost

Unless you pay your loan off within about three or four years, the negative points will yield the lender a sizable return from the extra interest it collects as a result of the higher rate you've agreed to pay. With a $200,000 loan, for example, your payment runs $1,468 per month at 8.0 percent. At an interest rate of 7.0 percent, you would pay $1,331 per month. The 8.0 percent loan costs you an extra $137 each month. If your cash closing costs would have totaled $4,250, the lender needs you to keep the loan for at least 31 months ($4,250 ÷ $137 = 31).

If you keep this loan for 84 months (7 years), the lender collects, roughly speaking, an extra $7,000.[2] Although the mid- to longer-term economics of a no-cost loan greatly favors lenders, cash-short borrowers and short-term borrowers still might find the loan attractive. If you're tempted to go for this trade-off, run the numbers. Figure out how long you must keep the loan before it turns against you.

In periods when interest rates are trending down, serial refinanceers love this loan—and profit from it—as they ride the trend down with multiple no-cost refinancings. But at some point, the trend reverses. That's when you want to bite the bullet, pay discount points and closing costs, and enjoy the lowest interest rate you can get—from now until the foreseeable future. Without a short-term exit strategy, you will pay a steep long-term price for your no-cost, higher interest rate loan.

SECRET # **86**

Can you prepay without restriction or penalty?

During the 1980s, prepayment restrictions almost died out. But by the late 1990s, they were back. Why? To cut down the number of borrowers who refinance and pay off higher rate loans. When rates trend lower, serial refinancers can cost lenders billions of dollars in lost interest and excessive loan origination costs—especially for zero-point loans, negative-point loans, and low teaser-rate ARMs. Lenders pay loan reps large sales commissions that they hope to earn back over the life of the loan. A quick refi means the lender takes an out-of-pocket loss. Your early prepay to refi at a lower rate cuts short the lender's expected long-term profits.

---

[2] To keep it simple, this example ignores principal reduction, which would slightly alter the numbers.

Types of Prepay Restrictions

Most conventional and all FHA/VA loans do permit prepayment in full or in part without penalty. However, most subprime loans restrict or penalize in some way your right to prepay. Also, as a trade-off, some lenders will shave your interest rate by .25 percent or so if you will accept a prepay limit of some sort. If you plan to hold your mortgage for at least three years, I urge you to weigh benefits of this option. Here are a variety of prepay limits common to mortgages.

- *Complete prohibition:* No prepay permitted. Period! Although some-times found in commercial-investment mortgages, lenders rarely in-clude such restrictive clauses in mortgages issued to homebuyers.
- *Partial prepay:* These clauses permit you to prepay some stated per-centage of the loan each year—perhaps 20 percent.
- *Prepay penalty:* You may prepay at any time as long as you pay the lender for the privilege. These types of penalties may run as high as 5 percent of your loan's outstanding balance at the time of payoff, such as $7,500 on a $150,000 balance. Sometimes they may require, say, six months of extra payments.
- *Penalty phaseout:* Lenders may phase out the penalty over a period of say, three to five years (or longer). On a five-year phaseout, a year-one payoff penalty could cost you 5 percent of the outstanding balance, and a year-five payoff might assess a 1 percent of mortgage balance penalty.
- *Prohibition phaseout:* Likewise, a "no payoff permitted" might expire at year three, five, or perhaps ten.

Read the Fine Print

In the early 1980s, I signed for a 10-year term, second mortgage at 16 percent. At the time I applied for the loan, I specifically asked the loan rep, "Will I suffer any penalty if I pay this loan off early?" (Given the high rates of that period, I wanted to refinance as soon as rates came down to more reasonable levels.) The loan rep responded, "No, none at all. There's no prepayment penalty." The lender (a major bank) also advertised these loans "no prepayment penalty." However, several years later when rates had noticeably dropped, I called the bank for its payoff amount. Their figure came out about $800 more than my calculations.

"Your numbers are wrong," I told them. "No, they're not," the bank responded. Alas, it turned out the lender was "right." Although the loan did not include any explicit prepayment penalty, it did impose a penalty for prepayment. (Yes, you read that correctly.) The fine print of the contract specified that the lender would calculate early payoffs according to the rule of 78s. This now less-frequently used method of loan amortization overloads interest payments into the first several years of the loan. Thus, lenders who use this technique (legally) cheat their customers. (The rule of 78s does not in any way increase the APR disclosure rate!)

Did I complain about fraudulent misrepresentation? You bettcha! Want to guess how well I succeeded in getting my payoff reduced? Zip, zero, nadda.

Learn from my mistake. Don't blindly trust a loan rep to address your concerns. Read the fine print of the contract. Every borrower wants to know, "Is it going to cost me extra to prepay this loan in part or in full?" Clearly, this bank knew its borrowers were concerned about this issue. That's why it advertised, "No prepayment penalty." The bank wanted to deceive its borrowers and found a lawful way to do so. No sensible borrower would have wanted to keep such a loan for its full 10-year term.

I can assure you, many lenders use the same tactics today. Rather than fully explain and address your real concerns, they might answer with partial truths that can subsequently be resolved in the lender's favor by pulling out the paperwork.

Not Just for Prepayment!

I emphasize again, learn from my mistake: Each time you ask the loan rep a question, refuse to accept a mere oral reply. Tell the loan rep that you prefer to see the written language that determines the issue. Apply this safeguard not just for prepayment penalties, but to other material issues such as loan caps, margins, indexes, adjustment periods, closing costs, rate locks, and the topic *Secret #87* addresses—assumption clauses.

SECRET # **87**

An assumable loan may offer less than you've assumed.

Here's another example from my experience—only this time I won, the sellers lost; and the bank pulled in more profit. The sellers had lived in their newly acquired home for nine months; then their employer told them to transfer to Denver.

To qualify for their loan, these sellers had bought down their interest rate for three years to 10 percent—against a market rate of 12.5 percent. Very expensive buydown! "At least," they thought, "we won't have any trouble selling our house. Thankfully, we can offer a buyer our assumable mortgage with that great, below-market 10 percent interest rate." They were right. As soon as I saw the deal they presented, I bought. Unfortunately for the sellers, the bank refused to honor the assumption language the sellers had advertised and incorporated into our agreement.

Assumable Loan, Yes. Assumable Rate, No.

Although the lender quickly approved me for the loan assumption, it refused to approve the below-market rate. "Sorry," the bank told the sellers, "we'll only go forward at the 12.5 percent mortgage contract rate." Outraged, the sellers responded, "What do you mean? We just paid thousands of dollars for that buydown less than a year ago. You're telling us that we just poured that money down a rat hole."

"Now, now, Mr. Seller, we at the bank are sorry you feel that way, but our hands are tied. The contract clearly states that we will approve assumptions only at the loan contract rate, not the buydown rate. I know headquarters would never let this assumption go through at 10 percent."

"Why did you emphasize to us when we got this loan that it was assumable if it couldn't be assumed at the 10 percent rate," the seller angrily contested.

"We don't recall you asking about that at the time. Did you?"

"No, I didn't ask," the seller shot back, "I just assumed that the rate we bought is the rate the buyers would get."

"Well, as we said, Mr. Seller, we're truly sorry about *your* misunderstanding. But there's nothing we can do."

What Happened?

My purchase contract with the sellers specified that (subject only to loan qualification) I could assume their mortgage at 10 percent. It did not give the sellers an escape hatch. To fulfill their obligation under the contract, they had to again pay the bank thousands of dollars to buy the rate down for me. They were not happy campers. They threatened to sue the bank, but in Dizzy Dean fashion, their lawyer warned that they had only two chances of winning: slim and none. In any event, legal costs would swamp any court victory—even in the improbable event that one was achieved.

The Moral: Don't Assume Anything about the Assumption Clause

Your loan rep may point out that the loan you're originating includes a much-desired feature. "It's assumable," she says. You respond, "Sounds good, but tell me more.

- At what interest rate?
- What credit and qualifying standards will apply to my buyers?
- What amount of assumption fee must the buyers pay? What other closing costs or settlement fees will be levied?
- Will the buyers retain the contract right to streamline refi if market interest rates drop?
- Will you require an appraisal for the property at the time of the assumption? If so, what's the maximum loan-to-value ratio that will gain approval?
- Is this assumption a one-time shot? Or, can the new buyers pass the loan along to their eventual buyers?
- Is the assumption only available to owner-occupants, or can investors also assume the loan?
- (If the loan is an ARM), will the buyers retain the right of conversion? Can the periodic or lifetime caps change for the new buyers?

"And while we're talking about it, would you please show me the contract terms, documents, or riders that specifically address each of my concerns and questions?"

To know that buyers can assume your loan is really to know nothing at all. The devil may lurk in the details. In times of higher market interest rates, tighter qualifying standards, or excess housing inventory, assumable mortgages provide sellers a competitive advantage. Their properties sell faster and at higher prices, but only if that assumable conveys benefits that new originations don't offer. (Note: As mentioned earlier, investment properties frequently carry assumable loans. So, if originating or taking over such a loan, review its terms and conditions closely.)

Assume nothing about your assumable. Verify facts.

SECRET # **88**

Appraised value doesn't necessarily equal market value.

Prior to funding a loan, nearly every mortgage lender requires some type of property appraisal.[3] To the detriment of their borrowers, lenders often play games with appraisers and appraisals. Understand that the lender's *appraised value* for a property can register above or below the property's *market value*. Moreover, neither appraised value nor market value says anything about the price you should expect the property to sell for in the future.

Credit, Not Property

For most mortgages on one- to four-unit residential properties, credit stands more important than property (*Secret #40*). To see how this fact applies to appraisals, let's eavesdrop on this conversation between a loan rep and an appraiser.

---

[3] Some streamlined refis omit this step. The topic of appraisals is discussed more extensively in my books, *Investing in Real Estate*, 5th ed. (John Wiley & Sons, 2006); and *The 106 Most Common Mistakes Homebuyers Make (and How to Avoid Them)*, 4th ed. (John Wiley & Sons, 2006).

"Hello, Ed, this is Frank over at Fidelity Mortgage. Look, we got a borrower with a 790 FICO. He wants a $640,000, 80 percent LTV loan to buy an $800,000 place in Mountview. The price sounds a little steep to me, but we would really like this loan to go through smoothly. See what you can do for us, okay?"

"Sure," appraiser Ed responds, "fax the appraisal order to us. I'll get on the job right away. Sales price does seem on the high side, but those homes in Mountview have been appreciating pretty well. I think I can come up with some comps. With a little fiddling, I suspect that we can get the number you need. I'll get back to you in a few days. And thanks again for your business. This will make the fiftieth appraisal job our firm has performed for you this year. Let's hope the market continues to roar."

Strong Borrowers Generally Get the Appraised (i.e., Appraiser) Value Lenders Want

You pay for the appraisal report, but you're not the client. The lender is the client. No appraisal firm that wants to stay in business can regularly provide value estimates that run against its lenders' wishes. That's why the appraisals for strong borrowers nearly always equal or exceed their purchase contract price.

Don't conclude that you're protected by the lender's appraisal. Do your own research. Satisfy yourself by expertly comparing properties, features, and sales prices. Some homebuyers fall in love with a property, agree to pay whatever price the seller is asking, and expect the lender's appraisal to bail them out if they've overpaid. Unless for some reason the lender wants to kill the deal, that won't happen. For the great majority of owner-occupied purchase/refi loans, credit trumps valuation, rarely the reverse.

(For subprime loans, lenders do reduce credit standards, but to offset risk, they set lower LTV ratios and/or greatly increase points, fees, and interest rates. Nevertheless, loan reps will still push appraisers to hit the value required to fund the loan.)

Electronic Appraisals

Increasingly, for high credit score borrowers, lenders may not even send an appraiser out to the property. Instead, they obtain the appraisal electronically from a data bank of recent property sales. If your contract price doesn't severely raise eyebrows, the property passes the appraisal test. Although appraisals based on statistical modeling have long been used by property tax assessors, they do not adequately substitute for close, detailed property appraisals performed by a competent and disinterested expert.

I have run dozens of properties through software valuation models. The results provide a basic data point, but I never rely on them as a final answer. Errors abound.

From a cost standpoint, though, electronic appraisals win hands down. A typical price for an electronic appraisal ranges from $3 to $15 versus the $250 to $450 that most appraisal firms charge. At sites such as zillow.com, you can even pull up free comp sales and value estimates.

If your lender does use a computerized appraisal, watch out for over-billing. Some lenders go ahead and bill you at closing for a standard appraisal fee. HUD says these types of markups (garbage fees) are illegal, but federal courts have ruled otherwise.

SECRET # **89**

Sometimes lenders signal appraisers to lowball their value estimates.

Verify all appraisals. Sometimes they push too high. Sometimes they come in too low to justify the amount of your mortgage loan.

"We had spent almost a year looking at houses," says Phil. "We liked a lot of them, but for one reason or other nothing quite excited our fancy. Then one Saturday we drove by a house we knew we had to have. It was priced right—or I should say, *we* thought it was priced right. Less than 10 days before closing, we learned the lender's appraiser had reported a different opinion. She valued the property $10,000 less than our purchase price.

"To offset this lower appraised value, the lender said we'd have to increase our down payment by $8,000. Or, instead, we could ask the sellers to reduce their price. We had bargained hard as it was, so we didn't think the sellers would agree to come down more. And they wouldn't. As for raising our down payment by $8,000—no way. So, the financing fell through and we had to begin our search all over again."

From time to time, lowball appraisals kill a sale. Sometimes lenders use low appraisals to turn down loans they do not want to make. At other times, appraisers respond to tightened government appraisal regulations. Either way, a lowball appraisal can wreck your planned LTV ratio and down payment.

Prevent Deal-Killer Appraisals

To help prevent this problem, research the sales prices (and terms) of similar properties in the neighborhood. Use these prices to guide your offer. Next, learn the name of the appraiser your lender plans to use. Identify for the appraiser (or ask your agent to) the comp sales you relied on to figure your offer. After the appraisal is complete, get a copy from the lender. (You are entitled to a copy of your appraisal under the 1991 Equal Credit Opportunity Act, various state laws, and regulations put in place by the Federal Reserve Board.)

If, because of a low appraisal, a lender rejects your loan (or requires you to pay more money down), a financing contingency clause in your purchase contract should permit you to recover your earnest money deposit. If you think the appraiser has lowballed you, schedule a meeting with the appraiser, or write out your objections to the appraisal and give them to your lender.

The appraiser can either accept or dismiss your comments. If he or she rejects them, you can ask the lender to send out another appraiser. If the lender wants your business, it will probably agree to obtain a second opinion. If the lender doesn't oblige (and you exceed the allowable LTV), you must increase your down payment, ask the sellers to reduce their price, or apply for a mortgage somewhere else. (To appease your frustrations with the appraiser, write a complaint to the state licensing board; however, that won't help you get the financing you need.)

Beware, though. If an appraiser refuses to hit the value you want, at least carefully listen to his reasoning. At times, buyers press appraisers to boost a property's appraisal only to learn later (and to their regret) they really did overpay. The appraiser's original estimate proved correct. As some property markets soften, appraisers should become more conservative. Remember, in a declining market, comp sales actually overstate current (and future) values.

In sharply rising markets, lenders, appraisers, homebuyers, investors, and, yes, speculators get careless. With eyes on the future, no one worries much about the price today because it's sure to climb higher tomorrow. (This ill-advised outlook reflects the view that "inflation cures all mistakes.") When you value a property, give due weight to the past, present, and future. Where are you relative to the real estate cycle?

Appraisals Exclude Personal Property or Atypical Seller Contributions

Appraisers limit their value estimates to the building, site improvements, and lot—that is, real estate. If your purchase price includes personal property (antique Oriental rugs, costly appliances, custom-made draperies, furniture) or if your seller has agreed to pay an atypically high percentage of your mortgage points and/or closing costs, the lender's appraiser will subtract these amounts from his or her value estimate. If the lower appraisal increases your LTV, the lender may cut back the amount it is willing to lend you—or increase your interest rate and/or the costs of your mortgage insurance. Before you write seller contributions into your purchase offer, learn lender rules; then figure out an advantageous way to get the loan you need to pay for any personal property and/or settlement expenses. Sometimes it's wise to write up a separate agreement to cover these items. Ask your loan rep or real estate agent for advice.

SECRET # **90**

Appraisals do not forecast the future.

Maria and Jorge Olson were sitting in the living room of the home they wanted to buy. Five other hopeful buyers sat nearby. Their desired home was listed at $390,000. The sales agent for the sellers came into the room. Tension hung in the air. "We're going to start the bidding now," the agent said. Offers started flying. Pandemonium broke loose.

"It was really wild," Maria recalled. "Then, after everyone had had their say and written up their offers, the agent and the owners left the room. When they came back, we just knew we'd won. We were right. The owners accepted our offer of $420,000. We celebrated that evening by going out to dinner at the most expensive restaurant in town. With home values increasing 20 percent a year, we felt that we got a great deal."

Two years later Maria and Jorge were in divorce court. They needed to sell their home and hired an appraiser. His value estimate came in at $385,000—about the same listing price that several real estate agents had suggested to the Olsons. (Several other agents had estimated much higher.)

Lawsuits against Appraisers Require Proof of Negligence

To say the least, the Olsons were distressed and angry. They wanted someone to blame. They decided to sue their lender, their real estate agent, and the appraisal firm that had appraised the house when the Olsons originated their mortgage. That appraisal valued the house at $425,000. The Olsons knew the market now was soft, but surely prices couldn't have fallen that much. Their lender's appraiser must have overvalued the home, or if prices were really going to fall that much, the Olsons argued, someone should have warned them.

The Olsons lost their court case for two reasons. Expert testimony showed that the original $425,000 value estimate wasn't completely off the wall at that earlier boisterous time. Although one could easily question the appraiser's judgment, the appraisal displayed no wildly objective errors. The court also ruled that neither appraisers nor realty agents could be expected to predict the future. Estimates of market value apply only to the date of the appraisal. Neither the Olsons nor other homebuyers, investors, or speculators should rely on an appraiser, their mortgage lender, or their real estate agent to tell them whether property prices are headed up or down.

Appraisers Don't Forecast Values

Throughout the United States, the ruling in this case generally holds. With limited exceptions, property buyers must make their own forecasts. At best, appraisers describe the current market. An appraiser might think, "Speculators are bidding up prices. Buyers are crazy. Within a year prices are going to fall faster than the NASDAQ crash of 2000." But appraisers won't put these kinds of comments into their reports of market value.

Likewise, when performing a market value appraisal, an appraiser wouldn't comment, "This is the best market for property investors that I've seen in years. Prices are sure to double within the next five years." You could ask an appraiser (or real estate agent) to give you his or her opinion about where the market is headed over the coming years, but for you to see the future as clearly as possible, study the market signals such as job growth, population demographics, the amount of new construction, time on market, number of existing properties up for sale, interest rates, qualifying standards, and foreclosure trends.

Many buyers think they are getting a great buy if they purchase a property for less than its current market value; however, tomorrow's another day. Answer these three questions before you buy: Do I really know the property's market value? What market signals indicate this property will be worth more tomorrow than it is today? And, what market signals spell D-A-N-G-E-R? Beware of landing upside down with overappraising and overborrowing.

Verify the detailed features of comparable properties. Evaluate the inventories of unsold new and existing properties. Are their numbers decreasing, stable, or increasing? How long are properties taking to sell relative to six months or one year ago? Overpay and you can wait several years to recoup your money. Buy right and the property will likely rank among your best investments.

CHAPTER 9

Achieve the Lowest Interest Rate Available

"**H**ello, this is Easy Money Mortgage Company. What can we do to you today . . . I mean . . . for you today?"

The caller responds, "Can you tell me the best rate you can give on a 30-year mortgage?"

Readers, please remember: Never "dial for dollars" when you shop for a mortgage. You set yourself up for fleecing.

"Okay," you say to me, "if that approach doesn't work, what does?"

I'm glad you asked, because that's the question this chapter answers. To start, let's look at interest rates from the lender's perspective to see why and how loan reps might underquote yet overcharge.

SECRET # **91**

Refuse to yield to oversized yield-spread premiums (YSPs).

Most mortgage originators want to sell you a loan to earn a commission. No loans, no paycheck. Plus, loan reps earn their highest commissions when they sell you higher-cost loan products. If your loan rep says, "The best I can do is a rate of 6.25 percent and 2 points," don't accept that claim as the gospel truth. Just like a car salesperson (or any other type of salesperson), the loan rep may be testing you.

If you agree, great. If you balk, the rep can say, "Oh, wait a minute, I've just thought of something else. Maybe I can get the lender to slice a point off those origination fees. Those folks owe me a favor."

To avoid overpaying, ask to see the loan rep's rate sheet. The rate sheet shows the "wholesale" cost of various loans. The bigger the spread between the wholesale price and the price (interest rate and points) you pay, the larger the loan rep's commission. Ask the rep, "What's your YSP on this loan?" For cookie-cutter Fannie/Freddie loans, a fair YSP should not exceed (in my view) $1,500 to $2,500. If more, ask the rep to explain and justify. Ask Realtors or other loan reps whether the quoted YSP seems fair and competitive.

Credit Blemishes

Mortgage lenders sometimes classify borrower profiles into categories of A, B, C, and D. The lower your grade, the more you pay for a mortgage. But just like in school, the grade you receive depends on who does the grading. Even with credit blemishes, one mortgage lender might give you an A-, another might downgrade you to B or even a C status—and, correspondingly, persuade you to pay a higher interest rate and fees. Generally, profile "grading" includes more borrower data than credit scoring. No precise distinctions apply because lenders differ in their approach to underwriting and loan pricing. Lenders also use categories called prime, Alt-A, and subprime.

If you get downgraded because you fall short of the perfect borrower profile, challenge that assessment. Ask why. Is the loan rep testing you so he or she can make more money? Or do you deserve your downgrade? Also, learn how long it will take—or what you can do—to reach A status. Maybe you should defer buying until you can qualify at lower rates and costs.

Talk with other mortgage companies. If your blemishes consist of nothing more than a few late payments, you can probably find an A grade mortgage. Even when you've suffered more serious setbacks, it's sometimes possible to provide an excuse that will at least get you Alt-A pricing.

One mortgage broker confessed to me that 30 to 40 percent of B and C borrowers could probably qualify (with a little tweaking) for an A or Alt-A pricing. If you deserve a B grade or lower, negotiate and persuade. Emphasize your strong points (the eight Cs). Ask whether a higher down payment of co-signor (or co-borrower) will gain you better pricing. Talk with an FHA or VA loan rep. These programs offer good pricing and benefits, yet with relaxed qualifying. (Many loan reps won't suggest these possibilities because they do not originate FHA/VA loans.) Provide compelling reasons. When asked, some loan reps will come down from their sticker prices when you bolster your borrower profile.

Prepayment Penalty Discount

A loan rep can receive an extra yield-spread premium (commission bonus) by slipping a prepayment penalty into a mortgage contract. Prepayment penalties deter loan runoff when interest rates fall. So, typically, a loan that restricts (or prohibits) prepayment can be offered at, say, .25 percent less than a loan that lacks such a penalty. But if the rep does not pass along the rate discount to you, the lender shares its gain with the rep.

Whether you should request the discounted interest rate in exchange for prepay penalty depends on the same rate/point questions that always come up: How long do you plan to keep the loan if interest rates don't move down? And, does either inflation (or disinflation) seem imminent, leading to higher (or lower) interest rates?

If the odds point to lower rates, skip the penalty. If higher inflation and higher interest rates look more likely, then you won't refi any time soon. So, if you accept the penalty for the rate discount, you can profit from the trade-off. (Remember, many mortgages omit prepay penalties. Therefore, this trade-off issue will not arise because accepting the penalty does not become an option.)

SECRET # **92**

Red and yellow, black and white, do lenders treat them all alike?

Critics often complain about two types of mortgage discrimination: stereotypical ("We don't make loans to _____. They're bad risks."), and discrimination through "neutral" rules or practices that adversely impact some identifiable groups of borrowers such as African Americans, Hispanics, immigrants, women, singles, single-parent families, and so on.

As company policy, lenders have nearly eliminated stereotypical turn-downs; however, studies indicate that some borrowers pay more for their mortgages than other borrowers—even when their borrower profiles look similar. (Of course, that fact stands as one of the principal themes of this book.) Nevertheless, borrowers who pay more fall disproportionately into some legally protected category. Does this suggest that lenders illegally discriminate? Not necessarily.

Instead, it suggests that some borrowers fail to negotiate interest rates and fees. When the loan rep says, "Gee, this is the best I can do," such borrowers accept the loan on the terms offered. They don't realize that they should respond with their own negotiating gambit, "Really, that's the best you can do? Well, Providence Mortgage quoted a better deal. Sorry, we're wasting our time with you." Or, "We saw much lower pricing on bankrate.com. Why is that? You're not trying to boost your yield spread premium, are you?"

Forget about your gender, race, religion, or politics; some loan reps will charge you higher interest and fees whenever you let them. If you fear the lending process, if you fail to aggressively negotiate, or if you fail to educate yourself about mortgage loan practices and products, you are limp prey for the predators. Warning: Predators come in all colors, ethnicities, and religions. Please do not place trust in your loan rep merely because you share some racial, ethnic, or religious similarities. Industry insiders know all too well that some loan reps use some shared feature to gain trust when no trust is warranted.

To protect yourself, assert yourself (politely, of course). When some loan reps sense a vulnerable victim, they make a killing. Once again: Trust, yes. But verify, too.

SECRET # **93**

Rate quotes: Fact or fiction?

Loans differ from most products. You won't know the price (total costs) of your newly originated mortgage until after you have agreed to buy it. This industry-wide practice encourages some loan reps to charge you more than you were originally told; but it also exposes you to risks when you deal with honest reps.

Even though you negotiate interest rates, costs, and fees with your loan rep at or around the time you apply for your loan, the rate you pay can still differ from the rate you both have agreed upon. Moreover, if market rates fall prior to your closing date, you could lose that rate drop—unless you protect yourself as *Mortgage Secrets* advises you to do.

Lowball Quotes

Lenders compete aggressively with each other. To draw in prospective customers, some loan reps deceptively lowball interest rates, points, or closing costs. Or if true, the quoted figures may apply to only a small niche of people. After you're a week or two forward in the mortgage process, the loan rep informs you about a previously overlooked glitch in your credit, employment, tax returns, or qualifying ratios. Often, a loan rep who wants to change deal terms can find a way to do so.

Bait and Switch

Once you learn that your loan won't go through as previously agreed, you could threaten to switch lenders. But, if you're obliged to the sellers for a 30-day close and you've already hit day 13, what do you do? If the loan rep talks a good story, you'll agree to switch to a less desirable loan product, or perhaps accept a higher interest rate or costs. Either way, a dishonest loan rep can use this sleight of hand to increase his (her) commission. If he's smooth, you will thank the rep for the heroic job he performed to save the deal and meet your closing deadline.

Your Defense

Don't shop price alone. Shop for integrity. Verify the experience, reputation, and dependability of the loan rep. Check references, of course, but more importantly, early on nail down the precise loan amount, costs, interest rate, and terms the loan rep is promising and why he thinks he can deliver on his promises. Listen carefully for hedging. You know the "Well, I'll try to do the best I can." Watch for mannerisms, eye movement, body language. Does the rep pass the comfort test, or does something not feel right?

When thinking over the times I've been sandbagged, one constant remains: The clues were lying in plain sight if only I had paid attention. Isn't that fact true for you, too? When asked, all honest loan reps will provide you written guarantees subject only to disclosed and explained potential changes. Seek not only a true good faith estimate (GFE), but also any possible reasons the final loan amount, costs, or terms might differ from that GFE.

SECRET # **94**

What rate will you get at closing?

Other than ARM teasers, mortgage assumptions, and seller financing, few lenders guarantee their rate *quotes*. The rate you get is set on (or near) the date you close. If you dislike such uncertainty, you can lock a rate. After you submit your application, you decide whether to float or lock. If you choose to lock, that opens this set of questions:

- *When to lock:* Generally, you can lock on the date of loan approval— or as early as the date of application—or anytime up until a day or two before closing.
- *How long:* Lock periods may run anywhere from 10 to 90 days, or longer if you arrange permanent financing for a new property before the builder completes construction.
- *How much:* The longer you lock your rate, the more the lock will cost you (or the lender). Although some lenders try to collect this fee up front, industry standards favor payment at closing.

Whether to Lock?

To help answer this question, return to the issue of qualifying ratios. If, during the loan processing period, rates move up .25 percent, would the lender still qualify you for the amount you need? If no, lock immediately. Why risk losing your loan or having to scurry around at the last minute to reconfigure your qualifying income and qualifying debts? If, however, you've plenty of extra cash to reduce the amount of your loan, then you might accept the risk as long as higher monthly payments would not wreck your monthly budget.

Most people who dislike risk prefer to lock, even if upward rate moves wouldn't upset their budget or disqualify them from the mortgage for which they've been approved. If you fall into this category, lock and sleep well. Of course, the downside occurs when rates drop and you kick yourself for worrying so much.

When to Lock

Even if you decide to lock, most lenders give leeway. Should rates drop the day you receive your loan approval, you might wait to see if drops continue. Ride the trend down and then lock after the next couple of upticks.

Obviously, the rate lock issue prompts you to forecast short-term interest rates. And anyone who perfects this skill can make millions as a bond trader, so don't expect flawless timing. Follow the rates, and act when you feel comfortable in the trade-offs among opportunity, risk, and regret.

How Long Should You Lock?

Are you counting on a 30-day closing or less? Are you already a week or two forward in the mortgage process? Does your loan approval depend on explanations, inspections, appraisal, or documentation? If so, how much time must you or the lender allow to remove these contingencies? Have you verified, corrected, and cleaned up your credit reports prior to applying for the loan (*Secret #44*)? Before you choose a lock period, realistically review what needs to be done and how long it will take.

Many borrowers lock too soon and for too short a period because they ballpark their closing date and fail to avoid glitches. As you saw earlier, when interest rates trend up, don't push against the timeline. To break your lock, the lender may delay closing. Without your rate guarantee, the lender can move you into a the then higher market rate.

How Much Do Rate Locks Cost?

The longer you lock, the more you pay. On a $200,000 loan, a 30-day lock could cost between $500 and $1,000. A 60-day lock could run up to $1,500 or more. Your lender may, for little or no charge, lock for 15 to 30 days. (Check whether your state regulates rate locks.)

Although longer term rate-lock fees shift up and down, they're seldom cheap. So, typically, you wouldn't add an extra 30 days "just to play it safe." Smart borrowers ride trends down, prepare to avoid glitches and contingencies, develop a realistic closing schedule, and lock a rate for the minimum number of days that safely protects until closing.

Market Floats Down

You could lock at a rate, say 6.5 percent and then rates fall. When that happens, will you enjoy the lower rate? Probably not, unless your lender has agreed to a rate lock with a float down.

Without a float down agreement, can you negotiate a lower rate? Sometimes, but your lender may have presold your 6.5 percent mortgage to an investor in the secondary mortgage market. That investor expects a 6.5 percent loan. If your lender delivers a 6.0 percent loan instead, it will lose money because the investor will discount the price it pays so that it still earns the 6.5 percent it bargained for. If you want a rate lock with a float down, negotiate for it early on.

Find a New Lender

If your lender did not agree to a rate lock with float down, you could possibly grab the new 6.0 percent market interest rate by jumping to a new lender. To quickly move forward with the new lender, the old lender must be willing to immediately transfer your application file. The new lender must agree to accept the file and close within 15 days. Otherwise, you must buy another rate lock, unless disinflation and weak economic growth signal further drops in interest rates, and you think floating presents an acceptable risk.

You would likely forfeit the application fees and costs you paid to the first lender, as well as pay additional application fees and costs to the new lender. Changing lenders halfway through the mortgage process seldom proves easy. Nevertheless, you might tactfully raise the possibility to your loan rep. The rep might at least give you some rate break. So, don't leave your float down to last minute negotiations. Ask for it before you need it.

If dealing with a mortgage broker, that rep might be willing to move your file to another of his wholesale lenders. Of course, a broker who pulls that tactic too often will find fewer lenders who will accept applications from his loan customers. Good mortgage brokers play fair with their lenders and their borrowers.

With refis, however, you hold more power because no sales contract imposes a closing deadline. Also, under federal law, you may rescind your refinance agreement within three business days after you close that refi.

SECRET # **95**
___

Achieve your best rate.

Typically, lenders honor their rate locks. But *Mortgage Secrets* advises you to leave nothing to good-faith oral promises. With shady loan reps, or in periods of heavy loan volume, those our-word-is-our-bond rate locks often prove insecure.

Confirm the Lock and Price in Writing

You decide that it's time to lock. You telephone the loan rep; she checks rates and fees. You tell her to lock. She says, "It's done. We've got you 6.5 percent for 30 days. That should give us plenty of time with several days to spare."

You then ask the loan rep to fax or e-mail the agreed terms of the lock. Alternatively, fax or e-mail the loan rep your "understanding." Request a response. In fact, this "confirm-in-writing" precaution works to prevent disagreement in all types of discussions that take place orally. Profit from the lessons I've learned, often the hard way. I once suffered a world of grief when I acted on a lawyer's erroneous advice given orally. Later, he lied and denied it—just what you would expect from a lawyer. After that experience (which cost me more than $100,000), I now scrupulously confirm in writing.

Don't Let Your Lock Expire

You can bust your own lock if you don't timely fulfill your loan rep's (or loan underwriter's) requests for documents, explanations, or other paperwork that's necessary to move the loan forward. Anticipate, clarify, research, and prepare. Learn what's expected of you. Meet these obligations promptly.

Sometimes, though, lenders don't meet the deadline for one of three reasons:

- *Third-party failure:* Your closing depends on the work of outside parties that the lender doesn't control (credit repositories, appraisers, title insurers, surveyors, property inspection services, and so on). When these people err or delay, the loan process stalls. In many instances, real estate agents can use their influence to speed up third-party providers. Agents hold the power of future referrals.

- *Lender mistakes or neglect:* Before a third party delivers, the lender must place the order. Sometimes they forget, or the lender misplaces documents, ignores necessary verifications, or employs too few file handlers to expedite its overflow of applications. Sometimes the loan underwriter decides at the last minute he requires another document, explanation, or verification.

- *Improper intent:* When interest rates jump .5 percent or more above the locked rate, the lender could lose money on that loan, or if the lender can deliver the loan at a rate substantially above a locked rate, it may gain thousands of dollars in overage. Bottom line issues can seriously test the lender's ethics. A loan rep only needs to find some quasi-legitimate last minute reason to delay. "We're really sorry, but the underwriter now insists that you (or the seller) repair that leaky roof before closing."

When you know why locks expire, you can head off trouble. Remain involved in the loan process. Don't badger the loan rep every day, but do ask for a flow chart of who, why, where, and when. Track the scheduling. Verify that all steps are moving forward on time. Where you see foot-dragging, push for cooperation—even if it means that you (or your realty agent) call third-party providers and diplomatically insist on service.

By the time you lock your rate, the lender should have scheduled the commitment process and set a tentative closing date. Ask the loan rep whether the lender will honor the locked rate if it causes the delay. If so, include that promise when you confirm your lock's terms and fee. If not, you're forewarned. Speed the process along—or pay a penalty for the lender's ineptness (that is, if interest rates go up during the loan processing period).

Finally, if you sense purposeful delay, stand firm. Insist that closing take place as scheduled or you'll use every consumer right and regulatory complaint procedure available. Should that fail, insist that the lender honor the otherwise expired rate lock. Also, search for alternative ways to remedy the cause of the delay. For example, rather than require preclosing repairs, you or the sellers could post a sufficient sum of money into a repair escrow account, or the lender could withhold funds at closing pending repairs. Think through a problem. You can discover multiple ways to solve it and close on schedule.

What Does the Lender Mean by "Market Rate"?

Some lenders will lock in your mortgage interest rate, yet will give you a float down if rates fall between the time you apply and the date your loan closes. "Good news," your loan rep tells you, "rates have fallen and we can now close your loan at 6.75 percent instead of 7.0 percent. You're going to save $56.30 a month."

Yes, that's good news, but it may not reflect the full drop in rates that has occurred. If market rates are really at 6.5 percent, by getting you to accept 6.75 percent, your loan rep will pocket an extra $1,000 or so in commission. Even with float downs, verify that you receive the full float down that you are entitled to. (For example, compare your rate to the ones shown at bankrate.com.)

SECRET # **96**

Industry pros and government agencies need your help.

To a large degree, the tricks of the mortgage trade continue because they give lenders and loan reps ripe opportunities to profit at the expense of their borrowers. Although various housing, banking, and consumer regulations govern lenders and loan reps, these regulations seldom protect effectively. With many regulations, form trumps substance, bureaucratic rules trump common sense, and good intentions trump concrete results.

Even worse, U.S. Senate hearings in March 2007 revealed a "chronology of regulatory neglect," said Christopher Dodd, chairman of the Senate Banking Committee. The *Wall Street Journal* and *New York Times* have followed up these hearings with many articles such as "Regulators Are Pressed to Take a Tougher Stand on Mortgages" and "Regulators Scrutinized in Mortgage Meltdown."

More specifically, this Senate investigation found (just as I warned against in the 2003 edition of *Mortgage Secrets*):

- Millions of borrowers are led into bad loans.
- Bonus compensation for loan reps who persuade borrowers to take higher-cost loans.
- Hidden (undisclosed) prepayment penalties that prevent or deter borrowers from refinancing high-cost loans.
- Overuse of "exotic" mortgages with increasing payments.
- Excessive fees and costs.
- Unsuspecting borrowers are pushed into mortgages they cannot afford.
- Lenders conspiring to originate "liars loans" (a term of widespread usage in the mortgage industry that refers to mortgages supported by fraudulent statements of borrower debts, income, assets, property value, or some combination thereof).

To sum up testimony heard at these hearings, Senator Richard Shelby queried Sandra Thompson (director of supervision for the FDIC), "So, we're just touching the tip of the iceberg. Is that a fair statement?"

"That would be a fair statement," responded Ms. Thompson.

Industry Initiatives to the Rescue?

In a 2002 issue of *Mortgage Banking*,[1] John Robbins wrote:

As mortgage bankers, we know that integrity, trust, and honesty are simply the rules of conduct by which we should all live. . . [government

---

[1] *Mortgage Banking*, "Integrity," April, 2002, pp. 17–18.

and industry] are currently targeting many unethical practices such as flipping [repeated] refinances that result in fees for lenders without any benefit to borrowers . . . inflating a home's appraised value, packing loans with unnecessary credit insurance, and charging extended prepayment penalties that trap homeowners in high interest rate loans. . . .

It is commendable that some mortgage banking and brokerage firms are initiating voluntary consumer disclosures on their own. These disclosures detail the loan fees a borrower can expect to pay and how much other settlement costs should total. Some companies also disclose in advance of settlement if closing fees will exceed the initial good faith estimate. Mortgage applicants possess the power to demand similar information from lenders who are not now offering these extra disclosures.

As multiple 2007 congressional hearings show, neither lenders nor mortgage applicants have conquered this challenge. All industry observers agree that mortgage lenders, and yes, borrowers, too, have failed to meet their responsibilities.

Upfront Mortgage Broker (UMB)

To spearhead full upfront disclosure of costs, fees, commissions, bonuses, yield-spread premiums, and other types of lender charges and loan rep compensation, Jack Guttentag (mtgprofessor.com) has created the Upfront Mortgage Broker's Commitment (see Figure 9.1). UMBs believe that full disclosure will force reform.

Essentially, UMBs want mortgage lenders to behave more like professionals who work for their clients' best interests while charging a fully known, agreed-upon fee. With true client representation and fixed compensation, the loan reps can design and search for the optimal solution to a borrower's funding needs and wants. When incentives to gouge the borrower are removed, loan reps will walk the straight and narrow. Loan customers will receive better service. Everyone will live happily ever after.

◆

1. The broker will be the customer's representative or agent, and will endeavor to act in the best interests of the customer.
2. The broker will establish a price for services up front, in writing, based on information provided by the customer.
3. The price may be a fixed dollar amount, a percent of the loan, an hourly charge for the broker's time, or a combination of these.
4. The price or prices will cover all the services provided by the broker. This includes loan processing, for which customers always pay a broker or lender.
5. On third party services, such as an appraisal, ordered by the broker but paid for by the customer, the broker will provide the invoice from the third party service provider at the customer's request. Alternatively, the broker may have the payment made directly by the customer to the third party service provider.
6. Any payments the broker receives from third parties involved in the transaction will be credited to the customer, unless such payments are included in the broker's fee.
7. If the broker's fee is 1 point, for example, and the broker collects 1 point from the lender as a "yield spread premium," the broker either charges the customer 1 point and credits the customer with the yield spread premium, or charges the customer nothing and retains the yield spread premium.
8. The broker will use his best efforts to determine the loan type, features, and lender services that best meet the customer's needs, and to find the best wholesale price for that loan.
9. The wholesale prices from which the broker's selection is made will be disclosed at the customer's request.
10. When directed by the customer, the broker will lock the terms (rate, points, and other major features) of the loan, and will provide a copy of the written confirmation of the rate lock as soon as it has been received from the lender.
11. If a customer elects to float the rate/points, the broker will provide the customer the best wholesale float price available to that customer on the day the loan is finally locked.
12. The broker will maintain a web site on which its commitment to its customers is prominently displayed, along with any other information the broker wishes to convey.

Figure 9.1 Commitment of an Upfront Mortgage Broker (UMB)
(Courtesy of Jack Guttentag)

Borrower Savvy Still Needed

The UMB commitment can't work by itself. Consider this analogy: Lawyers owe strong fiduciary duties to their clients, yet anyone who has watched closely knows that lawyers often abuse their clients' interests to line their own pockets.[2] Mere fee disclosure in a fiduciary relationship doesn't vanquish chicanery, duplicity, and incompetence. Lawyers can triumph over their clients and the social good because most people lack knowledge about the law, the rules of procedure, and that oxymoron, legal ethics.[3]

Likewise, you will pay too much for too little unless you gain the knowledge to assert yourself forthrightly and intelligently. Only when consumers ask the pertinent questions—and demand factual, well-reasoned answers—will they achieve their best loan at the lowest costs and pricing available.

Until then, match the ideal of John Galt. Become part of the competent minority who refuses to humble yourself with, "Well, we will do whatever you think is best." With *Mortgage Secrets* as your guide, insist on the service and disclosures that will distinguish you from the sheepish borrower who prefers a pleasant, run-of-the-mill loan rep—someone who won't confuse their decisions with multiple choices. No doubt, most loan reps are not willing or able to meet this challenge.

This same situation holds true for real estate agents. During most of the twentieth century, realty agents disparaged knowledgeable buyers. And many still do. Increasingly, though, buyer knowledge (partly due to a plentiful selection of books on homebuying and real estate investing) has forced an upgrade in agent competency, although it is still far below the standards agents should meet.

Nevertheless, as more homebuyers and investors expect honest competency, real estate firms are slowly edging out the fast talkers whose only goal is to make a sale. This same trend influences mortgage lending. To foment a revolution, we just need to enlist more foot soldiers. Won't you

---

[2] See, for example, the books, *Double Billing, A Nation Under Lawyers, A Feast for Lawyers, Divorced from Justice,* and *Injustice for All,* to name just a few exposés on this topic.

[3] Can you name one other occupation whose ethics books include a chapter entitled, "Promoting Falsity," along with instructions on how to do so?

join up? At the end of the day, consumers determine the ethics, competence, and professionalism of the people who serve them.

SECRET #

How to (almost) vanquish tricks of the trade.

You may think that you should avoid loan reps who live by sales commissions, bonuses, and overages. Rather than take a chance, play it safe. Talk only with salaried loan reps at your bank or credit union. Not a good solution. Here's why:

- *Less competency:* Most savvy, stand-out-from-the-crowd mortgage professionals prefer commissioned income. Paper-shuffling, by-the-book loan reps prefer guaranteed salaries in bureaucracies. Of course, even salaried loan reps must meet loan production quotas and often earn bonuses for meeting or exceeding bank goals.
- *Higher price:* Because many people believe that banks provide safe harbor in the cutthroat world of commerce, their loan departments can charge a premium. Banks rarely offer the lowest interest rates or fees; however, credit unions may prove a better choice—especially for plain-vanilla products. Credit unions typically incur lower operating costs than banks. Their income-tax-free status enables them to pass along savings to their borrowers if they choose to.
- *Limited choice:* Rather than sell you what you need, salaried reps may push their employer's favored products; or they may push only those products (typically, the 30-year fixed-rate mortgage) that they find easy to explain.
- *Performance standards:* Salaried reps must meet their employer's volume and profit goals. Although you can hire a mortgage broker to work as your buyer's agent, the salaried reps can never represent you. They are obligated to pursue the interests of their employers—subject to laws and regulations, of course.

An Innocent Slaughtered: Bank Malfeasance

In helping my friend Sue with a refinance, I reviewed all documents that pertained to her current loan that she had obtained 10 years earlier from one of the largest and most reputable banks in the state. This loan carried a 7.75 percent interest rate. Sue had taken out this loan as a refinance of her purchase loan three years earlier, which had carried a 9.75 percent interest rate. After working through the numbers, I could not believe how the bank had overcharged her (for the wrong product, no less) either through loan rep ignorance, deception, or both. During the past 10 years, that supposedly trustworthy bank's loan rep had cost my friend more than $20,000 (loss of home equity buildup, excessive fees and interest charges). And this extra $20,000 in costs was against an original loan payoff balance of only $58,000!

Specific Goal

At the time of her refinance, Sue told the loan rep that she chiefly wanted a loan that would get her house paid off as quickly as possible. Sue stated that she was specifically interested in a 15-year, fixed-rate loan.

The loan rep told Sue that, given her income level, she would not qualify for a 15-year loan. Then the rep proceeded to advise Sue to sign up for a no-cost [sic], 30-year fixed-rate loan. Accordingly, Sue accepted this advice. After all, the loan rep's the expert, isn't she? When Sue closed this loan, she owed $62,100 with a 30-year term. When she walked into the office, she had owed $58,000 with a remaining term of 27 years. The loan rep had sold Sue the worst mortgage possible, given Sue's specifically stated goals. But that loan (in term, fees, and interest rate) ranked high in profitability for the bank.

Obvious Misdeeds

Either through ignorance or deceptive intent (probably ignorance), Sue's loan rep erred in at least the following ways:[4]

- *Qualifying:* Although Sue's total debt ratios (the back ratio) would have exceeded conventional guidelines (15-year term), a little

---

[4] Of course, I'm speaking from Sue's perspective. From the bank's perspective, the loan rep earned five stars.

financial planning could easily have restructured those figures to match the conventional underwriting guidelines for 15-year loans.

◆ *Compensating factors:* For the preceding three years Sue had paid every mortgage payment on time, in an amount that exceeded the sums required by a new 15-year loan (at the then lower interest rates). In addition, Sue had perfect credit and displayed numerous strong compensating factors such as a secure job, low housing cost ratio (the front ratio), low living expenses, dependability, and stability.

◆ *ARM possibilities:* At the time of the refi, many ARM lenders offered attractive interest rates. The loan rep never mentioned these choices.

◆ *High interest rate:* 15- and 30-year fixed-rate loans in Sue's market were readily available in the 6.0 to 7.0 percent range. At 7.75 percent, Sue's rate was far higher than she should have paid.

◆ *High costs:* Unlike most "no-cost" loans that trade off costs for higher interest, Sue's loan carried costs in excess of $4,000 (on a $58,000 refi!). Sue's loan product was falsely advertised as no-cost when, in fact, it was merely no cash due at closing. Her costs included points of 3-1/8 percent.

Neat trick when a lender can do it: High interest rate, high costs, and low amortization (equity build-up). About the only thing good about this loan was its lack of a prepayment penalty and few garbage fees. But with 3-1/8 points, who needs garbage fees?

Who's Responsible: The Lender or Sue?

If questioned, the bank would admit no wrongdoing. It complied with every required rule, regulation, and disclosure. Sue's file folders for this mortgage brimmed with all necessary signed documents. Although this loan rep probably was not commissioned, the bank may have paid a bonus for originating no-cost refinances such as this one.

When I asked Sue why she chose this lender, she said she had responded to its advertisement. Did she call any competing lenders? No. Did she call the mortgage company that serviced her current mortgage to learn what they could do for her? No. Why not? Because the advertised bank enjoyed a good reputation and claimed status as the largest mortgage lender in town. If you can't trust a salaried employee of a large bank to give you a good deal, whom can you trust?[5]

Who Can You Trust?

The cynic says, "Trust no one." To the contrary, *Mortgage Secrets* advises you to trust yourself. Gain the knowledge and savvy that will enable you to negotiate the optimal loan. But also think through your goals and priorities. What loan best puts you on the path to achieve the financial goals that are most important to you? Then trust your loan rep, but only after he or she earns your trust. He should question and clarify your goals, needs, wants, and capabilities. How can someone serve you who doesn't learn who you are and what you plan to achieve? The professional will rank priorities. Only after an introductory interview can the loan rep explain and recommend loan programs.

Affordability, budgeting, qualifying ratios, credit and credit scores, type of property, interest rate/point trade-offs, family issues, equity buildup, these factors and many more combine to impact your choice of a mortgage.[6] Too few borrowers and loan reps comprehend how the property and financing choices you make today will impact your life and your wealth 5, 10, and 20 years into the future.

So, whom can you trust? Trust those professionals whose behavior and demonstrated competence leave no doubts about their motives. Trust those who adopt your goals as their own—and then exercise the due diligence and expertise to help you achieve what you want and what you can realistically afford while charging a fair YSP.

---

[5] In speaking with an investment trust [sic] officer of a major bank, I queried, "You're telling me that you only sell your customers funds and investments that carry heavy front-end expense loads?" *Trust* officer response: "Of course, the bank has to make a profit. I've got to make a living."

[6] For example, you ask, "How much will you loan me?" The loan rep replies, "probably around $350K." The rep (without thinking) gives you a figure that applies to single-family homes. He omits the fact that if you bought a two- to four-unit property, you might qualify for a loan amount of $500,000 or more. Without asking, most reps merely report single-family home figures.

CHAPTER 10

Manage Your Property and Financing for Maximum Return

J ournalists routinely quote financial planners who advise homeowners, "Your house is a roof over your head—not an investment!" As to stocks, journalists chant this enthusiastic litany, "Hang tight and you will be rewarded. Over the long run, stocks can be expected to outperform all other investments."

If you wish to build wealth and maximize the return on your assets and investments, you will ignore this journalistic babble. Despite the push for stocks and 401(k)s, 403(b)s, IRAs, and Keoghs, home equity remains the largest source of wealth for the great majority of Americans, and home financing remains their largest liability. Moreover, since the end of World War II, the data clearly show that investments in real estate have yielded much higher and more dependable returns than stocks.

Jack Guttentag, finance professor emeritus at the Wharton School, who now writes a nationally syndicated column on mortgages, received this question from one of his readers: "Why do the media obsess over the stock market while giving relatively little attention and advice to the wealth-building issues that relate to homes and home financing?" Professor Guttentag replied,

"Emphatically, the media give more attention to Wall Street because they believe that consumers actively manage their stock portfolios, and therefore want continuous information about what is happening in the stock market. Whereas, mortgage borrowers drop their attention once their loan closes. But this media view no longer holds true. More than half of the mail I receive is from consumers who ask questions about managing their existing mortgages."

Professor Guttentag has identified an emerging trend. Americans do need to manage their property assets and liabilities to enhance their returns. Informed housing and home finance decisions will pay returns far larger than any amount you can reasonably expect to receive from stocks, bonds, or other investments.[1]

SECRET # **98**

Treat your home and your financing as an investment.

If you read those personal finance articles in magazines and newspapers, you've seen articles that tell you to exclude home equity from your projected net worth at retirement. Financial planners or the journalists who quote them say that homes make for relatively poor investments; and because you will still need a place to live after you retire, money tied up in a house won't add to your spending power.

Mortgage Secrets refutes these statements. Regardless of what the media report, homeownership and investment properties have helped more Americans build wealth than any other asset class. Yet, since the end of WWII, the media have missed the wealth-building power of property and instead have chosen to repeatedly warn of housing peaks and bubbles. Take this quick review of headline stories and so-called expert advice from the past 60 years.

- The prices of houses seem to have reached a plateau, and there is reasonable expectancy that prices will decline. (*Time*, December 1, 1947)

---

[1] For proof, see my book, *Value Investing in Real Estate* (John Wiley & Sons, 2002).

- Houses cost too much for the mass market. Today's average price is around $8,000—out of reach for two-thirds of all buyers. (*Science Digest*, April 1948)
- If you have bought your house since the War . . . you have made your deal at the top of the market. . . . The days when you couldn't lose on a house purchase are no longer with us. (*House Beautiful*, November 1948)
- The goal of owning a home seems to be getting beyond the reach of more and more Americans. The typical new house today costs about $28,000. (*BusinessWeek*, September 4, 1969)
- Be suspicious of the "common wisdom" that tells you to "Buy now . . . because continuing inflation will force home prices and rents higher and higher." (*NEA Journal*, December 1970)
- The median price of a home today is approaching $50,000. . . . Housing experts predict that in the future price rises won't be that great. (*Nations Business*, June 1977)
- In California . . . for example, it is not unusual to find families of average means buying $100,000 houses. . . . I'm confident prices have passed their peak. (John Wesley English and Gray Emerson Cardiff, *The Coming Real Estate Crash*, 1980)
- The era of easy profits in real estate may be drawing to a close. (*Money*, January 1981)
- The golden-age of risk-free run-ups in home prices is gone. (*Money*, March 1985)
- If you're looking to buy, be careful. Rising home values are not a sure thing anymore. (*Miami Herald*, October 25, 1985)
- Most economists agree . . . [a home] will become little more than a roof and a tax deduction, certainly not the lucrative investment it was through much of the 1980s. (*Money*, April 1986)
- We're starting to go back to the time when you bought a home not for its potential money-making abilities, but rather as a nesting spot. (*Los Angeles Times*, January 31, 1993)
- Financial planners agree that houses will continue to be a poor investment. (*Kiplinger's Personal Financial Magazine*, November 1993)
- A home is where the bad investment is. (*San Francisco Examiner*, November 17, 1996)

◆ Your house is a roof over your head. It is not an investment. (*Everything You Know About Money Is Wrong*, 2000)

In the late 1940s, $8,000 to $10,000 seemed like an outrageous amount to pay for a house. In the late 1960s through the mid-1970s, $30,000 to $50,000 seemed well beyond anything reasonable. In the early 1980s, popular belief held that at $100,000, home prices in California could only go down. Today, similar comments about peaks, bubbles, and busts fill the press. But just as past voices now sound foolish, so too will current opinion as we look back from the future.

Can some home prices soften or decline in the short-run? Sure. They have done so before and will do so again. Local economies ebb and flow, but over periods of 5, 10, 20, or 30 years, well-selected properties will continue to register high-profit appreciation.[2]

Financing Magnifies Returns

Here's a simple example: You invest $10,000 in a $100,000 property. You finance your purchase with a 30-year, $90,000 mortgage at 7.75 percent. After eight years you will have paid down your mortgage balance to $81,585. With 4 percent a year appreciation for eight years, your property's value will have grown to $136,860. If we subtract the balance of $81,585 from this $136,860, you see that your original $10,000 investment has increased more than fivefold to $55,275. That result yields an after-tax annual rate of return of around 24 percent (see Table 10.1). During the early- to mid-2000s, lower rates of interest and higher rates of appreciation produced rates of return on invested cash that far exceeded 24 percent.

Stocks Typically Yield Lower Results

Depending on whose numbers you use, stocks have supposedly yielded average *pretax* returns of between 9 and 12 percent a year over the longer run. On an *after-tax* basis, a 10 percent a year return on stocks is considered very good. In fact, over the long term, fewer than 2 percent of professional

---

[2] Potential homebuyers: For more extensive discussion of this issue, see Chapter 3, "Home Ownership: How to Make It Your Best Investment," in my book, *The 106 Mistakes Homebuyers Make—and How to Avoid Them*, 4th ed. (John Wiley & Sons, 2006).

Table 10.1 **Property Appreciation Yields High Returns**

Today

Property purchase price	$100,000
Original Mortgage	90,000
Cash invested	10,000

Eight Years Later

Market value @ 4% appreciation	136,860
Mortgage balance	81,585
Equity	$55,275

Equity Growth Rate

$10,000 $55,275

```
|   |   |   |   |   |   |   |   |
0   1   2   3   4   5   6   7   8 years
```

Annual growth rate of home equity = 24 percent. Proportionately increasing the down payment and purchase price would still yield a 24 percent rate of return.

fund managers have been able to consistently earn after-tax returns on stocks of more than 10 to 12 percent a year.

At the end of 1965 the Dow Jones Industrial Average (DJIA) stood at 969.26. At the start of 1982 this index of blue-chip companies actually stood lower, at 884.36. During this entire 16-year period, the DJIA closed no higher than 1051.70, and it fell to as low as 577.60 in 1974.

If you compare stock gains during the *unprecedented* market boom that ran from 1993 (DJIA at 3,500) to early 2000 (DJIA at 11,700), you'll find property wealth multiplying even faster. In the small college town of Gainesville, Florida, a home bought in 1993 for $100,000 could have been sold in 2000 for $150,000. Assuming a $10,000 down payment, that $50,000 gain in price returned a fivefold increase in investment—not counting mortgage paydown.

If instead, you had put $10,000 or $20,000 into a property in a boomtown such as Portland, Oregon; Austin, Texas; Boston; Seattle; San

Francisco; Park Cities, Utah; Denver or Boulder, Colorado; or Sarasota, Florida—or any one of dozens of other hot housing markets—you would have enjoyed a tenfold (or greater) increase in your original down payment investment, compared to the approximately threefold gain in the stock market.

Summing Up

You can reasonably expect your property investments to outperform the stock market. With a property you gain the benefits of leverage. You invest a 5, 10, or 20 percent down payment, yet you receive returns based on increases in the total value. That's why even a 4 percent annual rate of appreciation will nearly always outperform the price gains you might receive from stocks. And not only does property ownership present less risk than stocks, but stocks won't keep you dry when it rains or warm when the weather is freezing cold. Nor will they give you an amount of income (dividends) that comes close to the amount of income (rents) that an investment property can yield.

As you grow older, diversify your wealth into various types of investments. But don't naively accept the false idea that other investments will yield higher returns or lower risks than property. (For more historical investment results and explanations, see pegasusdialogues.com or garyweldred.com).

Future Uses of Property Equity

The financial planners dismiss housing as an investment not only because they claim (erroneously) that you can earn better returns in stocks, but also because your equity is illiquid. Wrong again. Equity lines of credit (HELOC), refinances, and reverse annuity (now called Homesaver) mortgages all provide tax-free money from your home.[3]

As your housing needs change, you may choose to downsize. Sell the higher-priced family home and move into a lower-priced empty-nester home. You and your spouse will pocket up to a $500,000 tax-free gain. In contrast, the IRS will tax the money you withdraw from your 401(k) and

---

[3] *Mortgage Secrets* discusses when and whether you should withdraw these monies later in this chapter.

other tax-deferred retirement accounts at your highest marginal ordinary income tax rates, even if a large part of those funds actually accrued through capital gains such as stock price appreciation.

Lack of Diversification

Today, in addition to "stocks for the long run," financial planners preach the virtues of diversification. "Never put all of your eggs into one basket," they say. There's merit to this advice. But it doesn't apply to real estate in the way the stock enthusiasts think it does.

"Most experts argue—correctly, in my view"—writes Jonathan Clements of the *Wall Street Journal*, "that if you own your own home, you already have plenty of real estate exposure." And from *Barron's Guide to Making Investment Decisions*, the same Wall Street line: "We will argue that one's own home is probably enough exposure to the real estate market for the average individual investor. If you're thinking about buying [a home], please, at least consider the alternatives."

Why this hostility to real estate? According to the clichéd critique, real estate fails the test of diversity. If you maintain your job, your home, and your property investments in the same community, you're placing too many eggs into one basket. If your employer, your industry, and your community slide into recession, your finances could take a triple hit.

In a know-nothing manner, this critique of property investment confuses the short run with the longer run. It also mistakenly assumes that housing prices yo-yo up and down like the prices of stocks and bonds. Yet, in most areas, in most times, property prices rarely slide down—and in those cases when a big down cycle does hit, rebounds nearly always occur within three to five years. In contrast, when stock prices hit down cycles, they can stay down for 10 to 20 years (e.g., 1907 to 1921, 1929 to 1953, 1966 to 1982).

The Short-Run Error

Unless you develop short-term ownership strategies such as fix and flip, think of property as long-term wealth, not wealth that you check three times a day by tuning into Bloomberg reports. Sometimes local economies sag. Job growth falters. On occasion, homebuilders build too many houses, condos, and apartments. Unsold inventory gluts the market.

Nevertheless, these localized downturns rarely last for more than a few years. In fact, severe downturns such as occurred in California in the early to mid-1990s provide enormous opportunities to create home equity wealth by trading up. I know California homebuyers who, in 1993, bit the bullet and took a mild loss on their $200,000 home. They then bought a $400,000 home that had sold three years earlier for $550,000. Today, that house is worth $1.2 million; they've accumulated around $900,000 in equity, and their monthly payment (due to refinancing into lower interest rates) is only 15 percent higher than they were paying in 1990.

Volatility

If you own stocks, you must diversify your holdings even if you invest for the long run. Stock prices and profit performance of even the best companies can plummet and remain down for decades. Name-brand highfliers of earlier eras can end up in bankruptcy. (To name just a few: Polaroid, Enron, United Airlines, World Com, U.S. Steel, Pan Am, and Pennsylvania Railroad.) Owning stocks of just one or several companies can expose you to financial ruin—*especially* when you plan to hold those stocks forever.

Property owners suffer no similar risk. Do you know of any decent property that would sell today for less than it sold for 5 or 10 years ago? Check the historical prices in so-called less-desirable neighborhoods. You will find that even these properties have appreciated. Certainly, individuals can let their properties run down, but I do not know of any neighborhoods in the United States where market values have declined from where they stood 10 years ago, unless the local job base (e.g., Detroit) has severely declined. Obviously, you should not *invest* in property that's located in a declining economic area, though you might speculate, if that suits your risk profile, and hope for a turnaround or revitalization.

Plan to Build Property Equity Wealth

Most retirees have gained greatly from the increased value of their property equity, but most of them haven't had to tap into it. Today's retirees still draw substantially from social security, company pensions, and, yes, the historically unprecedented bull run in stocks of the past two decades.

You, though, can't count on the same degree of income support from social security, pensions, or stocks. No one predicts huge increases in social security payments. Most companies have abandoned pensions. And who knows where stock prices might land 10, 20, or 30 years from now. Further, what will happen to stock prices when tens of millions of boomers try to liquidate their 401(k), 403(b)s, and IRAs to raise cash to pay for their living expenses?

In an uncertain world, one constant remains: If the United States continues to grow its population and its economy, housing values and rent levels will continue to go up. Unless you know that you can secure your finances in other ways, don't leave your equity gains to chance. Choose your properties and financing with a *calculating* eye on the future.

SECRET # **99**

Monitor opportunities to refinance.

With newspapers and magazines widely publicizing the refi boom of the early to mid-2000s, you might be surprised to learn that millions of Americans still hold mortgages with interest rates above 7.5 percent. Even among the people who recently refinanced, more than 50 percent held mortgages with interest rates greater than 8 percent. This is amazing. People will drive across town to use a $5 coupon, but they consistently miss out on opportunities to save tens of thousands of dollars through refinancing.

Granted, no one likes to apply for a mortgage, so people procrastinate. A friend of mine who refinanced a 9 percent mortgage on an investment property had placed this task on his "to do" list three years ago. During that period of procrastination he could have profitably refinanced two or three times. His savings on interest and additional equity buildup would have totaled $15,000. That's a steep price to pay for tardiness.

Mortgage products and interest rates change continuously. Your future plans may change, too. Maybe, you begin to consider a move. Maybe you decide to stay put. Either choice might warrant a change in your property financing. So, at least every few months, compare your current financing and costs (in light of your current plans) to the then available financing alternatives. Not only manage your asset (the property), manage the liability (your mortgage). Manage both and you accumulate wealth faster.

Run the numbers. Calculate your cost savings and increased equity. Think how you might invest some of that money. Translate that gain into a dollars-per-hour figure. A refi can net you more than $1,000 an hour. Unless you're a CEO or an investment banker, that's not bad pay.

Facts, Not Rules of Thumb

Return to the story of my friend Sue with her 7.75 percent mortgage that originated 10 years earlier (*Secret #97*). She could have refinanced earlier at 6.5 percent and saved a vault load of cash. Why didn't she? She believed the 2 percent rule, which says, "You can't profitably refinance unless you lower your current rate by at least two points." Dear reader, you may be able to refi profitably even if your rate drops by just .50 percent. To answer the refi question, always calculate. Never rely on rules of thumb or back of the envelope guesstimates. Compound interest can easily play tricks with casual conclusions. Talk periodically with your *trusted* loan rep. Stay abreast of changing products and rates.

Equity Build-Up, Not Merely Lower Payments

Return to that so-called "no-cost" loan (*Secret #97*). A friendly loan rep calls with a "Have I got a deal for you" pitch. "How would you like to drop your monthly payments by $200 a month—and it won't cost you a cent in fees or closing costs."

Do you realize that a good part of that $200 a month savings results because the lender wants to put you back into a 30-year term? Assume you owe $200,000 at 7.5 percent with 21 years remaining on your mortgage. Your payments run around $1,578 per month. The loan rep says, "I can get you into a 7.0 percent loan that will drop your payments to $1,331. And it won't cost you any money out-of-pocket."

Who could turn this deal down? Seems like found money of $247 a month. But later on, this free lunch will cost you a large check, or, to be precise, 108 large checks. This refinance dramatically slows your equity buildup.

What you saved in monthly payments, you more than lost in equity buildup. Plus, your new loan runs for 30 years, whereas your then existing

Table 10.2 **Equity Buildup Comparison**

	Interest Rate	Current Remaining Term	Current Balance	Equity after 10 Years
New loan	7.0%	30 years	$200,000	$28,325
New loan	7.0%	20 years	$200,000	$66,545
Old loan	7.5%	21 years	$200,000	$58,451

loan would pay off in just 21 years. If you really wanted to use a no-cost loan, you could refinance profitably into a 7.0 percent (or maybe 6.75 percent) 20-year loan. Your equity would build even faster—after 10 years, you would owe $133,459. Table 10.2 shows how the three loans compare after 10 years. (The equity shown includes only mortgage paydown—not appreciation.)

Why do loan reps push the 30-year refi? Because the immediate monthly savings look so great. With the 30-year loan at 7 percent, your payment drops by $247 per month. With a refinance into a 20-year loan, the payment slips just $28 to $1,550. Regrettably, most Americans think in terms of low monthly payments now. As a reader of *Mortgage Secrets*, you know better. Whether you choose to finance or refinance a property, pay as much respect to equity buildup as you do the amount of the monthly payments.

(Caveat: If you diligently invest that $247 savings each month at 8 percent interest, your equity plus accumulated savings could exceed the equity buildup of the 20-year loan. Investors who try to maximize returns may purposely elect this lower payment alternative so they can attempt these greater gains. Most refi folks, though, squander the $247 and end up with less wealth and higher debts.)

The Equity Killer: No Cash Closings

As you saw with my friend Sue, many of these supposedly no-cost refis actually charge large amounts of fees at closing and add them into the mortgage balance. When this add-on occurs along with a renewed 30-year term, equity buildup is set back for years. Never sign up for such a loan. The money you lose will far exceed your monthly "savings." Get the loan rep to run payoff schedules for your loan alternatives, or click on to any of the mortgage calculator web sites. Compare the equity buildups. Make your loan decision with the facts in front of you. How much will that lower payment cost you in future equity? (Same caveat: If you diligently invest, add in your accumulations. However, remember that mortgage payoff not only offers risk-free gains, for most people it provides psychic rewards.)

SECRET # **100**

Use refinancing to create other benefits.

Although most people refinance to lower their monthly payments, as noted, you might refinance to achieve other cash management and wealth-building purposes, such as:

- *Equity buildup:* As many as 50 percent of all refi borrowers select shorter-term loans. Lenders are originating record numbers of 10-, 15-, and 20-year mortgages. As *Secret #15* reveals, shorter-term loans build equity much faster than the more common 30-year amortization period. After just 5 years of payments, a 15-year loan shows a lower balance than a 30-year loan shows after 10 years.
- *Pay off credit cards:* Use lower-interest mortgage money to pay off higher interest credit cards and installment accounts. Execute this plan only if you possess enough self-discipline to stymie your high interest borrowing. Increasing numbers of people take out bill-payer refis. Then they run their credit card balances right back up to where they were before their refi. They've racked up more debt, *and* they've spent their equity. Such people help account for the growing number of property foreclosures.
- *Eliminate mortgage insurance:* In some circumstances, the law permits you to cancel your PMI and stop paying those $50 to $150 a month premiums (see *Secret #103*). If your home has appreciated, or if you've created value through improvements, you can refi your

balance at the new higher property value, which could drop your LTV below 80 percent. Thus there is no need for PMI.

- *Switch an ARM to a fixed-rate mortgage (FRM):* If inflation appears to be heating up, you might go to the safety of a fixed-rate mortgage. Also, if you financed with a short-term horizon that now appears longer term, the FRM might prove the better choice, especially if FRM rates sit relatively low. As short-term ARM indexes jumped considerably during 2005–2007, hundreds of thousands of ARM borrowers switched to FRMs.

- *ARM to ARM:* This strategy can work well when ARM rates are hitting lows. You can refi into another ARM with lower caps, a slower moving index, a slimmer margin, or more liberal terms of assumption. Even if your current payment doesn't decrease, you win if the new ARM includes more favorable features.

- *FRM to ARM:* If you're just a few years away from selling a property, switch from an FRM to an ARM. Because you no longer need long-term interest rate protection, you save money with the ARM. If your new ARM includes a good assumption clause, this feature could enhance the sales appeal of your property. This tactic doesn't work in periods of flat or inverted yield curves—for example, 2006–2007. Also, you might hold onto a low interest, assumable fixed-rate mortgage if it still shows a high LTV.

- *Streamline refi: Mortgage Secrets* reminds you that FHA and VA mortgages include a unique and desirable feature called streamlining. When rates fall, FHA/VA borrowers can refinance without an appraisal, credit check, income verification, or qualifying ratios. In the refi boom of the early- to mid-1990s, many Californians could not dump the high-rate mortgages they had originated in the 1980s because the value of their homes had temporarily dropped, or they were unemployed or underemployed and could not meet qualifying standards. Thanks to streamlining, no FHA/VA borrower faced that frustrating dilemma.

- *The good life:* Although many homeowners squander their home equity on new cars, trucks, boats, jet skis, European vacations, and junior's college expenses, *Mortgage Secrets* cannot abide such frivolities. You cannot build the wealth you will need later if you eat your seed corn today. As to junior, tell him to pay college expenses with part-time (and summer time) job money. Please, no student loans. Debts from college are destroying the finances and wealth-building potential of millions of college grads—and dropouts. The student loan racket has now excited Congressional ire. Deceptive loan practices aren't limited to mortgages.

In addition to the previously mentioned benefits, a refinance can serve at least one more important purpose: It can generate funds for additional investment.

SECRET # **101**

Refinance and invest the proceeds.

Promoters of every type of cockeyed scheme and speculation claim to offer investment opportunities. Peddlers of financial products, purveyors of financial services, pandering politicians, and even car dealers tell us to buy what they are selling because they offer us a good investment. Commodities, jewelry, condo timeshares, baseball cards, and old Mason jars all are marketed as worthy investments. Even luxury goods (i.e., wealth-destroying extravagances) such as $5,000 wristwatches and $80,000 cars are now advertised as investments.

Wealth-Building Investments

If you borrow against your home equity to invest, choose assets that yield both a growing stream of income and a near certain increase in value. *Mortgage Secrets* favors property. In terms of cash flows, no other asset beats income-generating real estate. In terms of inflation protection, no other asset beats income properties. Yet when inflation falls, interest rates fall. Property cash flows go up because you can refi into lower mortgage payments. Values go up because buying power increases. With rental properties, you win when inflation runs rampant; you also win as it declines.

In addition, rental properties provide tax advantages such as tax-free, cash-out refinances (to further pyramid your wealth); noncash tax deductions for depreciation; tax-free trade-up exchanges; and deferred taxes on capital gains through the use of installment sale contracts.[4]

Double Leverage

To pursue this investment strategy, use a cash-out refi (or a home equity line of credit) to raise $25,000 or $50,000 (perhaps more). Apply that money as a down payment to acquire a rental property.

Your interest costs (at today's rates) should total less than 7.5 percent, but the rental income plus appreciation of your property should yield (after expenses) 10 percent to 20 percent on the amount of your invested capital. With this spread between borrowing costs and yield, your leveraged rate of return proves wise. If you choose your rental property according to sound investment principles (as explained in my books on real estate investing), you could achieve these high returns with little risk. *Mortgage Secrets* would never advise you to gamble your home equity with risky ventures.

If you live in a high-priced housing market, invest in areas of the country (or world) that yield higher cash flows per dollar of investment. In recent years, for example, many Californians have bought property in Nevada, North Carolina, Arizona, Texas, Mexico, and Costa Rica.

What About Stocks?

During the 1990s, some financial writers and advisors urged homeowners to cash out their home equity and invest it in the stock market. In his 1997 book, *The Strategy: A Homeowner's Guide to Wealth Creation* (Key Porter Books), Garth Turner painted a wealthy, risk-free future for homeowners who would borrow against their home equity to buy stocks:

> Imagine, wealth virtually without risk. It's now possible thanks to the amazing convergence of low interest rates, solidly rising financial markets in the long run and an economic rebound in North America that will last well into the new millennium. . . . Today you can dip into your

---

[4] For more details, see my book, *Investing in Real Estate*, 5th ed., (John Wiley & Sons, 2006).

real estate equity and put that money into financial assets with confidence as long as you invest for the long term.

Turner goes on to tell his readers, "The new rule of real estate: [a home] is now just shelter, not an investment. . . . What you ultimately want and need is wealth, not a house. . . . Your future lies with financial assets, not real estate."

Indeed, hundreds of thousands of United Kingdom homeowners bought into this idea through a financial product known as endowment mortgages. To learn about the wealth-destroying disaster that ensued, google "U.K. endowment mortgages."

In his influential book, *Stocks for the Long Run*, 3rd ed. (McGraw-Hill, 2002), Wharton School professor Jeremy Siegel enthuses over stocks as the salvation for all investors who will keep the faith.[5] "Buy and hold through the market's ups and downs," Siegel advises. You will become wealthy. It's virtually guaranteed. Like Garth Turner, Siegel suggests (though not so emphatically) that homeowners leverage up their home financing and put their cash proceeds into the stock market.

The Reasoning

From a casual perspective, this technique to build wealth seems reasonable. Borrow mortgage money at a tax-deductible rate of 6 to 8 percent. Use that cash to buy stocks. Stock fund promoters claim that over the long run stocks yield returns of 10 to 12 percent a year—albeit with bumps and jolts along the way. Hang on for the ride and you eventually end up with far more money. What a wonderful opportunity to borrow home equity money cheap and invest high.

Sounds pretty good, and it could work. If stocks for the long run do yield a near certain 10 to 12 percent annual return, this strategy pays off big as long as your retirement—or other need for the funds—does not occur during one of those long periods of down markets, for example, 1966–1982.

---

[5] For a detailed discussion of Siegel's faulty analysis and conclusions, see Gary W. Eldred, *Value Investing in Real Estate* (John Wiley & Sons, 2002).

The Fallacy

Unfortunately, that 10 to 12 percent stock return figure does not warrant confidence. Stock market volatility creates more destabilizing uncertainty than the enthusiasts admit. If your retirement years coincide with a bear market, you could end up flipping burgers at McDonald's or greeting customers for Wal-Mart. Facts oppose the claims of the stock enthusiasts. Financial assets display major long-term risk. That's why *Mortgage Secrets* favors long-term investing in real estate rather than stocks: Safely leveraged real estate returns exceed the stock market's (overstated) yield of 10 to 12 percent. Yet real estate (housing) experiences fewer, milder, and shorter downdrafts while providing near certain upside potential over periods of five to ten years. (For historical data on stocks, bonds, and housing, see pegasusdialogues.com and garyeldred.com.)

Less Risk with Real Estate

For proof that property investments experience fewer and less severe price slides than stocks, try this experiment. Call several mortgage lenders. Ask them if you can borrow 90 percent of a property's purchase price for a period of 15 to 30 years at a fixed rate of interest. Of course you can. Now, ask those same lenders—or even your stock-touting brokerage firm—if they will make you a similar deal on a portfolio of stocks. "What? Are you crazy," they'd respond. Or just as likely, they'd tell you to pay cash for your stocks with money borrowed with a *low interest rate home equity loan.*

This simple, commonsense approach to risk assessment speaks volumes. If stocks were less risky than real estate, why won't banks accept stocks as collateral for loans with the same terms and costs that are widely available for property? (Remember, too, unlike stocks, property loans do not require a margin call.)

More Income with Real Estate

Rental properties outperform stocks as an *investment* because they yield a dependable and growing flow of income. Over time, rents for well-kept houses and apartments trend up. In contrast, at current market valuation, most stocks pay dividends of only 1 to 3 percent a year. More than 125 companies in the S&P 500 pay no dividends at all. By any reasonable standard, income yields do not support current stock prices. For the most part, stocks remain speculative because you hope to later sell them for a higher price to someone else—and of course, your buyer feels the same. But when confidence in the "greater fool" theory wanes, the bear strikes. Stock prices free fall.

All true *investments* must yield enough expected income to justify their current price. If you pay for future price gains without a commensurate level of income, you're speculating, not investing. Most speculators do not build a long-term, solid foundation of wealth. (See the classic exposition of this point in John Burr Williams, *The Theory of Investment Value*, Harvard University Press, 1938.)

Of course, I am speaking in terms of averages and tendencies. Undoubtedly, some stocks offer great promise for income and growth. Some properties are overpriced money traps. No matter which assets and asset classes you choose for your investments, due diligence must prevail. Anyone who merely assumes that any given property (or stock) will prove itself profitable should rethink those assumptions.

Good Idea: You Choose

Garth Turner writes in *The Strategy*:

> The greatest threat facing North Americans is not having enough capital to finance decades in retirement. And one of the greatest assets you have for fighting that threat is your home. It can help save you, but only if you follow The Strategy.

Undoubtedly, a shortfall of savings and investments does endanger millions of people. And you can profitably use 6 to 8 percent mortgage money to build wealth when you *invest* in assets that dependably earn more than your cost of capital. But if you do adopt this strategy, evaluate your investment alternatives in terms of their reasonable potential for income, appreciation, and risk. Your home equity sets the foundation for your wealth. Don't spend it for vacations and new cars. Don't throw it into ill-fated investment schemes.

SECRET # **102**

Never buy biweekly baloney.

After closing a mortgage, some lenders go back to their borrowers to extract even more money. Preying on their borrowers' inability to perform compound interest calculations, these lenders promise to prepare a new early payoff system that will permit their borrowers to save thousands in interest—for a small fee of just $395. Under these plans you pay 50 percent of your scheduled monthly payment 26 times a year (biweekly) instead of the full payment 12 times a year.

Mortgage Secrets calls this type of scam biweekly baloney, not because you can't profit by prepaying your mortgage. You can. Rather, it's because you need not pay your lender (or some other soliciting company) a fee to do so. Unless your mortgage includes a prepayment penalty, you can pay any time you want in any extra amount(s) you choose.

How to Achieve an Early Payoff

Your lender (or your mortgage servicing company) wants you to believe that setting up a new payment schedule and processing all of those biweekly payments deserves an extra administrative fee. It doesn't. You can write a check for your scheduled monthly payment; then enclose another check for $500 (or whatever amount you choose). Through a written note, tell the lender to apply that extra amount to principal.

Financial Tables, $29.95 Calculator, or Web Sites

Under the biweekly plan, you (in effect) pay one extra monthly payment per year. That prepay slices the term of a 30-year, fixed-rate mortgage down to about 22.5 years. Under the payment system proposed by *Mortgage Secrets*, you can create the same result by dividing your regular monthly payment by 12, then using that amount to supplement your monthly checks.

If you want to pay more or less than one-twelfth of your regular payment, you can easily calculate how quickly your loan will pay off and how much interest you will save. Nearly all major bookstores stock books that show compound interest tables. Simply multiply or divide the appropriate numbers, and you can evaluate the results of any proposed schedule of prepayments. (Note: Buy *compound interest tables* that show the interest rate factors, not precalculated mortgage payment books.)

Although some people still rely on a book of compound interest tables, most others use either a financial calculator (which you can buy at an office supply store for $29.95 or less), or the mortgage calculators available on web sites such as hsh.com, bankrate.com, and mtgprofessor.com). Even modest prepay sums regularly made will save you years of mortgage payments and tens of thousands of dollars in interest.

Should You Prepay?

Lenders report that several million Americans regularly prepay their 30-year mortgages. Many of these people are not saving as much money as they could (*Secret #15*). Rather than regularly prepay their 30-year loans, these homeowners should refi into a shorter-term mortgage. In addition to achieving early payoff, they could save big dollars in interest each year because 15-year loans typically (though not in periods of flat yield curves) charge a lower interest rate than 30-year loans. On a $400,000 loan the lower interest rate could save the borrowers $1,000 to $2,000 per year—unless interest rates have turned against you, that is, the current refi interest rate for 15-year loans equals or exceeds the rate you now pay for your existing 30-year loan. Of course, if market rates now sit lower than your existing rate, your 15-year loan could really put dollars in the bank account as well as equity into your home.

Qualifying and Flexibility. You might prefer a 30-year loan because you believe it's easier to qualify for a 30-year loan. That's true only if you borrow similar amounts. But as *Secret #15* shows, if qualifying presents a problem, reduce the amount you borrow. A less expensive property financed for 15 years can build equity faster than a more expensive property financed for 30 years.

You might choose to combine prepay and a 30-year loan because you want flexibility. "Yes, we're prepaying now, but if times get tough, we want the flexibility to cut back." That's not unreasonable. But, remember, "flexibility" costs you a steep price. Instead, you might use an interest only loan to achieve this same objective.

Loss of a Tax Deduction. Some advisers argue against prepayment and, for 30-year loans, recommend keeping the tax deduction for interest as high as possible. In responding to a published query, financial planner Marty David urged a homeowner couple (both age 52) to dump their 15-year mortgage that's now within 8 years of payoff in favor of a new 30-year loan. "I would recommend refinancing and getting a 30-year fixed mortgage," said David. "This insures that you will be paying mostly interest for the first 10 years, and get the largest tax benefits of mortgage interest. Think of it this way: The federal government has promised to pay you 30 percent of any interest payment you make (assuming you're in a 30 percent tax bracket). If you reduce your [total] interest payments, then the checks from the government will stop coming sooner."

Folks, that's precisely the wrong way to think about it. Yet, I repeatedly see this misguided view. These people are 52 years old! They need to build as much wealth as possible now. To correctly address their dilemma, one need only calculate how much their net worth will differ in 10 years. Using the financial planner's approach, the couple will be far poorer than if they had stayed with a shorter-term mortgage (see *Secret #15*).

They *may* have paid less in income taxes, but never try to minimize taxes *per se*. Tax-shelter promoters lure many investors into financial ruin while baiting their hooks with that appealing promise. Rather than minimize taxes, maximize after-tax wealth.[6] Regrettably, investors and financial advisers alike confuse these two very different—and often conflicting—objectives. Shorten the term of your mortgage through prepay if it enhances your net worth. Forget trying to minimize taxes as a goal separate from building wealth.

Alternative Investments. Ultimately, your decision to prepay turns on whether you can earn a higher risk-adjusted rate of return on your investments. Throughout the 1990s, investment writers said, "Leverage the house to the hilt and put the cash into stocks." Essentially, the prepay issue revisits the pros and cons discussed in *Secret #86*. Fairly considered, stocks, bonds, and rental properties do typically offer a riskier use of home

---

[6]The wealthiest 10 percent of all Americans pay more than 80 percent of total IRS income tax collections.

equity funds; however, when choosing between home equity, rental properties, stocks, or bonds, *Mortgage Secrets* recommends that wealth builders choose investment properties—as long as you retain a cushion of home equity and cash reserves. For wealth preservers—that is, for those people who have accumulated the wealth and security they need—*Mortgage Secrets* recommends prepay.

SECRET # **103**

Cancel your PMI—Get a refund from FHA.

If you now or in the future pay mortgage insurance premiums (PMI, MIP/FHA), you're wasting money that could otherwise slice your principal balance and build your equity. You want to eliminate this expense as soon as possible.

Although the rules for canceling PMI whip through some twists and turns that can confuse, these basics should put you on the right track.

Cancel Your PMI

For conventional loans (non-FHA) closed after July 29, 1999, upon your request lenders must cancel your PMI premium payments once your outstanding mortgage balance drops to 80 percent of your home's original purchase price. Should you fail to ask, the lender must automatically cancel when your outstanding mortgage balance falls to 78 percent of your original purchase price; however, on a 30-year loan your paydown to 78 to 80 percent won't occur for more than 11 years. You need to look elsewhere for faster relief.

The Market Value Test

When your loan has been sold to Fannie Mae or Freddie Mac, you get a break. Fannie and Freddie apply a market value test:

- ◆ *Two-year mark:* Once your loan passes the two-year mark, you may cancel PMI anytime as long as your loan balance totals no more than 75 percent of the *current* market value of the property.

- *Five-year mark:* Once your loan passes the five-year mark, you may cancel anytime as long as your loan balance does not exceed 80 percent of the property's *current* market value.
- *Appraisal required:* To cancel PMI under either of these options, provide a competently prepared market value appraisal to Fannie or Freddie as well as the originating lender.
- *Credit:* Excellent payment on your mortgage. No 30-day lates within the most recent 12 months. No 60-day lates within the past 24 months; however, the lender will not pull your credit report or credit score.
- *Second mortgage:* If you owe on a home equity loan, lenders apply stricter review standards for your credit and LTV.
- *Rental property:* Stricter review and lower LTV ratios also apply to nonowner-occupied properties, even if the property previously served as your home.

Given the fact that PMI premiums can cost anywhere from $75 to $200 a month or more, plan to terminate this coverage as soon as possible. Here are three ideas:

1. *Improvements:* You need not wait for market appreciation to boost the value of your property. Improve it. Borrow, say, $7,500 to $10,000 to create value; then pay off the loan with the money saved by canceling the PMI premiums.
2. *Prepayment:* If you lack ready cash, borrow money to pay down the mortgage balance. Execute an 80-10-10 plan retroactively.[7] Pay off the loan with your mortgage interest and PMI savings.
3. *Refinance:* On occasion, you might find it profitable to refi out of your mortgage insurance. Tom Warne, president of Majestic Mortgage, recently told how one of his customers refinanced at the same interest rate, yet by dropping his $168 per month PMI premium he still managed to save money.

---

[7] Beware, though of teaser ARMs or other deceptive gimmicks lenders use to lure unsophisticated borrowers into unwise home equity loans. At least PMI premiums will not increase as might an ARM or some type of deferred interest, negative amortization product.

If you could get stuck paying PMI for four or five more years, figure a way to meet the cancellation rules. PMI costs you real money. Yet after you close your loan, you gain no benefit from PMI that justifies its cost. Execute a plan to end it.

Portfolio Lenders

If a lender holds your loan in its portfolio, you're at the mercy of that lender. You can wait out the time necessary to drop your loan balance to 80 percent of your original purchase price, prepay as you gain extra cash, or accept whatever cancellation rules the lender makes.

When you apply for a mortgage (if your loan requires mortgage insurance), ask whether the lender will sell the loan to some firm other than Fannie or Freddie. Will the lender keep the loan in its own portfolio? Pin down what hoops you must jump through to remove the PMI as quickly as possible.

FHA Benefits: Cancellations and Refunds

FHA has cut its closing cost MI premium from 2.5 percent to 1.5 percent. For loans originated after January 1, 2001, FHA will automatically terminate the monthly MIP when the loan balance drops to 78 percent of the property's purchase price. Not as good as the rules of Freddie or Fannie, but still an improvement—and FHA promises more cuts if borrower defaults and foreclosures don't push its insurance fund into the red, as happened during the 1980s.

Borrowers who pay off their FHA loans through sale or refinancing also receive a bonus from FHA of $700 on average. Unlike PMI companies, FHA shares its mortgage insurance fund surpluses (if such surpluses accrue) with borrowers whose long-term payment record prior to payoff shows no serious delinquencies.

SECRET # **104**

Should you negotiate out of escrow?

Nearly all lenders require low-down-payment borrowers to pay homeowners insurance premiums, HOA fees, and property tax payments into a lender-managed escrow fund. Even some low LTV borrowers are required to pay taxes and insurance into escrow accounts. Account balances can reach $5,000 to $10,000 or more. Yet many lenders pay no interest on these funds. Even worse, I've seen lenders charge borrowers administrative fees for the privilege of letting the bank keep their money for them. Although lenders may claim otherwise, in fact no law or regulation requires borrowers to pay into an escrow account. I recently saw an escrow statement with this heading:

Initial Escrow Account Statement

Required by Section 12(c)(1) of

Real Estate Settlement Procedures Act (RESPA)

RESPA requires the account statement; it does not require the escrow account. It is your loan agreement that may impose that requirement. As such, you are free to ask the lender to withdraw its demand. Borrowers with strong credit profiles and low LTVs can press their cases hardest, but if the lender won't remove the escrow requirement, ask for a respectable rate of interest to be paid on escrow balances. Or, you could buy a certificate of deposit in an amount that exceeds all sums needed for the escrow account, then pledge that CD to the lender and pay your taxes, insurance, and HOA fees yourself.

HUD receives piles of complaints about escrow. Here is a sample:

- *Escrow waiver fee:* Some lenders charge several hundred dollars to waive their escrow account rules. Don't pay it. Pure garbage.
- *Overcollection:* HUD limits the amount that lenders can collect and hold in your escrow account. Generally, lenders may hold a two-month reserve *plus* accrued pro rata total expenses (usually 1/12 each month) for disbursements that year. To calculate legal maximums, go to the FAQ section on escrows at hud.gov. You'll find an easy-to-use fill-in-the-blank worksheet.
- *Discounts and late fees:* Your insurer, property tax office, or HOA may offer discounts for early payment and assess late fees against tardy debtors. At present, no law requires lenders to pay your bills according to a time schedule that guarantees you the available discounts. When the lender snoozes, you lose. Until proposed federal

legislation passes, you must cajole and complain to make sure you don't pay more than necessary.

♦ *Return of escrow money:* No law or regulation currently requires lenders to return your money in a timely manner after you pay off your loan (refi, property sale). Often 30 to 90 days may pass before a clerk in mortgage servicing decides to cut you a check. This, too, may change with new laws. Until then, cajole and complain. Certainly, try to get your check at closing. But to see it, you must request it.

"Why worry over a few hundred dollars?" you might say. But would you complain to your grocer, dentist, and dry cleaners if their practices cost you an extra "few hundred dollars" a year? Sure you would. So, display the same moxie when dealing with your mortgage lender.

One final point: To make escrow accounts more acceptable to borrowers, in exchange, some lenders offer to drop the borrower's mortgage interest rate by 1/8 or even 1/4 percent. Now that's an offer worth taking. Ask your loan rep about this possibility.

SECRET # **105**

Just say no to home equity loans.

"Cash out your home equity while rates are low." "Use your home equity as a checkbook." "Take that vacation you've always wanted." "You've earned it, now use your home for the good things in life you couldn't enjoy before." "Pay down your credit card balances, buy a new car, consolidate loans—just 3.9 percent interest."

You've seen the ads. They're everywhere: radio, television, newspapers, and dinner-hour telephone calls. During a typical month, I receive a dozen or more junk mail offerings, nearly all of which use some type of deceptive bait.

Today's trick offering: "Need a fixed mortgage payment? How about 2.2 percent for five years?" After reading the fine print, did I learn that the lender really would charge me a fixed-interest rate of 2.2 percent for five years? Of course not. In fact, the loan was variable rate with negative amortization. See how the ad copy is written: "fixed mortgage payment," not fixed-rate interest. As a smart reader of *Mortgage Secrets*, you probably noticed that sleight of hand. But many borrowers aren't that perceptive. That's why the ads pull in the gullible.

Lenders push home equity loans with reckless abandon. Americans have endangered themselves with more than $1 trillion in home equity debt. In fact, to call it home "equity" debt stretches the semantics because a growing number of Americans are flipped upside down with second, third, and sometimes fourth mortgages. Millions owe more than their home is worth. They're chained to debt for as far into the future as they can imagine. Or they face the peril of foreclosure and/or bankruptcy.

The Wealth Destroyer

Just 25 years ago, most homeowners optimistically counted the years and months that would pass before they paid off their home loans. To celebrate this happy event when it finally arrived, "free and clear" homeowners would invite friends and neighbors to a mortgage-burning party. Take out a second mortgage (as home equity loans were then called)—unthinkable! Only dire emergencies could force such imprudent borrowing. That's why nearly all members of the Greatest Generation crossed into retirement as home*owners*—not debtors.

From Fiscal Watchdogs to Selling Loan Products

Sometime in the mid- to late 1970s, banks changed. Loans became products that banks wanted to sell. They reversed their long-established role as fiscal watchdogs. Rather than counsel people against the evils of needless borrowing, bankers blitzed the public. Banks mass-mailed unsolicited credit cards to people they had never seen or heard of.

"Spend, borrow; borrow, spend," the bankers urged. "No credit, slow credit, bad credit, no problem. If you own your own home, we've got a loan for you. No equity needed." No wonder bankruptcies have climbed to levels 10 times higher than they were several decades ago. Likewise, mortgage delinquencies, defaults, and foreclosures are climbing in response to the 2001–2006 orgy of lending to borrowers who did not understand—or could not afford—the loans they were given. Of course, loan reps earn their fees and commissions from bad loans as well as good ones.

Weakness of Will and Financial Discipline

In adopting the sales approach, the bankers knew their marks. They knew that millions of people would jump at the chance to spend and borrow now—then worry over the destructive consequences later. You may have read news articles that talk about "the shrinking middle class." In its place we see great growth in families and households with little or no positive net worth. But the opposite is true, too—great growth in the number of people who are prospering. And no, income differences do not satisfactorily explain the wide disparities in wealth.

What does account for these discrepancies? Stanley and Danko (*The Millionaire Next Door*) coined the terms UAWs (under accumulators of wealth) and PAWs (prodigious accumulators of wealth). The critical distinction: spending and borrowing versus saving and investing. On a scale of 1-10, UAWs score 8-10 on spending and borrowing; 0-3 on saving and investing. PAWs reverse those scores: 8-10 on saving and investing; 3-6 on spending and borrowing.

Just Say No

Home equity borrowing vanquishes your capacity to build wealth. If you do use it, use it only for productive investment that offers low risk for good returns. Never eat seed corn. Yet, the data on home equity loans show overwhelmingly that most borrowers waste this money with imprudent spending (which includes *ill-considered* home improvements, such as the faddish—yet absurdly expensive—granite countertops, hot tubs, swimming pools, and $5,000 outdoor grills). If you pay cash for extravagances, okay—if you like to throw money away. But to build wealth, never squander your home equity to buy such luxuries.

What about bill consolidation, or paying off high interest rate credit card balances? Again, prudence says no.

Rather than pay less interest, borrowing to pay bills most often leads to even larger payments for interest and higher amounts of debt. Why? Because borrowers who wrap their credit card balances and other bills into home equity loans (or refinances) temporarily minimize the pain of debt. Yet, with a longer term and lower payments, the debt generates higher long-term costs. Even worse, many borrowers run their credit card balances up to where they were before. "Uh-oh, better increase the HE-LOC limit or refi again. Thank goodness the home went up $25,000 in value last year." Wealth destruction continues.

What to Look for in Home Equity Loans

If after review of the numbers you still decide to load up with debt, examine the terms of your home equity loan (lump sum borrowing) or home equity line of credit (spend your equity directly through the checks or credit card the bank gives you). Borrow with the same savvy you would apply to any other home finance agreement that you enter into. No matter what misleading advertising ploys the lender coins, a home equity loan carries the same types of terms, conditions, obligations, and rights of foreclosure as does any other mortgage.

No, let me revise that statement. Don't merely borrow with savvy; borrow with magnifying-glass scrutiny. Lender hype and fine-print gotchas multiply with home equity loans.

Most people pursue purchase mortgages or refinancing out of need. These loans are bought as much as they are sold. This is not true of home equity loans. Ninety percent of the time, lenders *sell* these loans. Relative to their dollar volume, lenders spend far more to promote and market home equity loans. Also, predatory lenders stalk the jungles of home equity lending in fierce competition with other members of their species.

Specifically, here are several of the more important terms and conditions to watch out for:

- *ARMs:* Adjustable-rate mortgages account for most home equity loans. Scrutinize caps, adjustment periods, and margins.
- *Teaser rates and payments:* Nearly two-thirds of home equity loans start with teaser rates. How long will it last? How high can it jump? Also, I have noticed a trend toward "teaser payments." Lenders know people care more about the amount of their required payments than the level of their interest rate. So, ads tout "fixed low payments" and slip negative amortization through the back door.
- *Prepayment penalties:* Great teaser rates often come with prepayment penalties. Lenders don't want you to grab a below-market rate

for three or six months and then bail out before they've extracted their pound of flesh.

- *Balloon payments:* When does the loan fall due? Is it callable prior to that date? If you wish to renew, must you requalify? Must the lender order a new appraisal?
- *Loan fees:* Usually not as bad as with purchase/refi mortgages, but some lenders will sting you if you're not swatting as necessary.
- *Maintenance and inactivity fees:* Some borrowers set up home equity lines of credit only to be used in emergencies. The lender may require you to either borrow some stated minimum amount, or pay a fee for the privilege of refraining.

An open line of home equity credit—whether used or not—can reduce your credit score. If you plan to refinance or buy another property anytime soon, place this borrowing within the context of your total credit profile. The AU/credit-scoring program could conclude that you're over-extended.

SECRET # **106**

Trouble, trouble, what to do?

Given the high tide of delinquencies, foreclosures, and bankruptcies rolling over the country, mortgage lenders have decided to approach troubled borrowers with a velvet glove and an olive branch rather than the iron fist of lawyers and legal process. The *Mortgage Banker* has published a variety of articles with titles such as "Compassionate Servicing," "Rescuing Latepayers," "The Delinquency Story," and "Wells Fargo Implements [Freddie Mac's] Early Resolution System."

Borrowers Won't Listen

Borrowers all too often rebuff their lender's peaceful problem solving. They won't open their mail or answer their telephone. They turn tail against anything or anyone that looks like or sounds like a collection effort.

To counter this head-in-the-sand tendency, First Nationwide Mortgage disguised its "please come in and talk with us" letters. Instead of offensive pink past-due notices, First Nationwide placed its pleas for workout in envelopes that look like wedding invitations.

Even that effort gained only a 13 percent reply rate. Creative collection beat the ordinary response rate of 2 percent, but 13 percent still leaves a majority of troubled borrowers neck deep with the water rising.

What to Do

When you suspect that you might encounter financial difficulties, call your mortgage servicer. Better to put on a life jacket before you need it than wait until your lungs are filled and you're going down for the third time.

"If you know you're going to face emergency bills, we can suspend your payments until you recover," says Paula Edwards, a workout and loss mitigation official with Countrywide Home Loans. "But we can't do anything if we don't know. I've helped all sorts of people—mechanics, doctors, judges, professors. But only when they call."

Although early beats late, late beats never. Among all borrowers who seek peaceful resolution, 85 percent could nearly see the courthouse steps. By then, their legal costs, past-due payments, late fees, and escrow shortages had piled up to magnify the difficulties of resolution.

To succeed in workout, a borrower needs two things: a willingness to eventually pay, and some foreseeable and provable steady source of income. For a look at major workout alternatives, please read through Figure 10.1.

In any workout, the lender will weigh many factors. "We don't want to set you up to fail," says John Plaisted, a workout specialist with Countrywide.

But to achieve a workout, loan counselors must discover the reasons for the delinquency. They must judge whether the borrowers care enough to keep their property. They must talk to borrowers.

Lenders fight toughest when they are forced into battle. To avoid hostilities and begin a peaceful—though often stressful—workout, borrowers must candidly, truthfully, and realistically disclose all personal and financial events that are likely to impact their life during the foreseeable future.

◆

Before a lender enters into a mortgage workout, it will first try to learn the real cause of the problem. It will then judge whether the borrower can recover. With this assessment, the lender chooses one or more workout alternatives:

- *Forbearance.* This alternative can succeed when the borrower suffers a temporary setback. Normally, a lender will agree to reduce or suspend payments for 6 to 24 months; then when the borrower can afford it, a new payment is figured that eventually gets the borrower caught up.
- *Modification.* When good faith borrowers suffer a permanent setback, lenders might rewrite the loan to extend the terms, lower the interest rate, or both. This loan modification will reduce monthly payments so that the borrower can meet the new budget.
- *Advances.* When a borrower has missed fewer than 12 payments on an FHA/VA loan, the lender may advance funds to bring the loan current. In return, the borrower signs a note promising to pay back the advance—but without interest.
- *Deed in lieu of foreclosure.* Rather than suffer the stigma, costs, and stress of foreclosure, some deep-in-debt borrowers convey their property to their lender. If the lender accepts, it releases the borrower from personal liability under their mortgage and promissory note.

  In some cases, the FHA will pay borrowers $500 to $1,000 to move out of a property and deed it to FHA.
- *Short sale (short payoff).* Borrowers might want to sell their property, but they owe more than the property is worth. To facilitate a sale, a lender may accept a payoff that's less than the outstanding balance on its loan.
- *VA refunding.* The Department of Veterans Affairs (VA) sometimes buys delinquent VA loans from lenders and takes over the servicing. The VA then tries to structure a loan plan that the delinquent borrower can handle.

Figure 10.1 Alternatives for Workouts

If at some time you find yourself unable to pay your mortgage(s), immediately notify your lender (i.e., the mortgage servicer). Do not try to make ends meet by running up cash advance balances on your credit cards. Far better, ask your lender to help you craft a solution that will conserve—not destroy—your finances and your life.

Conclusion: You Can Live on the House

As discussed, conventional wisdom preaches that the U.S. stock market yields the highest long-term rates of return. Homes? Buy one if you must, the pundits advise, but only as a comfortable place to live. Certainly, don't think of it as a bank account with a white picket fence. "There's no liquidity in property. You can't take that unused bedroom to the supermarket to buy groceries," says *BusinessWeek* in quoting financial planner Thomas Grzymala.

The New Rule of Personal Financial Management

Although such clichéd advice still gains applause from the financial cognoscenti, it ignores six facts about investments in property:

1. *Leverage magnifies returns:* Homeowners and investors can magnify seemingly low rates of property appreciation into high rates of return without long-term chance of loss. (Unlike the historical record for stocks, each decade brings higher property prices.)
2. *Equity exceeds all other assets:* Even at the top of the late, great bull run in stocks, the overwhelming majority of Americans owned more wealth in property than they ever had owned in stocks. Contrary to Wall Street hype, property stands—and will continue to stand—as the largest asset for most individuals and families.
3. *Cost of financing:* Closing costs, interest, and mortgage balances remain the largest offset to incomes and net worth. Managing debt—especially mortgage debt—can build or destroy your wealth.
4. *Tax advantages:* The tax advantages of property ownership surpass those of any other asset. Tax deductibility of interest and depreciation (home office, investment properties); tax-free, cash-out refis; tax-free capital gains for homeowners; and tax-free pyramiding of

— 259 —

gains for investors provide benefits for real estate over stocks. Remember, upon withdrawal, the IRS will tax 401(k) and IRA capital gains at ordinary high rates of taxation.

5. *Boosting home equity gains:* When you own stocks, the fate of your appreciation rests on the hoped-for performance of CEOs and their acolytes. With property, you can add value yourself through property improvements and neighborhood upgrade.[1]

6. *Bedrooms will buy groceries (and many other things):* Even home equity wealth need not remain idle (or "dead," as the stock enthusiasts like to say). You can use it to increase your standard of living and quality of life in future years. (See next section.)

Make no mistake: Your home, your investment properties, and the financing techniques you employ will dramatically affect your future net worth. No savvy wealth builder can rely on social security, company pensions, or so-called financial assets. Property—even if you choose only to buy a home—can enhance your wealth and increase your spendable income. Here's how.

Living in *and* on the House

Let us count the ways that home equity can add to your well-being: Live rent free, live rent free and collect an income for life, downsize tax free and invest the difference to supplement your income, create an accessory apartment, and/or operate a share-a-home or bed and breakfast.

Live Rent Free

When the financial press tells you not to count your home as an investment, they omit the number one reason to own a home free and clear—or even with a mortgage. Homeowners will never see another increase in rents. Read any news story about the plight of seniors who do not own their own homes. These articles lament the financial trials seniors must navigate to contend with the (supposed) greed of landlords.

---

[1] I thoroughly discuss these topics in my books on real estate investing. Also see my book *Make Money with Fixer-Uppers and Renovations* (John Wiley & Sons, 2003, 2008, 2nd ed.). Of course, not all home remodeling adds commensurate value to a property. My books focus on productive, value-creating improvements.

In contrast, homeowners who pay off their mortgages invest early to avoid future rent payments that will continue to go up. Even long-term homeowners with mortgage balances gain because inflation shrinks the real cost of their monthly payments, and, unlike rent, these mortgage payments will end at some point. More promising, the reverse annuity mortgage (RAM) allows homeowners to not only live in their homes but also to live on the house. (Now called the "Homesaver" mortgage by Fannie Mae.)

The Reverse Annuity Mortgage (RAM)

Nikki Wendt, a retired widow, is a member of the house-rich generation. "I wanted to travel more, and I wanted to help my kids," says Mrs. Wendt, "but I couldn't do it. I had all this equity tied up in my house, but I couldn't do anything with it. It was like having a pile of money in the bank but not being able to touch it."

Then Mrs. Wendt learned about the reverse annuity mortgage. The RAM differs from other types of refinancings because it doesn't need to be repaid until the borrowers die or eventually sell their homes.

Like Mrs. Wendt, many older homeowners refuse to borrow against their paid-off homes because they don't want monthly payments. The reverse annuity mortgage solves that problem. Under the RAM financing plan selected by Mrs. Wendt, her lender agreed to pay her $900 per month for as long as she lives. With the extra money, Mrs. Wendt has taken a trip to Hawaii, paid for some surgery to improve her hearing, and remodeled her kitchen. "Everything is better now," reports Mrs. Wendt. "I'm not just getting by anymore—my reverse mortgage is providing me a new life."

A good source of information on reverse annuity mortgages is the booklet *Home-Made Money*, put out by the American Association of Retired Persons (AARP). To obtain a copy of this booklet, go to www.aarp.org/revmort/. Also FHA sponsors a variety of reverse annuity programs. With RAMs, you can have your cake and eat it, too.

Downsize Tax-Free, Invest the Difference

As *Mortgage Secrets* has noted, married homeowners can realize up to $500,000 tax free ($250,000 for singles) when they sell their homes. Future homeowners who choose this alternative can pay cash to right-size their home and invest the difference in income-producing assets such as rental properties, annuities, high-dividend paying stocks, bonds, and so on.

Create an Accessory Apartment

Seniors who remain in their current home can create an accessory apartment or a mother-in-law suite to generate income. (Homeowners can use "bedrooms to buy groceries.") Of course, this possibility for income doesn't apply only to seniors. You can use this technique to build equity faster during the years that you're paying off your mortgage. A variety of publications (cited earlier) explain how to put this income-generating idea into practice.

Share-a-Home or Bed and Breakfast

Have you seen reruns of the Golden Girls? These sixtyish women shared a home. Traditionally viewed as an affordability tactic of the young, house sharing actually cuts across all age groups. Some investors in Florida, for example, now operate large houses that are marketed specifically as senior share-a-homes.

How about another television example? Do you recall the Bob Newhart show where he abandoned the big-city rat race to open and operate a country inn? This, too, reflects an emerging trend, and you don't even need to move to the country. *The New York Times* reports:

¶ Increasingly, New York homes, from hi-tech lofts in Soho to Victorian brownstones in Brooklyn to prewar apartments in Queens, are being opened to travelers. Visitors are offered comfortable surroundings, continental breakfasts, and a whole new way to see New York: as paying houseguests of real New Yorkers, rather than simply as tourists.

Valerie Griffith, a freelance writer and consultant has enjoyed this creative source of income. "It's been really wonderful," she says, "It's almost never empty. . . . We were cautious in the beginning, but in more than three years, we've never had a problem."

If a country inn/bed and breakfast (B&B) doesn't appeal to you, how about converting some excess space for use as a rental office or studio. Consider this ad that ran in a Berkeley, California, newspaper:

¶ Beautifully converted large garage. Very quiet. Large skylights. Windows looking out to a Japanese garden. Excellent workspace for writer or artist. $650 per month. Call 765-4321.

I telephoned the day after this ad first appeared. The property owner had already rented the space.

Financing: A Means to an End

Most people believe that property financing exists to help them buy real estate. They're only right by half. When used constructively, financing helps you to accumulate a higher net worth through equity. Yes, buy and finance a home to enjoy that "comfortable place to live," but, keep in mind, the properties you buy, the mortgage type(s) and amount(s) you choose, and the costs and interest you pay throughout your life can add hundreds of thousands of dollars (even millions, if you work at it) to your later income and wealth.

I hope that *Mortgage Secrets* has provided you with insights and knowledge that help you achieve and enjoy the more prosperous life that lies within your reach. As I write, the property and mortgage markets are going through some cyclical adjustments—as do all markets. Nevertheless, experience and reason clearly show that leveraged (OPM) property purchases remain the most safe and certain way to build long-term wealth.

Should questions arise as you buy and finance your properties, please give me a call at 352-336-1366 or visit my web site, garyweldred.com.

Index

More from your favorite Best-Selling author Gary Eldred

INVESTING in **REAL ESTATE**

0-471-74120-5, $19.95

9123-5, $16.95

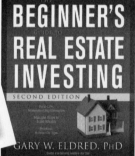

9780470183427, $15.95
Available March 2008

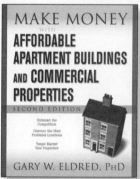

97804711917274, $21.95
Available Now

9780470183441, $19.95
Available April 2008

9780470183434, $19.95
Available April 2008

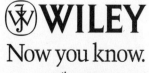